TRIUMPH
B O O K S

RISING

FROM THE

DEEP

RISING
FROM THE
DEEP

The Seattle Kraken, a Tenacious
Push for Expansion, and the
Emerald City's Sports Revival

GEOFF BAKER

TRIUMPH
BOOKS

This book is available in quantity at special discounts for your group or organization. For further information, contact:

Triumph Books LLC
814 North Franklin Street
Chicago, Illinois 60610
(312) 337-0747
www.triumphbooks.com

Printed in U.S.A.
ISBN: 978-1-63727-062-2
Design by Patricia Frey
Photos courtesy of the author unless otherwise indicated

CONTENTS

PART FOUR: SPRINT TO THE FINISH

FOREWORD

As a young boy growing up in Detroit, I was fortunate to discover three things that not only inspired me but altered the course of my life. When I was six years old, my uncle gave me a secondhand Argus camera, a fascinating contraption that triggered my lifelong love of photography. I tinkered around with it for hours on end and took pictures of just about everything. By the time I was in high school, I had turned our basement into a makeshift darkroom, printing my own photos and even collecting a few awards along the way.

It wasn't long before movies entered the picture. At eight years old, I saved enough money to go to the Mercury Theater for a double feature matinee, and my life was never the same. Sitting in the front row of that magnificent setting and looking up at the images of John Wayne and Rita Hayworth was pure magic. That experience opened up a different world of fantasy, adventure, and imagination. It also fanned the flames of my future career as a storyteller.

But like other Detroit kids, especially during the freezing Michigan winter months, I also dreamed of Gordie Howe, Terry Sawchuk, and Ted Lindsay wearing the red and white of our beloved Red Wings hockey team.

The Red Wings weren't just any team. In the early 1950s they were the best in the world. I followed them religiously and started collecting

Parkhurst hockey cards, a hobby that had a catastrophic fate: after I left for college, my mother threw them away.

When I was 10, Tony Leswick scored his Stanley Cup overtime winner to beat Montreal. It was the best feeling a young boy could have.

But even better were the days my father came home from his long hours at work with hockey tickets to see the Red Wings play at the old Olympia. The two of us would head downtown to Grand River and McGraw and climb the arena's steps right up to the ceiling rafters. Although the seats were nowhere near the action, that didn't matter. I got to spend quality time with my father as we ate hot dogs and cheered on future Hall of Famers. Soon, I was intrigued by every aspect of the game.

I began teaching myself to skate—a task that wasn't easy since my skates were two sizes too big. This obstacle didn't seem to faze my mother at all. She told me we couldn't afford new ones, so I'd just have to grow into them!

And then there was the outdoor rink itself. It was otherwise known as the 8 Mile Drive-In. During the winter months, the slope of the parking lot created a gully that froze over, thus transforming it into a makeshift ice rink. Regardless of its major imperfections, for me, this was heaven on earth.

Soon, I began to gather up my friends and organize neighborhood games until we eventually joined a local league. Like most kids our age, we just couldn't get enough of hockey, and we played long after dark, never wanting to stop.

These pastimes could have become insignificant footnotes in an ordinary childhood, incidents that faded into one's memory. But even at a young age, one thing was clear: my obsession with photography, film, and hockey was destined to play a major role in my future.

Not everybody's dreams materialize, but I was lucky enough to refine my photography skills into an advertising career that eventually took me to New York, and that success created another opportunity to move to Hollywood and produce movies and television. This career has spanned 50 incredible years and I still love it as much now as I ever did. Ironically, this also honors my dad's advice. He said to pick a job that I loved. Don't spend your life looking forward to a two-week vacation.

When dream No. 1 and dream No. 2 had come true, it was time to revisit an old passion. And for me, the final unfulfilled dream stemmed from those first encounters with hockey. They had grabbed ahold of me and never let go.

During my first years in California, hockey was not at the forefront of my life. But that changed when "the Great One" was traded to the Los Angeles Kings. I immediately bought season tickets and became an avid Kings fan, attending as many games as possible and becoming interested in the operation of the various teams. In the meantime, I organized games with retired NHL players and Hollywood celebrities and even created an annual hockey tournament with some of these same players.

But it's one thing to dream of a hockey team, and quite another to create one.

And for that transitional leap, I needed a little help from my friends…

One such friend is Harry Sloan, a successful entrepreneur and avid sports enthusiast who was aware of my love of hockey. Through the years we had endless discussions about the possibilities of owning a team. At one point, Harry—probably weary of hearing me talk about it—said, "Let's just do this!"

Finally, it was time to take the big dreams and bring them to life.

Our first notion was to find an existing NHL hockey team we could buy or, secondarily, to identify a city that didn't have a team. These plans began to take shape when Harry introduced David Bonderman, "the Wayne Gretzky of finance," as a new partner.

For several years, we continued the search for the perfect scenario. But it soon became clear that indeed the best strategy was to focus on a city without an NHL team. We flirted with numerous possibilities, including Las Vegas, but nothing clicked. Throughout our journey, Seattle was always my top choice. It was the place that had it all: vitality and excitement, the beauty of the great Northwest, and best of all, enthusiastic sports fans.

Seattle became a reality when my longtime friend Tim Leiweke, co-founder and CEO of the Oak View Group, approached us with an inventive plan to build a new facility underneath the original roof of the historic KeyArena. This was no small accomplishment, as we knew we were facing a daunting engineering challenge.

Nonetheless, having this blueprint, plus the addition of the brilliant Tod Leiweke to run the entire operation, catapulted our game plan to a higher plane. We now had a team of people who were not mere friends and business partners, but forces of nature. With their skills and determination, we were one step closer to a deal.

On October 2, 2018, we were seated outside a conference room in New York City. With hundreds of details and hours devoted to this project, we were finally ready to present our vision to the nine most powerful NHL owners in the next room. Those owners would decide that day whether to let the league's full board of governors meet later to vote on giving us a franchise. If they said yes, the remaining 22 owners would almost surely follow. But if they said no, the discussion was over.

My role in this meeting—a rather terrifying one—was to conclude the presentation, the one that would take us across the finish line. Here I was, face-to-face with my dream, feeling the pressure of this monumental task. What magic words could I possibly say that would persuade this group to seal the deal? Finally, I settled on my childhood memories. What better way to reach them than to share my personal story, the very one I am telling you now?

Fortunately, what emerged from that room was an ultimate vision fulfilled: the birth of the Seattle Kraken.

In the grand scheme of things, my mission has always been to entertain people. Whether it involves photography, film, or hockey, I aim to transport them from their everyday lives to another reality. This is what I have spent my life doing. And now, I am honored to contribute this knowledge to my sports partners—David Bonderman, Tim and Tod Leiweke, and the rest of Seattle's ownership group. We are devoted to finding innovative ways to energize our fans and restore the fun of good, old-fashioned hockey of generations gone by.

The spectacular Climate Pledge Arena and the Kraken Community Iceplex make that job rather easy. The successful opening of both facilities has exceeded even my lofty expectations. The crowds that rushed to the arena on opening night and the families that are flocking to the Iceplex are proof that we have given Seattle something special and unique. After one visit to the Iceplex, seeing the smiles on the faces of families, children, and friends, all united in the quest to have fun—that lone experience makes all our efforts worthwhile.

Geoff Baker's fantastic reporting will take you behind the scenes of how we were able to bring the Kraken to the city of Seattle. Our hope is that the entire Seattle Kraken organization and experience will entertain and thrill our fans for years to come. We are committed to reimagining the hockey experience, to elevating it to a higher level of enjoyment, to building a winning team, and to bringing the Stanley Cup back to Seattle, Washington.

We are so happy you are along for this thrilling ride.

Thank you for sharing the dream.

Jerry Bruckheimer
Seattle Kraken owner
April 2022

PART ONE

The Seeds of
Loss and Rebirth

Chapter 1

LIVING IN PURGATORY

Four years since he'd last been seen in public, former Seattle Mayor Ed Murray sat down with me in a near-empty pizza joint on a rainy winter afternoon in the city's Capitol Hill neighborhood. Gone were the immaculate suits, cuff links, and silk ties from his days in office, replaced instead by a powder-blue, zip-collar sweatshirt. For safety reasons, Murray prefers remaining somewhat anonymous these days as he walks the surrounding neighborhood streets near his home, though people do occasionally recognize him even with his baseball cap and obligatory COVID-19 mask on. When that happens, he scurries past quickly. He and his husband have hired private investigators to probe random threats to their safety, not trusting the city's police department.

He's attempted suicide. Gone through extensive therapy. His finances are a mess and getting worse. But Murray can't get a job, even a volunteer gig to pass his time. And as universally loathed as he senses he will be living out the remainder of his days, his biggest enemy now is boredom. At age 67, he literally has nothing to do. So, he'll walk the neighborhood streets, sometimes with his new rescue dog in tow. His closest former associates won't call him up to say hello or check on him and Murray prefers it that way, not wanting to tarnish their careers with his own radioactivity. No one seeks his advice, even on political and municipal issues he once specialized in with shining results. His life's work of shaping and enacting public policy, first as a Washington state lawmaker and later as the city's 53rd mayor, is over and done with. Those who've held his titles have gone on to lucrative consulting and university teaching careers. He's been refused what he terms "janitor jobs" trying to earn whatever money he can.

Murray has been "cancelled" and knows it. The life he once led is over. And the new one he'd like to start won't ever get out of the gate. In September 2017, he'd woken up looking forward to the next chapter. But by nightfall, that future was dead.

"It's never going to change," he told me. "And that's taken me four years of mental health expenditures to figure out."

There is no future for Murray now, only a present, isolated existence with the few people left in his life. He lives it, as the sports cliché goes, one day at a time. But his life isn't a cliché—more a cautionary tale about consequences. In Murray's opinion, those consequences are undeserved. Still, he knows better than to argue he was wronged. If his therapy taught him anything, it's that some hoped-for vision of "justice" in his favor will never happen. And that's because too many people beyond Murray, save for his few closest loved ones, believe justice went easy on him. That he'll never be punished enough.

So, he looks for things to do, to stimulate his mind and keep his existence from submitting completely to his state of purgatory. Given that reality, it isn't surprising that, on this particular afternoon, Murray seemed eager to discuss his role in helping the city he once ruled land a National Hockey League franchise.

I'd reached out to him knowing he hadn't given a single interview since the day he'd resigned from office. Part of me hoped the passage of time would make him more open to speaking. No other mayor had presided over a period of such turbulence and progress in Seattle's long-festering arena debate. We'd met on a handful of occasions during that time. Murray in power had once told me, in a line he'd repeated for others as well, that he longed to be the country's first openly gay mayor to help bring major professional sports to a city. So, it had to have stung when even that was ripped away from him during his mighty fall. A final reminder that nothing would ever be his again.

But you can't "cancel" history, though many try. And Murray was part of the history I was seeking to chronicle, regardless of whether he now walks his neighborhood streets a ghost. I'd often wondered what his ruined life had become. Heard the rumors he might head back to Northern Ireland, where he'd spent his teen years with family in Belfast. Now, I'd see it first-hand. Upon entering the restaurant, his first words to me were, "I was surprised that you'd want to hear from me."

But speak we did for the better part of an hour. Casual niceties at first while we ordered veal parmigiana half-sandwiches and salads, but then with the recorder he'd encouraged me to turn on so the official storytelling could begin.

Murray spent the hour spelling out intricate details of arena negotiations he'd been privy to as mayor. Things he would never have told me back when he wore his custom suits to work and dined in restaurants with maître d's and cigar rooms instead of sandwiches. There were meetings with NBA commissioner Adam Silver and NHL counterpart Gary Bettman. With billionaires and opportunists that curried his blessing. With political enemies looking to sabotage his efforts to resolve an arena impasse that had cost Seattle its NBA team and any hope at future winter sports to fill that void.

Mainly, he talked about having wanted to revive the Seattle Center public park where the 1962 World's Fair had taken place when he was a boy. Within that park sat city-owned KeyArena, an aging venue Murray said he'd long hoped could be salvaged within his grander Seattle Center vision. As time passed, he told me, he'd realized the city's dilemmas with

KeyArena and with gaining a new major sports venue to attract the NBA and NHL were one and the same.

Slowly, our talk turned to the beginning of his end. About how 2017 had started with such promise, his re-election that coming November having once been a foregone conclusion. We discussed the Request for Proposals process his office helped orchestrate, in which global arena management czar Tim Leiweke and his fledgling Oak View Group were chosen to build the equivalent of an entirely new venue at the KeyArena site. A new arena, mind you, that would preserve KeyArena's historically protected roof built a half-century prior by prominent Northwest architect Paul Thiry.

It was during that RFP process, in which Leiweke's then-new company battled his former Anschutz Entertainment Group goliath for the KeyArena rebuild rights, that the first sexual assault allegation against Murray surfaced.

It came in the form of a lawsuit by a 46-year-old man, Delvonn Heckard, claiming Murray had raped and sexually abused him starting in 1986 while he'd been a drug-addicted teenager on Seattle's streets.

The *Seattle Times* reported on the lawsuit and on two earlier cases with similar allegations. In those cases, Jeff Simpson and Lloyd Anderson told the newspaper they'd met the future mayor as youths in an Oregon home for troubled teens when Murray was working as a counselor there while also attending Portland University.

Both claimed to have been sexually abused by Murray as minors in the 1980s when he was in his twenties. Murray even took Simpson in as his foster son for two years when some of the abuse is alleged to have occurred. Simpson talked to a social worker and police detective at the time, but no criminal charges were filed.

Murray denied all the claims as false. Then, a month later, a fourth accuser, 44-year-old Maurice Lavon Jones, came forward claiming Murray paid him for sex when Jones was a teenage drug addict and prostitute. He made the claim in a sworn jailhouse declaration to Heckard's attorney as part of his lawsuit filed against the mayor. Murray dismissed the claim as a media stunt by those wishing to discourage him from running again.

None of the allegations against him involved actual criminal charges. By then, the statute of limitations for those had run out, so there was still just the lone lawsuit against him as well as the out-of-court accusations by the three other men.

But provable or not, the accusations were causing Murray significant political damage. A week after Jones came forward, Murray announced on May 9, 2017, that he was dropping his re-election bid but would serve out his term the remainder of that year.

Devastated at being denied a second term, Murray told me he nonetheless moved forward determined to prove his innocence and cement his political legacy. After all, he'd enjoyed a highly successful term to that point, enshrining a $15 hourly minimum wage for the city and advancing its politically progressive populace's push for police reform. Murray had also joined the growing chorus of Washington state politicians making a name for themselves nationally by standing up to the bully tactics of one U.S. President Donald Trump.

Surely, there'd be a bright future for him someplace on the other side of this. He'd begun exploring opportunities to put his political and municipal policy experience to use. And with seven months to go in his term, he threw himself into "the hard stuff" on his plate—the arena file being one such priority. Now was the time to get such things done, he reasoned, knowing he didn't have to worry about the next election.

Plus, he loved being "in the game" on projects involving complex negotiations, myriad moving parts, and an assortment of power players all seeking common ground. The arena file was certainly that and the energetic Murray found the hard work got his juices flowing.

By June 2017, the lawsuit filed by Heckard was dropped. And though Heckard stated he'd refile it after Murray's mayoral term ended, that never happened. The day Heckard pulled his lawsuit, Murray held a news conference declaring he'd been vindicated and challenged reporters to dig into his accuser's background. Eight months later, Heckard was found dead of a drug overdose in a local motel room, his lawsuit against Murray never refiled.

With the lawsuit gone, Murray swung into his arena work with renewed vigor. He was determined to have an arena deal hammered out with Leiweke's group and approved by the city council by year's end. Murray shrugged off a mid-July report that Oregon child welfare investigators had believed foster son Simpson's initial abuse accusation in 1984, but charges were never filed because the prosecutor didn't believe the case would hold up in court. And by late summer 2017, a memorandum of understanding was taking shape. Leiweke had agreed to assume all construction costs and any overruns and pay for needed transportation infrastructure upgrades.

And he would do it all while keeping the arena's roof intact.

Never mind the astounding architectural feat that would entail, which Leiweke had committed to take on. Murray knew Leiweke's pledge, expected to cost at least $600 million, represented arguably the most generous arena deal a city had ever received from a private developer. A deal that would rescue taxpayer-owned KeyArena from being rendered obsolete and flattened by a wrecking ball.

A press conference was called for September 12, 2017, to announce the deal. It would take place in an outdoor plaza adjacent to KeyArena, with Murray and Leiweke standing side by side.

Murray had awoken that morning with optimism he hadn't felt in some time. The sun was shining and so was his future, one that would see Murray achieve his goal of launching the repurposing of Seattle Center through its arena. And the part he'd played in this straight male, macho world of pro sports would prove that he, a gay man, could also be a power player. He picked out a suit, knotted his silk tie, and headed to his plush-carpeted downtown office on the sixth floor of Seattle's city hall building. It was a brief stop to go over his day's agenda. The big item was the press conference, his first duty that morning. Already, his aides were gathering at the site. Television and still cameras were being positioned while print and broadcast reporters mingled.

Leiweke and his entourage had arrived as well. They'd gathered in an adjacent staging area where they could see the activity from a distance while awaiting Murray's chauffeured SUV to meet them.

In his office, Murray had already phoned to ready his driver and was throwing on his jacket for the 10-minute ride. His phone buzzed. It was one of his assistants. "You'd better check out this link I sent you."

Murray did. A new *Seattle Times* story had been posted. In this one, his younger cousin, Joseph Dyer, alleged Murray had sexually abused him when he was only 13. They'd shared a bedroom in the 1970s when Murray had returned from Northern Ireland as a young adult and gone to live with Dyer's family in New York.

Once again, Murray proclaimed innocence, figuring this allegation would be the easiest to beat back. He also assumed the press conference with Leiweke would still take place. Not happening, the aide said.

"He told me, 'Mr. Mayor, those folks don't want to be seen with you,'" Murray said.

Leiweke and his entourage, he was told, were leaving. This fifth accuser was apparently more than anyone was willing to take. The chairs and podium were being packed up as stunned media members pieced together what was happening. Murray asked him whether the arena deal was still on.

"I was told the deal was still there," Murray said. "But it wasn't happening if I was still around."

Murray knew what that meant. Him waiting another three and a half months to leave office could torpedo several deals he'd worked on, particularly the arena plan. Delaying things that long could cause Leiweke's group to grow antsy and seek more city concessions. The incoming mayor, whoever that was, might decide the city needed more from Leiweke. And the city council had yet to approve anything. With this latest tarnish, Murray knew, it certainly wouldn't be bowing to pressure from him.

"This was a big deal to me," Murray said of the arena plan. "And it was always touch-and-go. So, I knew it was fragile."

An hour later, Murray made his decision. On his own, he said, without pressure from his inner circle. He left his office that day and never came back. A statement was issued shortly after. His life, as he'd known it, was over. And about to get much, much worse.

The arena deal wasn't yet as dead as Murray. But it was no longer the sure thing it appeared to be when dawn broke. Nothing about Seattle and arenas ever came easy.

Chapter 2

A CITY IN TRANSITION

There's nothing quite like an aerial view of the snow-capped, 14,411-foot-tall majesty that is Mount Rainier. Especially as the sun bounces off that high-altitude snow, causing it to glisten with a jeweled radiance befitting the nicknamed "Emerald City" below. Pilots are constantly pointing it out to awestruck airline passengers rolling up their window shades in preparation for the final descent into Seattle-Tacoma International Airport.

Unfortunately, the air might be the only place a short-term visitor sees the dual wonders of Washington state's tallest peak and that ball of fire known as the sun. Once the aircraft dips below the cloud line, all bets are off. It's been known to rain in Seattle, which means the accompanying clouds form barriers that occasionally block views of the city's famous mountain. Sometimes, especially during hockey season, those clouds sit for weeks and the only way to see Mount Rainier is by cracking open a local Rainier beer with the snowy peaks pictured on its aluminum can.

Now, the somewhat defensive aspiring meteorologists otherwise employed as engineers, baristas, storeowners, realtors, and IT workers among the city's 741,000 inhabitants will without provocation recite statistics showing more annual precipitation in Boston, New York, and even Miami. All of it true, except rainfall in those places comes in periodic deluges, whereas Seattle's is more an omnipresent "drip, drip, drip" commonly associated with forms of torture.

Truth be told, Seattle rain often amounts to little more than a drizzly mist. But with about 150 days of it yearly, the accompanying gray skies will alter the mood of many a resident, some of whom happen to be sports fans.

Sure, it beats shoveling six feet of East Coast snow. Mind you, six inches of white stuff can paralyze Seattle for a week and even topple a mayor from office. While snow might be a thing atop Mount Rainier, its occasional appearance on Seattle's hilly streets must be waited out to melt as the city's handful of plows struggle to get to it. But at least those plows now have some help. For the longest time, the city mostly avoided the use of road salt to help melt the snow and ice. The salt, it seemed, risked infiltrating neighboring waterways and harming the resident fish. Seattle's environmentally conscious populace wouldn't stand for Nemo, Dory, and their buddies getting killed off by salt and so sand was accepted as an alternative, albeit a rather poorly performing one.

Then came the great Seattle snow disaster of 2008. The worst storm in a decade effectively paralyzed the city for a week. Two charter buses carrying students in the Capitol Hill neighborhood skidded on the sand-covered, icy roads, crashed through a barrier, and nearly plunged off an overpass down onto the interstate below. Citizens were outraged. Mayor Greg Nickels vowed the city would reverse course and use road salt going forward. But it was too late to save "Salt Nick" from electoral primary defeat the following spring. To this day, that loss remains largely attributable to his administration's performance during the 2008 storm.

So, rain in Seattle is generally seen as a more pleasant alternative to snow, even though the perennial misty days make viewing Mount Rainier outside the July through September months more of a treat than an expectation.

And then there are the gray days with no rain but merely the threat of it. Nothing tempers optimism more than planning a family picnic under constant clouds threatening to empty themselves at any moment. But, troupers that they are, Seattle residents grin and bear it and head out with blankets and baskets, determined to get lucky but knowing they probably won't. It's an attitude that permeates the city's daily existence.

And it explains why true Seattleites, when venturing out on gray days, won't be carrying umbrellas. Instead, they'll don hooded fleece-and-Gore-Tex jackets from The North Face in preparation for rain, mist, or whatever the clouds dump that day while pretending it's a fashion statement rather than a pre-emptive move. And should the sun happen to trick everybody by popping out unexpectedly, the North Face–wearing fashionistas won't be caught looking foolish carrying an umbrella around on an otherwise perfect afternoon.

It all starts to make sense once you've lived in the city long enough. Sort of the way it makes sense to spend $430 million building an NFL stadium now known as Lumen Field without including a retractable roof to protect football fans from those misty gray elements—or worse. Not that those fans would bring umbrellas. No, the "12s," as they call themselves, would rather be soaked to the bone than umbrella-block their fellow patrons from seeing now former Seahawks quarterback Russell Wilson scramble for his life without an offensive line to protect him.

That's just the way it is in Seattle. You hope for the sun to pop through the clouds at halftime to finish your Dungeness crab chili dog in a rare display of dry November warmth gifted from the heavens. But that hoodie will always be there to pull over mist-soaked hair should the weather and life inevitably turn for the worse.

Some who've lived in Seattle long enough have even trained themselves to embrace the rain as a soul-cleansing ritual. Forget San Diego and sunny optimism. Or powdery, hammocked Mexican beaches in television commercials touting watery beer with a lime wedge jammed in its bottle lip.

Seattle has its cans of Rainier. It has the Seahawks and a roofless stadium, one that has soaked taxpayers in more ways than one. But that's life. That's Seattle. Optimism be darned. Sooner or later, everybody gets wet.

This artful balance struck between Mother Nature, realism, and getting through the day seemed to be working out just fine. But then, slowly at first, things changed. Word got out that Seattle had a real nice mountain behind all those clouds. It also had houseboats that people lived in and this real neat music called grunge.

Sure, these revelations came mostly in Hollywood movies, and it was always pouring buckets true *Blade Runner* style in those. But the mountain, Tom Hanks, Meg Ryan, and the prospect of a cool, undiscovered place where folks wore hoodies to work and hiked on weekends seemed appealing. Not to mention there were jobs in Seattle. Well-paying tech jobs, first with Microsoft in the 1990s but later with a multitude of companies across various industries, all harnessing the power of computers to cause disruption.

But as these newcomers kept arriving, at first mostly from California but later all parts of the United States, Canada, Asia, and elsewhere across the globe, the Seattle that locals had known and loved wasn't the same. Not every newcomer embraced the rain, for one. Some complained about it and even toted umbrellas to work on what later became perfectly sunny afternoons.

Before long, Seattle was caught in transition between the dive bars of its hardscrabble, seafaring roots and the glitzier, modern cocktail lounges springing up to service these new tech workers. Older brick buildings gave way to luxury high-rises. Restaurants that served family-portion plates at affordable prices were closing, replaced by wannabe fine-dining eateries automatically incorporating 20 percent tips and additional service charges into their three-digit tabs.

Soon, the streets became crowded with umbrella-toting transplants driving their cars with California license plates through two-lane roadways that never anticipated so many people using them. Suddenly, the decades politicians had spent punting on decisions about implementing subways and other commonplace mass transit were called into question.

Something called "Link Light Rail" was finally approved by voters in 1996. Not quite a subway, more an above-ground version, light rail was deemed better suited to a city surrounded by water. Rather than pass though underground tunnels that would inevitably bore into a lake or bay, the light rail trains used tracks built atop outdoor platforms and bridges. They were also best suited to the rock-salt-shunning region's more progressive politics, powered by environmentally friendly overhead electrical wires rather than burning fossil fuels.

The only problem with Seattle's light rail was its $54 billion cost and the 47 years it would take to build all those platforms, bridges, and tracks. In the interim, while awaiting the 116-mile light rail circuit being built in three phases, Seattle drivers old and new continued clogging the city's roads and nearby highways.

While fewer than 750,000 people live in Seattle proper, the greater metropolitan area counts 3.4 million. Much of that metro area is more far-flung than in other cities. And by the start of the new millennium, Seattle was still relying on an aging floating bridge section of highway to link the city with its burgeoning east-side suburbs.

The city itself was also sprinkled with drawbridges giving priority to commercial ships and recreational yachts that only magnified the traffic chaos above. Getting to Seattle, or around and out of it, was not easy. And staying away from its downtown core, especially at night, became a more palatable option each passing year.

IN SHORT, though Seattle's population kept on growing, it became less a city built around a thriving core and more a collection of neighborhoods.

Not that there was anything wrong with Capitol Hill, Ballard, Fremont, Queen Anne, Magnolia, Greenlake, South Lake Union, Belltown, or any other neighborhoods forming the city's core. The issue became that, while the greater Seattle metro area was comparable in population with mid-sized U.S. cities such as Denver or Minneapolis, Seattle itself was still a rather small city, difficult to access from distant burbs. This became a critical talking point for professional sports in terms of fans accessing venues to see teams play.

For years, the prevailing wisdom was that the South of Downtown industrial district—or "SoDo" to locals—was the best place to put a stadium or arena. Indeed, that's where the old Kingdome had been, since blown up and replaced by Lumen Field, home to the Seahawks and Major League Soccer Sounders. SoDo is also where the Seattle Mariners baseball team opened its new Safeco Field ballpark in 1999, now called T-Mobile Park.

The area had direct driving access to the city's downtown core plus additional highways in all directions. And, SoDo had incorporated light rail stations leading in from downtown and communities to the south. Mind you, the closest station was still a hefty 15-minute walk from both stadiums for your average middle-aged fan not used to hiking the region's surrounding mountains. Also, pre and postgame SoDo traffic typically saw sports fan drivers ensnarled with freight trucks hauling and unloading cargo to and from the neighborhood's port docks, leading to traffic chaos. But this was as good as Seattle was going to get and the locals put up with it as a price of fandom. Sooner or later, everybody gets wet.

Now, KeyArena had none of these things when the NBA Seattle SuperSonics played there. Built for the 1962 World's Fair as part of a Seattle Center public park, it had no light rail nearby. Instead, it was nestled in a part-urban, part-residential location with narrow streets and one main arterial valve along Mercer Street that turned into a rush-hour parking lot. As the years passed and Seattle's population swelled, KeyArena and the surrounding area, like drivers with California plates, went from being tolerated to despised. In fact, for a good portion of Sonics fans, giving

KeyArena the Kingdome treatment with demolition explosives and building a new venue someplace else—say, in the SoDo district—seemed more than reasonable.

Amid this chaos of driving to and from work and sporting events, Seattle transitioned from a city run by Microsoft to one where Amazon was calling the shots. Being a company town was nothing new to Seattle, which had bent over backward to please aerospace giant Boeing long before computers changed the pecking order of its corporate scions.

In a city where Microsoft was still a significant force, along with satellite offices for Apple, Google, and Facebook and local upstarts Expedia, Zillow, and Redfin, Amazon became the dominant entity.

The e-commerce giant had been founded by Jeff Bezos in the basement of his home just across the city's floating bridge in the east-side suburb of Bellevue. By 2020, it had evolved into cloud computing, entertainment, sports streaming, and other technology ventures and counted 50,000 employees within a triad of skyscrapers and additional buildings in Seattle's flourishing South Lake Union district. Its annual sales easily surpassed local brick-and-mortar retail competitors, even those of legacy giants like the Nordstrom department store chain. And in many cases, it put those retail competitors out of business.

Seattle became an "Amazon town," with the city's government caretakers largely beholden to the company and its influx of workers. Those workers, bolstered by Amazon housing stipends, had sent Seattle real estate values skyrocketing and thus provided even more tax revenue from which to pay for bloated projects like the light rail plan.

But as one might expect, this Amazon-fueled change at lightning, tech-driven speed caused a greater strain than the city's previous growth. Seattle natives already resented the institutions of their childhood being shuttered and forgotten. Now, many complained of being unable to afford to live in their own neighborhoods. For a city proud of its progressive traditions, the corporate sprawl was becoming tough to swallow. Backlash was inevitable.

It didn't help that the locals weren't always the friendliest. Features of the appropriately named "Seattle Chill" involved a tribalism of sticking with one's close friends and family and revealing little to outsiders.

Unfortunately, Seattle was fast becoming a city of outsiders. They'd seen the Rainier mountaintop and wanted to stick around and shape their new home. A clash between "old" and "new" Seattle values was unavoidable. And like it or not, anyone planning major projects within the city would soon be ensnared in the tentacles of that fight. It didn't always make sense. Then again, it didn't have to.

This was Seattle. And sooner or later, everybody gets wet.

Chapter 3

SEATTLE FOUNDED AND PLUNDERED

Long before Seattle became a Boeing town, then a Microsoft town, and later an Amazon town, it was a mill town. Seattle natives tend to forget that the corporations monopolizing the city didn't just start when California invented license plates for its drivers to take north.

No, Seattle had been a company town almost since the very day its Denny Party settlers arrived in September 1851 on the shores of Alki Point. They erected a roofless cabin on land belonging to the Suquamish and Duwamish Native American tribes and somewhat optimistically dubbed their settlement "New York." Soon, perhaps doused to reality by pounding rain and bone-chilling winds blowing off the Puget Sound, they added "Alki"—a Chinook expression roughly translating to "before long"—to the name. And the following year, with their beachfront farmland still looking nothing like Manhattan, the "New York–Before Long" inhabitants wisely spread across Elliott Bay into a section of land adjoining a protected deep-water harbor better suited to the village of their dreams. This new place known today as Pioneer Square took the name Seattle to honor Duwamish tribal leader Chief Sealth, who'd been so helpful in allowing them to occupy his people's land.

Sealth would become famous for giving a speech about respecting Native land rights and showing environmental responsibility. Those themes—at least the bits about land ownership and not abusing the environment—would remain prevalent for future generations of Seattleites. Unfortunately for Sealth and his people, the Native rights part often got lost. Today, historians remain skeptical Sealth actually made the speech he's credited for. One thing Sealth's accommodation tactics certainly achieved was keeping his people out of future deadly gun battles between settlers and other Native tribes not so anxious to give land away.

Any new town needs an economic engine to survive. And long before the grandparents of Bill Gates, Paul Allen, and Jeff Bezos were even gleams in their own parents' eyes, the fledgling port city of Seattle had Henry Yesler and his lumber mill to keep it going.

Yesler was from Maryland and a complicated man of vision, albeit not always the brightest when it came to business. Still, in true Seattle fashion, none of that stopped him from making a lot of money by being in the right place at the right time. He'd paddled to the fledgling city by canoe hoping to capitalize on the vast natural resources of the surrounding countryside. A lumber boom was happening, and the steam-powered sawmill built by Yesler in 1853 quickly became the main supplier of jobs for nearly every male settler and numerous Duwamish alike. These workers would skid greased timber logs down a hilly slope to the port-side mill, where they'd be cut up and dispatched to San Francisco and smaller communities across the Puget Sound to build new homes for ever-growing populations.

Seattle quickly became a full-fledged boomtown and Yesler its wealthiest inhabitant. Like the self-made millionaires of Seattle's future, he dabbled in politics and immersed himself in municipal affairs to help the city's infrastructure. Yesler is credited with building Seattle's first water-filtration system, partly in response to complaints by residents that his greased log runs down the hillside were dirtying the drinkable water supply.

But just like future Seattle millionaires and even billionaires he'd never live to meet, Yesler didn't always display gratitude to the city whose resources he'd plundered for untold wealth.

In fact, by the late 1860s, he'd squandered his vast fortune by borrowing money to make bad land investments. Yesler and his wife, Sarah, had been ahead of their time in buying up large tracts of Seattle real estate just like their modern-day contemporaries. Unfortunately, their timing was off, as the market for Seattle land turned south just as they needed access to cash. Yesler was hit by more than 200 lawsuits in King County alone. One was filed by his former friend, John McLain, who'd loaned Yesler $30,000 to build his sawmill but had only been repaid $12,000.

The country's top credit agency declared Yesler an unsafe risk. When a global economic depression hit in the early 1870s, even Arthur Denny, one of the original "New York–Before Long" settlers from two decades prior, foreclosed on one of Yesler's mortgages. So, Yesler did what any self-respecting future Seattle corporate czar would when struggling for cash flow. He turned to local politicians to help him out. Yesler schemed to stage a lottery and use some of his increasingly devalued land holdings as prizes. Effectively, he'd get money for land no one otherwise wanted to buy. Unfortunately for him, as future generations of would-be entrepreneurs and sports owners would come to discover, Seattle and surrounding communities took a very unforgiving eye to gambling of any kind. Lotteries had been specifically banned and even if they weren't, they'd almost certainly fall under a broadly defined territorial anti-gambling ordinance.

But Yesler found a loophole. Or so he thought. The territorial law only barred unauthorized lotteries. So, Yesler headed off to the territorial capital of Olympia and asked lawmakers to approve his lottery. He agreed to donate 10 percent of proceeds to public schools, including the territory's lone university.

Somehow, through the backroom give-and-take of local politics, the schools promise got replaced by a pledge to fund the building of a wagon road between Yakima and King Counties. On the last day of that year's legislative session, a bill supporting Yesler's lottery was rammed into law.

By year's end, Yesler had a lottery license and began selling tickets for a drawing to take place July 4, 1876—coinciding with the nation's centennial celebrations. At the time, Yesler announced 5,575 prizes, including land parcels worth $300,000, or $7.7 million in today's equivalent. He'd later throw in additional cash and land prizes, some of the newer real estate paid for with revenue from selling his lottery tickets.

Yesler planned to sell 60,000 tickets total for $5 apiece. If successful, he'd earn most of the $300,000 he'd initially estimated his land was worth without having to go through the struggle of actually selling any of it.

Problem was, only 50,000 people lived in the entire territory, and just 3,500 or so in King County, where Seattle was located. Also, competing lotteries of dubious repute were now popping up and angering anti-gambling locals who'd thought only one had been approved. Yesler struggled to sell tickets and wound up postponing his lottery just two weeks before the drawings were to take place.

Angry citizens pushed authorities to charge Yesler and some of the other lottery operators with criminal offenses. A judge later ruled the lottery law passed in Yesler's favor overstepped its bounds and was null and void. Yesler was convicted in September 1876 of running an illegal lottery. But, not unlike some of his modern-day business counterparts, he got off light—a $25 fine and having to pay court costs.

No one really knows what happened to the money Yesler did collect from lottery-ticket sales. But Yesler, somehow, remained a popular figure and was elected mayor in 1885 and again in 1886. Along the way, much of the land he'd been clinging to soared in value when Seattle entered a late-1870s boom period. Yesler, ever the survivor, had again become one of Seattle's wealthiest residents. And he was now holding its top seat of political power, his financial mismanagement and lottery debacle of years prior a forgotten footnote.

Yesler lived out his remaining years in good fortune, dying in December 1892 at the age of 82. Today, he is remembered through Yesler Way, a 2.2-mile east-west thoroughfare running through Seattle's Pioneer Square district. The street is the same one where Yesler's greased logs had once slid down the hillside to his sawmill for cutting. Locals back then dubbed the street "Skid Road" in reference to the logs, though other cities soon adopted a generic "Skid Row" usage of the phrase for their own streets.

In more modern times, "Skid Row" seems a fitting metaphor for parts of Yesler Way as Seattle grapples with a serious homelessness and drug-abuse crisis. The Pioneer Square area, in the shadows of the city's adjacent NFL and MLB stadiums, has become the scene of shootings, stabbings, and property crimes. Once a vibrant tourist destination, its streets are largely lifeless and foreboding after dark. Shopkeepers complain of theft and robbery, of having to clean up used syringes and human feces left by homeless residents camped out in minivans or tents pitched on sidewalks.

It appeared during the first half of the last decade that part of the area might be revitalized. An entrepreneur named Chris Hansen pitched an idea to build a new NBA arena a few streets over in the neighboring SoDo district. There was hope that an entertainment district Hansen was rumored to be planning for the broader area surrounding the venue might spill over to the bars and restaurants of Pioneer Square.

But that never happened. Today, Yesler Way remains very much covered in squalor. And beyond superficial neighborhood aesthetics, the legacy of Seattle and its early pioneers would remain embedded in the city's psyche. Seattle truly was a place where corporate visionaries aspired to be like New York, a glimmering metropolis with all the trappings of a "big-league" city. That included big-league sports teams. But just as the early pioneers soon discovered, there was only one Big Apple and Seattle wasn't it. Today, the city's more realistic inhabitants largely content themselves with appreciating what they've got. Namely, the surrounding mountains and oceanic and forested beauty. Look hard enough, and you'll find the still-gritty nature of a second-city port town that hasn't yet sacrificed all to corporate consumerism. The longer one lives in Seattle, it seems, the easier it becomes to hearken back to the good old days of record stores, family-owned coffee shops, and restaurants where portions were big and the bill at the end of the meal wasn't.

But Seattle has also always been a boomtown. Its current tech wave is just the latest one, albeit fueling growth the likes of which the city hasn't seen since Yesler built his mill. But the past is never completely behind the increasingly modernized city. Perhaps that's a result of the behavior manifested by Yesler and other early settlers. The city's current inhabitants hold a healthy distrust of perceived "outsiders" coming in to plunder their resources while getting rich in the process.

They remain skeptical of how those wealthy entrepreneurs use local politicians to further their wealth. And they are ever conscious of the boom-and-bust cycle that's dominated the city's history. In essence, they know a wealthy person might not stay that way for long. And that promises of wanting to help the greater public good won't always be kept.

Chapter 4

ARRIVAL OF TIM LEIWEKE

Say one thing about Tim Leiweke; he immediately makes an impression. Not everybody is enamored with how the 65-year-old global arena czar can walk into a room, roll up his sleeves, and command attention for the next 30 minutes, hour, or even three hours. And I've seen him do all, whether at a one-on-one breakfast at the Four Seasons in downtown Seattle, at a newspaper editorial board meeting, or in his glass-enclosed boardroom at the Los Angeles headquarters of his Oak View Group arena management company.

No, Leiweke isn't for everyone. Right off the bat, I sensed he might not go over well with some of Seattle's more, shall we say, reserved folks used to taking their time. Leiweke treats time the way he would a loosened seat within one of his arenas—it's an enemy. Not used to waiting on things, he blew into Seattle like one of the tornados from his native Missouri. In our Four Seasons breakfast a few years back (omelets and coffee, if you're interested), he immediately asked whether I'd started watching the *Ozark* television drama on Netflix. I hadn't yet and was about to make some offhanded crack about dueling banjos when

Leiweke told me of how his stepmother, Pat Fontaine, an NBC television news pioneer, had moved with his dad, Jack, to a quaint, secluded spot in the Missouri Ozarks town of Lesterville. He had fond memories of spending time there with both.

It was an interesting foray into the Leiweke family story. It wasn't a tale of wealth and privilege, regardless of how Tim Leiweke's windowed office now commands a sprawling view of surrounding Westwood and downtown Los Angeles in the distance. Moreover, it was an early life that came to be dominated by sadness and responsibility. He'd been raised in modest surroundings, the fourth of six children to his insurance broker dad and homemaker mother, Helen, in the St. Louis suburb of Richmond Heights. And when Leiweke's mother was diagnosed with cervical cancer, health care coverage in the early 1960s wasn't yet picking up the cost of her chemotherapy as she battled the illness off and on for eight years. Leiweke watched his father struggle to pay medical costs. His mother died at their home in November 1968 at age 46.

A relative had taken Leiweke, then only 11; his younger brother, Tod, 8; and their siblings to a St. Louis Cardinals football game against the Pittsburgh Steelers at Busch Stadium while his father spent that afternoon saying his final goodbyes to their mother. It was a cold, blustery day with a sub-freezing wind chill, and Leiweke remembered a stadium usher summoning them with an urgent, second-half telephone message and how they were driven home and delivered the news. They buried their mother two days later.

Tim soon after began working at a bakery and deli to help his grieving father pay the family's staggering bills. "He definitely went through a lot of challenges," Leiweke said. "A widower with six kids."

Meeting Fontaine three years later in 1971 had given his father a reason to be happy again. She'd been a local celebrity in St. Louis doing weather and news at KMOX-TV. Her big break came in 1962 when she was hired for an 18-month news and features stint at NBC's *Today* show, appearing on camera with hosts Hugh Downs and Jack Lescoulie. Her interview guests included John F. Kennedy and his brother, Robert, along with playwright Tennessee Williams.

She eventually left the network to return to KMOX and spend more time with her children from her first marriage in Missouri. Her on-air replacement at *Today*? Barbara Walters.

Fontaine left KMOX after meeting Leiweke's dad, though she continued to do public relations, commercials, and radio talk show work. Lewieke was 14 when Fontaine became their stepmom and he regarded her as their second mother. Alas, his father and Fontaine were together only six years when she, too, was diagnosed with cancer in summer 1977. She died only two months later at age 53. Leiweke told me a bit of his father died with her. That he was never the same the rest of his remaining years.

So, Lewieke knows better than to wait until tomorrow to do what he can get done right away. Having spoken with him countless times in person and on the phone since that Four Seasons breakfast, including at his company's L.A. workspace, that much is obvious. He'd forsaken college for the insurance industry to keep paying his family's bills. From there, he'd broken into professional sports running a pair of indoor soccer teams in St. Louis and Kansas City. And he'd never paused for breath: quickly blazing a trail through the executive ranks of the NBA's Minnesota Timberwolves and Denver Nuggets, he forged a relationship with commissioner David Stern that served him well in ensuing years as the first CEO of the Anschutz Entertainment Group (AEG).

Leiweke and the company's mercurial billionaire owner, Philip Anschutz, blazed trails previously unseen. They built and managed venues for seemingly half the teams in the NBA and NHL. Later, working closely with NBA deputy commissioner Adam Silver, Leiweke and AEG built new arenas in Shanghai and Beijing. It was Leiweke's vision and execution that led to the L.A. Live entertainment district being created around Staples

Center in Los Angeles. His phone boasted a contact list that could get any league commissioner on speed dial within minutes.

But the energy and impatience that had served Leiweke so well in his ventures eventually led to a falling out with Anschutz over an aborted plan to build "Farmers Field"—a stadium that could lure an NFL team back to Los Angeles. Leiweke resigned from AEG in 2012 and then, stymied by a non-compete clause, parked his career in Toronto for three years as president of Maple Leaf Sports and Entertainment. While overseeing that parent company to the Toronto Maple Leafs, Toronto Raptors, and Toronto FC soccer team, he began plotting his next venture: a company to rival what AEG was doing.

By early 2016, Leiweke's new Oak View Group (OVG), co-founded alongside music mogul Irving Azoff, was taking off. It already had marketing deals with 22 NBA and NHL teams, some even before Leiweke had officially departed the Maple Leafs and Raptors. Leiweke leased a floor of prime commercial office space in a 22-story complex in Westwood. Soon after, he snagged an additional 20,000 feet on the 21st floor. Azoff kept some offices one floor below, but the legendary manager of the Eagles would pop up regularly to meet in person with his partner.

Another fixture at the offices was Leiweke's daughter, Francesca Bodie, whom he was clearly grooming as his successor. Leiweke had made her work lower-level office jobs at AEG in high school, as he'd once done. But she'd also been sent to Stanford University, a college dream Leiweke had been denied in the name of working to support his grieving family.

The Leiweke family had always been a close-knit clan, forced to rely on one another through childhood and teenage circumstances beyond their control. And that wasn't changing, with Leiweke's daughter now entrusted to more of the sports business decisions surrounding her father's fledgling company.

But that company still had one glaring hole. It had yet to build an arena. And Leiweke knew where he wanted the flagship venue to go.

There were only a handful of top-20 markets in the nation lacking a relatively new venue, even fewer such cities without an NBA or NHL team. Leiweke narrowed it down to Seattle; Long Island, New York; Austin, Texas; and San Diego. He'd eventually build in all but San Diego, with Seattle being OVG's first venture.

The decision to start with Seattle was helped by Leiweke's brother, Tod, having gone there in 2003 to serve as president of the NFL Seahawks. And Leiweke had plenty of experience with the market as well, having directly influenced two of the biggest moments in the city's sports history.

The first had been securing a Major League Soccer team for the city. Leiweke was pals with Hollywood producer Joe Roth, a former college soccer player at Hoefstra and Bowling Green who wanted to own an MLS franchise. Leiweke was chairman of the MLS board of governors at the time, representing the Los Angeles Galaxy on behalf of AEG.

Leiweke arranged for a meeting at the Palm Steakhouse in L.A. between himself, Roth, and Dan Beckerman, AEG's chief financial officer. Beckerman brought along a spreadsheet to show Roth the financials of owning a team. Roth was still interested, so Leiweke had him meet MLS commissioner Don Garber at a Galaxy game.

It was recommended Roth look at franchises in the Pacific Northwest. Leiweke knew that Seattle Sounders owner Adrian Hanauer was seeking MLS entry for his second-tier United Soccer League team and had spoken to his brother about a partnership. So, Leiweke flew up to Seattle with Roth and they met Tod for dinner at SkyCity restaurant atop the city's iconic Space Needle.

There, Leiweke's brother made an impassioned speech to Roth about how soccer would thrive and fill a void about to be created by the departure of the NBA Sonics for Oklahoma City. Roth bought in. He met Hanauer soon after and agreed to take a controlling stake in the Sounders. Hanauer's stake was a few percentage points lower. Tod Leiweke assumed the role as club president to go with his identical Seahawks title.

It was assumed MLS wanted a high-profile majority owner for its next expansion franchise and Roth certainly fit the bill, more so than Hanauer. MLS agreed, awarding the team in 2008 to begin play in 2009.

The Sounders in their initial years set MLS attendance records. And by 2014, the business arrangement with the Seahawks ceased as the Sounders gained confidence to go off on their own. Soon, Hanauer bought a small stake from Roth and became majority owner of the team.

As of mid-2022, the Sounders have won a CONCACAF Champions League trophy and two MLS Cup championships, have been to two additional league finals, and have not missed the playoffs.

The other Seattle sport in which Tim Leiweke's influence played a transformational role also involved his brother. Late in Tod Leiweke's stint running the Seahawks, it was decided that Jim Mora was not the ideal successor coach to icon Mike Holmgren. Mora had yet to be officially fired, but a search for his replacement quietly got underway. From the outset, Tod wondered whether Pete Carroll, having built a powerhouse University of Southern California football program, would be interested in taking another shot at coaching in the NFL. Tim Leiweke had known Carroll for most of his adult life, both having rubbed elbows throughout the Los Angeles sports scene and morphing into friends. So, he tracked Carroll down on vacation in Hawaii and tried to gauge his interest.

"I said, 'Are you walking on the beach?'" Tim recalled of their phone conversation.

Carroll replied, "Yeah."

"And I said, 'Good,'" Tim said. "'Because with what I'm about to tell you, you're going to want to sit down.'"

Carroll surprised him by not immediately rejecting the idea. From there, the conversation evolved, with Tim telling Carroll his brother would allow him to coach his way and do little to interfere with running the team.

But they weren't yet close to finalizing anything. And Carroll was worried about negatively impacting his USC relationships should word get out of his talking to the Seahawks. So, they decided to have Tod fly down to Los Angeles and conduct all meetings in the backyard of Tim's sprawling Mediterranean-style home in Brentwood. The back patio overlooked a sizeable in-ground pool and offered additional privacy from considerable plants and vegetation throughout the near-half-acre lot.

The only problem? The gardeners.

Tod flew in with Bert Kolde, the top confidant of Seahawks owner Paul Allen. The team's legal counsel, Lance Lopes, was also there. Tim's wife, Bernadette, arranged a dinner party for everyone with Carroll and his immediate entourage the guests of honor.

"We started in the backyard and I set them up back there because it was very private," Tim Leiweke said. "But unfortunately, my gardeners were there. And they only spoke Spanish, but one of them recognized Pete and I know it because I heard him saying his name. And I could tell Pete's like, 'Goddammit,' but I told him, 'Pete, he's fine. I don't think he's running out to the *L.A. Times*; I'll talk to him.'

"But we were under such high alert to not create any kind of speculation. And here I'd gone to great lengths to hide everything in my backyard—they couldn't go out to dinner, so we served dinner at my house. And it's just funny that the gardeners come walking through and they go, 'Ah, there's Pete Carroll!'"

Fortunately, the gardeners kept quiet. Mora was fired and Carroll left the Trojans three days later to join the Seahawks. Four years later, they captured their first Super Bowl over the Denver Broncos with Carroll at the helm.

So, yeah, Leiweke knew a thing or two about Seattle sports. Even before the city's sports fans knew who he was and what he'd contributed to the handful of pro championships in Seattle's name.

Few knew anything about Leiweke when, in October 2016, he declared his interest in rebuilding the city's crumbling KeyArena. Quite a few expressed open derision. Common wisdom locally had it that KeyArena, opened back in 1962 when the city had hosted the World's Fair, was unfixable. That major pro teams would laugh at the notion anyone could get the building up to modern-day standards.

But Leiweke and his brothers had never much cared for conventional wisdom. Perhaps it was their childhoods spent dealing with loss. The urge to keep moving forward rather than looking back. Whatever the reason, Leiweke had learned to do his own thing. And when he met with resistance, well, he just kept plowing straight ahead.

And in Seattle, he was about to meet plenty of resistance.

Chapter 5

FEEDING TIME

There's an old expression about never having too much of a good thing. And when it comes to Seattle and its sports franchises, the owners of said teams have historically had it very good when it comes to getting others to pay for the stadiums and arenas they play in.

No matter how independently wealthy, those owners knew they had friends at the city, county, and state levels who could green-light taxpayer dollars for their venues. By the late 1990s, the Seattle Mariners had persuaded the local governments to shell out $372 million in tax subsidies on a $517 million stadium to prevent the team from relocating to Florida, California, or wherever else it was threatening to move in any given month. That the team had been purchased in 1992 by Japanese billionaire Hiroshi Yamauchi was of little consequence. Yamauchi had made his fortune as the patriarch of the Nintendo video game empire. And the company that bred Donkey Kong, Super Mario, and Pokémon having its North American offices based in the Seattle suburb of Redmond, Washington, proved to be a big deal. The company included in its fold a powerhouse corporate lawyer named Howard Lincoln, who worked his way up to become company chairman. For the prior decade, Seattle-area business leaders had watched the Mariners be run into the ground, first by owner George Argyros and later Jeff Smulyan. By late 1991, Smulyan was threatening to move the team to St. Petersburg, Florida, unless somebody local stepped up to take the team off his hands.

Enter said business leaders, who included Microsoft executive Chris Larson, wireless communications maven John McCaw, and a host of others who would form the team's ownership group. Problem is, nobody had the money or will to become top dog. Bill Gates had turned the group down and Seattle itself back then only had so many billionaires ready to risk money on a team as bad as the Mariners.

Enter a longtime state senator and power broker named Slade Gorton, an avid baseball fan who'd never met a problem he couldn't find deep pockets to solve.

Through his previous dealings in the subject of IP theft and counterfeit goods, he'd been helped by companies such as Nintendo. So, Gorton phoned up old contact Lincoln, the company's chief legal counsel, and asked about Nintendo getting involved.

Not long after, Gorton was contacted by billionaire Yamauchi's son-in-law, who advised him that his wife's dad felt the Seattle region had greatly benefited his company. As a token of his appreciation, Yamauchi offered the local baseball owners $100 million to buy the team. It was later decided that Yamauchi would contribute $75 million and attain a 60 percent ownership stake while the local stakeholders would put in $50 million. That would give the group $100 million to buy the team from Smulyan and $25 million in working capital to pay for players, coaches, and all other things any good—or in this case, terrible—baseball team needs to survive.

A few hurdles remained; namely, Yamauchi was Japanese and America even in the 1990s still had hang-ups about that former World War II adversary trying to take over anything connected to Mom and apple pie. After months of back-and-forth between Gorton and the administration headed by President George H.W. Bush, the feds finally approved the sale under the condition Yamauchi retain only 49 percent voting rights on any team matters.

In other words, they would take his money but not his influence. And as such, Yamauchi never felt the need to fly to Seattle to watch his team play. Even when the Mariners opened the 2012 regular season in Tokyo against the Oakland Athletics, Yamauchi, by then 84 and in failing health, did not attend. He died in September of the following year.

By all accounts, Yamauchi was happy to view his majority ownership stake as a gift to the city of Seattle and little more. This rather unusual act of generosity would be mentioned time and again by the Mariners' minority ownership group, which actually went to games and had a controlling say in team affairs. Namely, the Yamauchi generosity bit would be mentioned whenever somebody asked why a baseball team owned by a man worth billions needed the public to subsidize its operations.

And it only took a few years after Yamauchi bought the team in 1992 for this to become an issue. By 1995, the Mariners and their new owners were running negative balance sheets at the team's Kingdome home. The Kingdome had opened in 1976 at a cost of $67 million, paid for by King County voters approving a bond measure to cover construction costs. Those costs wouldn't be paid off for nearly 40 years, when the final in a series of hotel and motel tax payments was made in 2015, long after the stadium itself had been leveled by explosives in a planned demolition.

The point being, as with most sports venues nearing their 20-year mark, the Mariners by 1995 felt the Kingdome no longer served their needs. Thus began the campaign for a new ballpark again paid for by taxpayers. That public push received a huge boost off the bat of one Edgar Martínez during a decisive Game 5 of the 1995 American League Division Series against the defending World Series champion New York Yankees.

With two on, one out, and the Mariners down a run against pitcher Jack McDowell, Martínez lined a ball down the left field line. The tying run scored easily and one Ken Griffey Jr., who, like Martínez, would one day be bound for the Baseball Hall of Fame, didn't stop as he rounded third base.

Somehow, the throw in from left field took forever and Griffey slid home safely, setting off a wild celebration by the 850,000 fans who today claim to have been in attendance. "The Double," as it's come to be known in Seattle lore, is typically No. 1 on most lists as the greatest sports moment in the city's history. It certainly became the defining moment in Mariners history. Not because it led to a championship; the Mariners were quickly dispatched by Cleveland in the ensuing playoff round and today remain the only current MLB club to have never qualified for a World Series. No, "The Double" became the greatest thing the Mariners ever experienced on or off the field namely because it helped push the team's quest for a public-financed stadium over the top.

A few weeks before "The Double," a ballot initiative seeking a sales tax increase of 0.1 percent had been narrowly rejected by King County voters. But with the celebratory roar generated by Martínez's double still ringing in their ears, the Washington State Legislature did an end-run around voter wishes and approved an alternative means of funding a new ballpark.

A food and beverage tax was instituted in King County restaurants and bars, along with a car rental surcharge in King County and a stadium admissions tax. Sales of special stadium license plates would be used as a funding mechanism. In addition, the baseball team was given a credit against the state sales tax.

Nine days later, the King County Council approved the funding package.

Lawsuits quickly followed but were dismissed by the courts. The Mariners had their public-financed ballpark and Safeco Field, today T-Mobile Park, opened July 15, 1999.

Meanwhile, just across the way at the old Kingdome, the NFL Seahawks couldn't help but notice all the public largesse being thrown the Mariners' way. Just like the Mariners, the Seahawks weren't setting any on-field records as a franchise and by the mid-1990s were sick and tired of their domed stadium as well.

Owner Ken Behring, taking a page out of the Mariners' playbook—his own team's plays thoroughly dismantled by opposing defenses at the time—threatened to relocate elsewhere unless taxpayers built him a stadium. On February 2, 1996, with the Mariners already counting up their tax subsidy and planning a new ballpark, Behring had moving vans start hauling equipment out of the Seahawks' training facility in the Seattle suburb of Kirkland. His plan? Relocate the team to Anaheim, California, from which the Rams had just bolted to St. Louis the prior year. The Seahawks players actually began off-season workouts at the old Rams' training facility while the front office and coaches did their business out of a Marriott Residence Inn in the Seattle suburb of Bellevue.

Amid the confusion, the NFL finally woke up and threatened to fine Behring $500,000 a day unless he stopped the silliness and reopened his Seattle-area operations. That he did, but the clock was ticking.

Behring, who'd bought the team in 1988, had initially claimed he wanted to move after seven years of middling stewardship because he didn't feel the Kingdome had been properly earthquake proofed. It seemed a ridiculous claim and his own son, David, the team's president, later told reporters his father didn't feel there was any chance at a new or properly remodeled stadium forthcoming.

There could have been one, of course, had Behring actually offered to pay for one himself. But this was Seattle, after all; the Mariners had just cleaned up, and Behring wanted his cut.

Things drifted on through 1996 without resolution and Behring made clear he wanted to sell. Once again, though, as the Mariners had discovered, there weren't a whole lot of billionaires in Seattle interested enough in sports to leap in to save the day.

Enter one Pete von Reichbauer, a longstanding King County politician with connections on all sides of the political spectrum. Behring had reached out to Von Reichbauer to find him a potential purchaser for the team. Von

Reichbauer searched far and wide throughout the Pacific Northwest, on both sides of the Canada–U.S. border, but came up empty.

Then, he arranged a meeting at the city's posh Rainier Club with Bert Kolde, a longtime friend and trusted confidant of Seattle billionaire Paul Allen. Also at the meeting were Bob Whitsitt, resident of the NBA's Portland Trail Blazers—which Allen already owned—and the billionaire's personal attorney, Allen Israel.

Von Reichbauer was acting as deal broker on Behring's behalf. He told the group Behring would only sell to a billionaire such as Allen who could pay for the team in one shot, without bank financing or minority investors to delay the deal. Also, he assured the group Behring wasn't trying to leverage a better deal from politicians in Anaheim to build him a stadium.

After some back and forth, Allen agreed in April 1996 to buy the team, but under one condition—taxpayers would have to pony up for part of the new stadium. This would not be an easy sell.

It didn't help that much of the public still resented how the Mariners had gotten tax money from the state legislature just weeks after voters had rejected giving the team any subsidies.

But politicians got a statewide funding proposal on the ballot for June 1997. Referendum 48 was all-or-nothing this time, as a deal for Allen to buy the team was close to expiring unless a funding mechanism for a new 72,000-seat stadium was approved.

It looked initially as if this second vote would end in defeat as well once early returns from eastern parts of the state went decisively against the measure. But then, slowly, as the ballots closer to Seattle were counted, the tide began turning. Finally, once all the votes from within the city itself were counted, the proposal to subsidize Allen's stadium project had passed with a slim 51 percent approval.

For the second time in less than two years, a billionaire sports owner had been given money to build a stadium despite a huge portion of the population opposing the idea. The new Seahawks deal saw taxpayers contribute

$300 million toward the new $430 million Qwest Field & Event Center, while Allen bought the team for $200 million and used $100 million of his own funds on the venue.

Today, what's known as Lumen Field houses a football team that went on to play in three Super Bowls under Allen until his death from non-Hodgkin's lymphoma in 2019. The Seahawks won one of those Super Bowls in January 2014. Another Lumen Field tenant, the Sounders, in May 2022 became the first MLS squad to win a CONCACAF Champions League title in front of a record 68,741 fans at the venue, while they also captured one of their two MLS Cup championships at Allen's stadium in 2019.

There are many in Seattle who argue that the sports franchises playing in both T-Mobile Park and Lumen Field have contributed greatly to the city's fabric and sense of community pride. To them, Yamauchi and Allen were "saviors" of the city's teams, stepping up to take charge when nobody else was willing.

But still others will and have argued that subsidizing sports venues for billionaires is not the business that local governments should be indulging in.

Less than a decade after Allen and the Seahawks got their stadium, the NBA SuperSonics and owner Howard Schultz would go looking for a public handout of their own to replace or rebuild their stagnating KeyArena home. But by then, citizen opposition to such corporate largesse had already taken root.

It wouldn't end well for Schultz. Nor the ill-fated Sonics. And the repercussions of Schultz's dual arena and franchise failure would reverberate for years. They'd be a major obstacle Tim Leiweke and his Oak View Group would have to overcome in pledging to build a new arena and land the city's first NHL franchise. They'd need to convince local politicians and a skeptical citizenry that they weren't trying to pick anybody's pocket. That this time, despite all those others before, things would be different.

Chapter 6

A VICTORY LAP CUT SHORT

There was nothing pretty going on weather-wise in Glendale, Arizona, the morning of February 1, 2015. And for Seattle Seahawks fans, it would only go downhill from there. The abnormally cool temperatures barely topped 50 degrees before noon and the skies that had dumped rain—yes, rain, in the desert—the previous day still carried an ominous, slowly dissipating fog. In other words, it felt more like Seattle than Arizona.

That had previously only been true in a metaphorical sense. Glendale is located just outside Phoenix. And the region's greater Maricopa County had long ago become a de facto suburb of Seattle, given all the second homes owned there by Washington state retirees and technology executives. So, it wasn't a surprise that thousands of Seahawks fans were in town to see the team play the New England Patriots in Super Bowl XLIX.

Actually, while in Arizona for the game, very few of those fans entered Glendale itself until right before kickoff. Nobody really goes to Glendale except for sports and entertainment flybys, to shop in its outlet malls or gamble in its casino. This point had come up repeatedly two years prior when the NHL Coyotes were threatening to leave the municipally owned

Jobing.com Arena to relocate to Seattle unless Glendale City Council gifted them one of the most one-sided lease deals in the history of professional sport.

The council acquiesced and promptly spent the next two years struggling to pay for police, firefighters, and other basic services. The arena lease simply sucked too much money out of the city's limited coffers. Glendale mayor Jerry Weiers was already making noise about getting tough on sports subsidies while that lease fight was ongoing. Handed the setback of actually having to keep the Coyotes, he'd been in no mood to negotiate when the NFL began telling him to strongarm local hotels into blocking room nights by the thousands to accommodate league executives and other VIPs for Super Bowl events.

Weiers' defiant stance gave the NFL all the excuse needed to move every major Super Bowl event to neighboring Phoenix, Tempe, and Scottsdale, leaving Glendale stuck paying for security and policing of the game itself with no spinoff events to recover revenue from. So, Glendale was not Seattle's karmic friend that February morning. And those Seahawks fans making the 40-minute drive to the game through traffic from their Scottsdale luxury vacation homes would soon experience the ultimate karmic devastation over four quarters of championship football.

Actually, the very worst day possible was likely had by the Seahawks fans who never even made it to the game. Ticket brokers, as per usual operating procedures, had pre-sold thousands of seats to the contest before having the actual tickets in hand. They'd planned to fly down the week of the game, buy the seats they needed on the secondary market or from their usual connections—as prices tended to drop once the game drew closer—and fill their orders at a tidy profit. That had been the way the Super Bowl ticket game had been played for years. The big problem this time was that a supply-chain disruption caused mainly by greed and partly by new NFL crackdowns would leave brokers still not having any tickets to fill their orders only hours before scheduled kickoff.

The usual ticket suppliers to brokers, consisting of current and former players, sponsors, league officials, and other ticket companies, had broken their handshake agreements to provide Super Bowl seats. In some cases, the shortage was the result of the NFL changing its Super Bowl ticket policy at the last minute and preventing players and alumni from picking up their allotted tickets until hours before gametime. One of the worst-kept secrets in the NFL is that players and former players receiving this ticket allotment often have no intention of ever going to the big game or partaking in Super Bowl week activities. They merely pick up their ticket allotment from the league at face-value prices, sell them to brokers for an inflated amount, and use the proceeds to supplement their meager retirement savings or pay medical bills to service broken-down bodies from their playing days.

The NFL was aware of this. The league by then was still learning how to best profit off resale of its own seats through NFL Ticket Exchange or taking a percentage of sales from other online platforms. In short, the NFL stood to benefit financially from Super Bowl prices on the secondary market being inflated by a ticket shortage.

And the resulting shortage of Super Bowl tickets on the "street" or open market in Glendale did indeed cause a spike in asking prices. Those holding tickets they'd promised to sell to brokers for $2,000 suddenly found they could unload theirs for five times that amount. And they made the capitalistic decision one might expect, leaving their broker pals out in the unseasonable desert cold.

Thus, Seahawks fans arriving in Arizona a few days before the Super Bowl expecting to pick up seats purchased online from StubHub, Vivid Seats, SeatGeek, or much smaller ticket brokers were getting turned away at prearranged meeting spots. It wasn't only Seahawks fans getting denied; a major New England brokerage firm had pre-sold seats to the well-traveling Patriots crowd and also had to admit they didn't actually possess those tickets.

In hindsight, the perfect storm of two fan bases known to travel with teams, plus the easy access to Arizona by Seattle fans who already owned homes there or had friends who did, probably would have created record street demand and prices anyway. But the additional circumstances surrounding broker "short selling" and a disrupted ticket supply wound up artificially driving prices toward the $15,000 range for a single seat anywhere in the stadium on game day.

Some panicked brokers skipped town altogether, unwilling to eat the astronomical costs of buying new seats at the last minute to fill pre-booked orders. They also feared being on the hook for the inflated flight and hotel room prices their clients had also paid to be able to attend a game they now wouldn't have tickets to.

Lawsuits would fly, state attorneys general would get involved, and some ticket brokers were permanently put out of business. It would take months for the biggest ticket "short-selling" scandal in the history of online brokerages to resolve itself. In the interim, frustrated, furious, and, in many cases, sobbing fans were stuck watching the game in their overpriced hotel rooms. And with Seahawks fans seemingly outnumbering Patriots supporters by a 3-to-1 margin both on the streets throughout the week and inside the stadium itself, it would be Seattle's faithful bearing the brunt of the scarring Super Bowl ticket fiasco.

As for Seahawks fans who didn't get burned on tickets, their suffering was only about to begin. A back-and-forth game unfolded. The Seahawks appeared to take second-half control, only to see quarterback Tom Brady put the Patriots back on top 28–24 with just five minutes to go. Brady had spent the entire week being hammered by the nation's media over his role in the "Deflategate" cheating scandal in which the Patriots were accused of deliberately keeping footballs underinflated and using them during offensive drives to give Brady a better throwing grip.

But now, Brady would get the last laugh. Or would he? The Seahawks and quarterback Russell Wilson began a late-game drive that seemed destined to stall. Then, with 1:06 to go, former Seattle homegrown football product and University of Washington standout Jermaine Kearse made a juggling 33-yard catch at the Patriots' 5-yard line. A catch that NBC analyst Cris Collinsworth described as "unbelievable" seemed destined to go down as one of the greatest Super Bowl moments.

The ball was spotted for a first-and-goal at the 5 and a Seahawks title repeat seemed guaranteed. After all, the Seahawks had Marshawn Lynch in the backfield. Lynch had led the Seahawks to their first and only title a year prior and the entire stadium knew he was capable of a five-yard run even with half the defense on his back.

On the very first play after the catch, he rambled for four yards to the 1 with just 58 seconds to go. By now, Seahawks fans were high fiving in the stands, discussing how best to score the go-ahead touchdown while leaving Brady as little time as possible to attempt a fruitless Hail Mary pass or two.

Lost in the discussion was the fact the Seahawks had already wasted a couple timeouts earlier on. This would become a running theme for head coach Pete Carroll and his offense in ensuing seasons, but on this Super Bowl night it proved lethal. Carroll was known as a deep thinker, but in this case, he likely overthought his plight. His Seahawks had a lone timeout remaining and the game clock was ticking down below a half-minute once the next snap occurred on a second-and-goal. Everyone assumed Lynch would get the ball again, overpower the four defenders who hit him, and roll into the end zone. But the Patriots had just subbed in their bigger goal-line defenders, and Carroll worried that if Lynch was stopped, he'd be forced to use his final timeout. And then, the Patriots would know he'd have to throw on third down, as the clock might expire if an ensuing Lynch run failed to get in.

So, Carroll made the most controversial call of his coaching career and threw the ball on second down instead of giving it to Lynch. Malcom Butler read the quick slant pass all the way, jumped the route, and intercepted the ball with 20 seconds to go.

A dynasty in the making was done before ever getting started. As I walked the dreary postgame tunnel to the Seahawks locker room, billionaire owner Paul Allen was being driven away on a golf cart. Allen's health had been deteriorating through a series of cancer treatments, but his face looked ashen and stunned into disbelief. And sad at the same time. It would be the final championship he'd live to see his team play for. Whether Allen knew it then is something only he could speak to; we'll never know.

But for Seattle sports fans, it marked the end of an all-too-brief era of being on top. Generations of loyal fans throughout the Puget Sound had been raised to believe they could not have good things. And now, after a brief flirtation with championship success at the major pro level, it had been snatched away. A year earlier, their team had crushed Denver for the title in the Meadowlands. The hit song "Can't Hold Us" by Seattle native Macklemore had ruled the pop charts and become the unofficial anthem of that championship march.

Now, the ceiling had caved in. Later that summer, the woebegone Mariners baseball team, after teasing for a second wild-card playoff spot through the final day of the 2014 campaign, crashed and burned through a disastrous 2015 in which their general manager was fired.

The Seattle Sounders, after winning their only Supporters Shield in 2014 for the best regular season record in Major League Soccer, would get bounced from the opening round of the 2015 MLS playoffs.

And in those early days of 2015, with an arena process deadlocked and nowhere close to being resolved, the prospect of a revived NBA Sonics team seemed impossible. Never mind an NHL squad. At that point, hockey was still being treated as an afterthought to the whole arena process.

Entering that dreary Super Bowl day in Arizona, breaking through the ceiling alongside Macklemore was on every Seattle sports fan's mind. The sky was the limit. This was a new sporting era for a city bashed many a time. But limping out of Glendale that evening and stumbling through the numbed aftermath in the months that followed, the floor was charging up on a wounded city and sports fans once again feeling they couldn't have good things.

Chapter 7

SEATTLE SYMBOLIZED BY A TROLL

Orlando has Walt Disney World. St. Louis boasts the Gateway Arch. San Francisco has a fantastic bridge suspended by cables and Washington, D.C., its obelisk monument. And within this universe of competing man-made American tourist attractions, Seattle punches its way into the field—quite literally—with a troll residing under a bridge.

That's correct. Sure, the city also has its Space Needle and Pike Place Market. But scroll down any top-10 compilation of touristy things to see not involving mountains, water, and other natural wonders, and the list is pretty short before one stumbles across the Fremont Troll. The 18-foot-tall, 13,000-pound behemoth was sculpted from concrete and is situated in the bohemian Fremont district beneath the north end of the George Washington Memorial Bridge, known locally as the Aurora Bridge.

Of Seattle's many neighborhoods, few are more artsy and eclectic than Fremont. Or, as longstanding residents have been known to suggest, it used to be that way before the outsiders came in and ruined everything.

But go for a stroll up NW 36th Street, past the cafes, the tattoo parlor, the "Weird and Whimsy" gift shop, and the shirtless guitar player smoking a joint, keep left at the giant statue of Vladimir Lenin, and—wait, um, what was that? Yes, that's correct. As if a giant man-made troll residing under a bridge weren't bizarre enough, the Fremont neighborhood also boasts its own Lenin statue. There aren't too many of those on this side of the planet—not north of Cuba anyway. After all, Senator Joseph McCarthy cursed his last "red" 65 years ago. True communism and Lenin, its best-known founding father, never quite went mainstream in America.

There are fewer than a half dozen Lenin sculptures or monuments believed to exist in the United States. One of them is on top of an East Village apartment building in New York, another in a space museum in Hutchison, Kansas—the Soviet portion, naturally. And there's one hidden in a Willimantic, Connecticut, scrap yard to keep red-blooded American patriots from laying waste to it.

But Seattle is the only place in this country with a full-on, 16-foot-tall, 7-ton bronzed statue of Vladimir Ilyich Lenin standing smack dab in the middle of a bustling neighborhood intersection. A hero to some, but to others a mass villain whose revolutionary actions led to millions of deaths, Lenin's statue somehow lives on more than a quarter century after its installation.

The statue was created in Slovakia by artist Emil Venkov in 1988 at the behest of the Soviet bloc nation's Communist regime. Then, after the regime's collapse, an adventurous Seattle traveling entrepreneur named Lewis Carpenter found it in a Slovakian town dump in 1993 and paid $40,000 to rescue it from melting demise and have it shipped home. Carpenter had hoped to install the statue in front of a Slovakian restaurant he'd toyed with starting but was killed a year later in a car accident before it could be reassembled. Eventually, the statue was put together, acquired in trust by the Fremont Chamber of Commerce, and erected in 1995 on private property at the intersection where it continues to loom over its passing subjects. It was put up for sale, but no one has offered to buy it. So, Carpenter's family remains the owner.

The statue isn't of some passive, contemplative Lenin as is often seen in artistic depictions worldwide. This one has Lenin in a more aggressive posture. Or maybe he's caught between personas and just being *passive aggressive*, which would befit the town he now calls home. Seattle isn't always known as the friendliest place, despite the customary pleasantries used to greet newcomers to the city. Those newbies often complain about never being smiled at again, especially if they insist on trying to pin down those open-ended dinner invitations from their initial greeters before at least 52, 104, or even 520 weekends have elapsed.

In a pique of passive aggression, somebody in the dead of night snuck over and slapped red paint onto Lenin's bronzed open hand, seemingly meant to suggest Lenin has blood on his hands. For now, he certainly does have dried paint on one of them. And some freshly added blue and yellow colors on his overcoat, pants, and shoes, meant to symbolize the Ukrainian flag and modern Russia's invasion of its neighbor. But that and the rest of Lenin's depiction live on in Fremont namely because pent-up local feelings of anger toward the statue haven't morphed into the full-on aggression seen in the toppling and destruction of such controversial items elsewhere. And even before the invasion of Ukraine, controversies recently flared over whether Fremont truly needs an ode to early 20th century Russian bloodshed drawing in even more tourists and newcomers bound to further erode the neighborhood's bohemian side. Still, nobody yet sees the need to hide Seattle's version of Lenin in a scrapyard the way they do in Connecticut.

Lenin enduring in the middle of a Seattle intersection while nationwide debates rage on about Confederate monuments from the Civil War sure does make it seem as if Fremont—and Seattle, by extension—is trolling the rest of the country. Something is certainly trolling somebody. And a prime suspect in that Fremont neighborhood is probably what you'll find a couple of hundred feet up a tree-lined side street once staying left and heading past where Lenin continues to live on long after his Soviet Union collapsed.

The first thing you notice walking up the hill from the Lenin statue toward the Fremont Troll is just how many people come there at all hours of the day to gawk at what's beneath the bridge. Parked vehicles line both sides of the street. And tourists, selfie sticks in hand, take turns posing for photos with the troll as their backdrop. There are no ticket booths or crowd cordons here. This all takes place under an active bridge. Those venturing by car must remain on the lookout not only for scarce parking, but also any wayward pedestrians paying too much attention to the giant troll as they dart in and out of oncoming traffic.

And it's easy to understand their distracted nature. The troll isn't just sitting there as a head bust. It also has a pair of oversized, clawing hands, one of which has supposedly plucked a car off the above bridge. The swiped vehicle is a concrete-sculpted Volkswagen Beetle and, naturally, sports a California license plate.

Local artists Steve Badaness, Will Martin, Donna Walter, and Ross Whitehead designed the troll as part of a local art competition in 1990 to revive the trash- and drug-infested underside of the bridge. They drew inspiration from Norwegian folklore, which apparently involves plenty of trolls living under bridges.

Norwegian and broader Scandinavian and Nordic influence is seen throughout Seattle. The Nordic Museum even opened a few miles west of the troll in neighboring Ballard in 2018. Immigrants from Norway, Denmark, Sweden, Iceland, and Finland moved to the region in vast numbers in the late 1800s, drawn by saltwater fjords, forests, agriculture, and mountains that reminded them of home.

By the early 20th century, Scandinavians made up 30 percent of Washington state's population and had become its largest ethnic group. But fishing, music, dancing, and crafts aren't all they brought with them.

They also brought trolls. And to hear some people tell it, not all those trolls reside under a bridge.

Critics of modern Seattle like to speculate that Scandinavian roots are behind the inward-looking, unfriendly vibe that newcomers to the city often sense from locals. Particularly, it's the Norwegians who are most blamed. But generally, a Nordic trend toward reserve, reticence, and guardedness is touted alongside Seattle's gloomy weather and an abundance of more intro-verted technology workers as a reason for the city's social awkwardness.

Making lasting friendships is said to be next to impossible; the passive aggressive, insular prevailing behavior of locals shunning expansion of friendship circles beyond those they'd grown up around. Dating within these constrictions is said to be an absolute mess. In junior high school, you'd call it "cliquish," but in adulthood, well, some just feel it's rude.

Whatever one might think of it, there's an actual name for the phe-nomenon: Seattle Freeze. And it's become the topic of much citywide con-versation, especially with the past decade's population explosion fueled by newcomers.

Having lived in Seattle for more than 15 years, I can confidently attest to there being merit behind the complaints. Not that I necessarily blame Norwegians for it. Though Norwegian culture is still celebrated, its popula-tion percentage within the region is far lower than it once was a century or more ago. Sure, it's possible elements of that culture were embedded within the city's mind-set, even among non-Norwegians. But I'm more inclined to believe the theory about a combination of factors being at play.

Traveling to cover sporting events on the East Coast, I'd forgotten how open and friendly random strangers there can be. Same in the Midwest, albeit in a different way. Starting conversations with people on the street really isn't that unusual in many of the cities I've been to dozens of times. In Seattle, two people walking past each other on the same sidewalk on a quiet street are more likely to stare down at their own toes than look up and acknowledge one another.

Now, granted, the city does have its friendly folks. I'm even friends with some and not all of them moved here from elsewhere within the past five years. But it takes work. I've never been one to crave a huge circle of friends and prefer to be selective. Still, I wasn't at all surprised when a former colleague I recently spent time with on the East Coast told me he and his wife had made more friends there within a few years than they had over multiple decades in Seattle.

Some who grew up here insist the Seattle Freeze doesn't exist. That people not used to making friends elsewhere are just blaming the city rather than gauging their own shortcomings. Others offer that if the newcomers don't like it, they can just head on back to Texas, Arkansas, Indiana, or wherever else people think it's cool and not slightly offensive to start random conversations on the street. And to a degree, they have a point. Seattle isn't the East Coast. If it were, so many from New York, Boston, Philadelphia, and elsewhere would just stay put. Instead, they are lured to Seattle by a scenic beauty that truly does exist once the rain goes away for a bit. There is a more relaxed pace to West Coast life as well. Sure, it can be competitive, especially in the tech industry. But it isn't New York competitive. The grind isn't the same. Combine it with some of the scenery, as opposed to the concrete jungles back east, and the allure of life in the Emerald City isn't a sham. It is very real.

But so are the real-life problems. Those don't go away by switching coasts. Financial stresses are there due to surging real estate costs. Homelessness and rising crime, particularly within the city's downtown core, are issues that remove some of the luster people often come to Seattle hoping to see.

And yes, the longtime residents of Seattle can be a bit different than found elsewhere. Most of the ones I've met take quiet pride in that. Never outward pride, though, because that's frowned upon. A popular expression in Seattle—not Norwegian, but Japanese in origin—has it that "the nail that sticks out gets hammered down." In other words, better to not draw too much attention to yourself.

But, yeah, of course Seattle is different.

There's a theory the city got through the COVID-19 pandemic with fewer issues than other parts of the country because its residents were already practiced in keeping to themselves. Regardless, it is a city with a little troll in it.

After all, it's a city that was unafraid of giving a collective middle finger to former U.S. President Donald Trump when he got a little too mouthy in telling it what to do. Some locals even declared during the hot summer of 2020—amid anti-police riots over the killing of George Floyd—that they were breaking off from the U.S. and forming their own autonomous zone in the city's Capitol Hill neighborhood. And local politicians didn't really try to stop them for weeks. It's hardly surprising that Jay Inslee, Bob Ferguson, Jenny Durkan, Pramila Jayapal, and other politicians who gained national attention telling Trump where to stuff it all hailed from Seattle. After all, it's where a Lenin statue has been flipping that same bird to the rest of the country unscathed for decades. And a place where a giant troll living under a bridge is actually paid homage.

No, the people in Seattle aren't about to automatically change just because some newcomers want them to. They were there first. They're quite happy living amongst the rain and the troll.

And any fast-talking, nail-sticking, vision-touting outsider hoping to waltz in and change things overnight, well, they'd best have a strategy planned. One that involves more than whining about how the locals won't invite them to dinner.

Especially if they're hoping to build an arena.

Chapter 8

SUPERSONICS WANT A HANDOUT

Keeping up with the neighbors is generally not recommended as a hobby that leads to anything good. Buying a fancy new car, installing an in-ground swimming pool, or adding a rooftop deck and hot tub might seem like a great idea at the time. But the bills quickly pile up and there are only so many hours in a day you can spend splashing in hot or cold water after a long, slow drive showing off the new vehicle before that initial shine starts to fade.

Not to mention, the psychology of a quick one-up purchase to offset the downside of being outhustled by your neighbor on something else becomes a roller coaster of mood swings without ever leading to true happiness. Once that neighbor puts the hot tub in his expanded living room and starts driving an RV with a boat on its trailer, all bets are off.

By 2004, Seattle SuperSonics owner Howard Schultz was not very happy. At least, not when it came to his basketball team. The players, especially superstar Gary Payton, didn't seem to like him. The fans hadn't much to cheer about, and Schultz appeared to be suffering from an acute case of neighbor envy. Perhaps he was drinking one too many caffeinated beverages from Starbucks, the former coffee bean store from Seattle's Pike Place Market he'd bought in 1987 and transformed into a global espresso-serving chain.

Whatever was fueling his angst, Schultz sure got impatient when glancing a few miles south at the brand-new, taxpayer-financed venues the Mariners and Seahawks were by then playing in.

The Seahawks had just opened Qwest Field a couple of years prior and now, with coach Mike Holmgren at the helm, seemed destined for bigger and better things. The Mariners? Well, they were coming off some of the best years in franchise history. Since opening Safeco Field, they'd made the American League Championship Series in back-to-back seasons in 2000 and 2001.

The 2001 edition of the Mariners had tied an AL record by winning 116 games. Two ensuing teams in 2002 and 2003 had put together 93-win seasons while missing the playoffs only because of record-setting wild-card squads in Anaheim and Oakland. But with more than 3 million fans per season now attending games, things were as good as they'd ever been for Seattle's hard-luck baseball franchise.

That wasn't the case for the Sonics. After losing a finals appearance to Michael Jordan and his dynastic Chicago Bulls in 1996, the franchise that had won the city's only major professional sports championship of the modern era in 1979 had fallen on hard times.

Schultz and a team of investors bought the Sonics and the Seattle Storm of the WNBA for $200 million from The Ackerley Group in 2001. He installed an "all heart, all ball" mantra along with a new Sonics logo and the promise of a return to the squad's halcyon days. Primarily, he'd hoped to infuse some of the highly successful corporate Starbucks culture within the basketball franchise.

That was his first mistake.

"What I did not appreciate at the time was that owning a public sports team is not the same as operating a private or even public company," Schultz later wrote in his 2020 book. "The obligations are different."

Schultz got himself in early trouble by pledging to "bring back respect for the game"—suggesting the NBA was too about self-promotion, money, and ego. Some of his players resented the public criticisms. And fans quickly soured on an owner appearing to be all talk without putting a winning product on the court.

It didn't help at all that the team's KeyArena home by the early 2000s was showing its age. Built for the 1962 World's Fair, the arena only a decade prior had undergone a mid-1990s renovation for $92 million, with $74 million of it coming from public bonds.

Unfortunately, those familiar with modern NBA arenas and their lavish club seating and luxury suites figured it would cost at least $200 million to bring KeyArena up to speed. The phrase "lipstick on a pig" got thrown around a lot in reference to the 1994–95 renovation and the prevailing opinion was that the comparison was grossly unfair to swine.

Schultz wanted to partake in that loser's game of keeping up with his neighbors. But he was no dummy. Oh no, he was a winner. Still one of the better-respected business leaders about town. And as a non-dummy, widely respected, winning businessman, he knew spending his own money on a new sports venue to keep up with the neighbors would only lead to headaches and stress. So, Schultz came up with the Seattle billionaire's instant fix—let the taxpayers refurbish him a new $200 million arena equivalent.

After all, they'd ponied up for Seahawks owner Paul Allen and Mariners counterpart Hiroshi Yamauchi. Why should he be the only billionaire owner getting stiffed with the tab? He was owed something, wasn't he? It was common knowledge that sports venues had an increasingly limited lifespan. The Kingdome had taken less than 20 years to get on the nerves of tenant teams. KeyArena's renovation was only a decade prior and already was insulting pigs and making Schultz nervous.

Alas, the local mood for such corporate welfare had greatly changed by 2004. A good deal of blame for that had to do with the Mariners and Seahawks. The Mariners had gotten money for a new ballpark just weeks after voters had expressly rejected the idea of giving them any. And the Seahawks? Well, their own ballot initiative had squeaked by like a fourth-and-inches credit card measurement by the referee.

Nevertheless, Schultz plowed ahead looking for his rightful cut.

And like any plow underestimating the avalanche forming directly ahead, the burial would not be pretty.

Chris Van Dyk, a longtime, self-described "political operative," lived a half-hour ferry hop across the Puget Sound from Seattle on Bainbridge Island. In 1995, just as the Mariners were seeking public funds to build their new ballpark, Van Dyk formed a nonprofit called Citizens for More Important Things. The sole purpose of this group was to prevent sports teams from receiving public subsidies.

Van Dyk's group proved highly successful even with a limited budget. It got the Mariners' request for funding onto a statewide ballot initiative, which it then narrowly defeated. Unfortunately for Van Dyk and his group, the Mariners at that point were in the process of completing a historic comeback to win the American League West Division over the California Angels.

"We would have been able to enjoy our win had the Mariners not gotten into the playoffs," Van Dyk said.

The Mariners would go on to defeat the New York Yankees in a decisive Game 5 of the Division Series on a walk-off double by Edgar Martínez. At that point, with the baseball team's popularity at an all-time high, state lawmakers found a way to approve an alternative funding mechanism in spite of the vote results weeks prior.

Then, in 1997, another statewide vote to approve a funding package for a new stadium to house the Seattle Seahawks and new would-be owner Allen just barely passed. Many voters were still upset the Mariners' plan had gotten approved despite the referendum results and the Seahawks ballot had been far closer than initially envisioned.

There had also been cost overruns plaguing both projects.

And so, by the time Schultz came calling for a subsidized Sonics arena, public sentiment for these types of handouts was at an all-time low.

"Schultz, he was just tone deaf," Van Dyk said. "His people were tone deaf. They came back and it was like 'We want our share now.'"

But the bar proved formidable. So much so, Schultz couldn't gain traction. He kept demanding the state of Washington provide $200 million to at least refurbish KeyArena. The team would kick in $18 million. But politicians told Schultz to take a hike. And they weren't advising him to explore Mount Rainer or some of the region's beautiful ranges on foot. No, they just meant a hike out of their offices. Schultz quickly became *persona non grata* and he wasn't happy about it.

He was so upset he gave up on his idea of keeping the Sonics and put them up for sale. As had been the case with the Mariners and Seahawks, local investors weren't exactly lining up around the corner to offer Schultz a pile of cash. Even future Los Angeles Clippers owner Microsoft CEO Steve Ballmer stayed on the sidelines as Schultz conducted his search.

Ballmer in later years would join forces with entrepreneur Chris Hansen in an attempt to build an arena in the city's South of Downtown, or "SoDo," District. Later, he'd drop $2 billion on the Clippers, which was about $500 million more than anyone else figured they were worth. But when it was time to buy the Sonics in 2006, Ballmer was nowhere to be found other than the rumor mill and the minds of wishful thinkers.

But there were buyers interested in the Sonics. When Hurricane Katrina devastated New Orleans in 2005, its sports teams had to scramble to relocate. In the case of the Pelicans NBA team, they found a temporary home a few hundred miles north in Oklahoma City. Their stay was such a resounding success, it seemed for a time that the Pelicans might never return home.

Of course, though, they eventually did. And by 2006, Oklahoma City was just another mid-sized American burg with a glitzy, modern arena used by minor professional teams. So, some well-heeled corporate citizens set out to do something about it.

Led by Clayton L. Bennett, an Oklahoma City group set out to purchase the Sonics. And by July 18, 2006, they did just that, for a cool $350 million. Naturally, the Schultz sale to an outside group from a city that had just hosted an NBA franchise and was seeking one of its own quickly set off alarm bells throughout Seattle. But Schultz, not wanting to be viewed as a traitor that gave away the town's NBA team, rushed to reassure worried fans he'd secured guarantees the team would not be relocated.

And for a while, Bennett and fellow investors that included Oklahoma oil man Aubrey McClendon went along with that scenario. But it soon became apparent they had conditions attached—build them a new arena or they would be gone and take the Sonics with them.

Chapter 9

REAL ESTATE RULES

For more than eight decades, the 90-foot-tall tulip tree next to Rodgers Park in Seattle's fast-growing Queen Anne neighborhood had withstood gale-force winds, the rare occasional snowstorm weighing down its mighty branches, and even the great Nisqually Earthquake of 2001. But it didn't have a chance against the city's insatiable hunger for real estate and development.

And so, the day after Christmas in 2019, as shoppers elbowed each other out of the way for in-store deals, the unmistakable sound of a chain saw tore through the neighborhood and soon, the 44-inch trunk of the tree as well. By day's end, as stunned bargain shoppers returned to their homes, a gaping hole lay on the property next to a 104-year-old house, which had been the true target of developers all along.

Though the tulip tree enjoyed "exceptional" protection status under city bylaws, developer Alex Mason of MGT Builders had argued months earlier that it needed to be felled. Mason told a city examiner's hearing he planned to demolish the adjacent, dilapidated home and build a three-story, three-unit rowhouse on the land. It was exactly the type of affordable, multiunit housing desperately needed by fast-growing Seattle. The city's expanding population was being increasingly pushed farther to its fringes. Mason argued, rather convincingly it would appear, that if the tulip tree remained intact the land's development potential would be reduced from 3,048 square feet to 1,297 square feet.

A city hearing examiner granted permission to topple the tree. But MGT Buildings didn't do the deed. Instead, it sold the land to another developer, Filthy LLC. The sale was for $1,650,000, which was $530,000 more than MGT Buildings had paid for the property. Nothing had yet been built on the land, but the permission to cut down the tree had been granted. And that alone, it seems, was worth a half-million bucks.

Seattle real estate is not for the faint of heart, nor wallet. The median price of a home within city limits was $1,019,950 by April 2022, while the median for all of King County was $995,000. Even neighboring Snohomish County to the north was at $839,298, while Pierce to the south was at $579,980.

These aren't mansions commanding those mid-to-high-six-figure amounts. Some aren't even fully intact houses anymore, like the one in the Beacon Hill neighborhood that burned down. It had sold for $315,000 in mid-2016. Then, after being gutted by fire, the unsalvageable wreckage on 6,000 square feet of land sold for $549,000. The idea being that somebody else could remove it, build something better, and hope to someday turn an even bigger profit.

One mold-infested house with unstable floors and ceilings in West Seattle sold for $427,000 in May 2016 after 41 offers were submitted and doubled its asking price. The home was later demolished, rebuilt, and sold again for about $1 million.

In coveted Seattle neighborhoods such as Capitol Hill, Queen Anne, or Magnolia, four-bedroom single-family homes of 4,000 square feet can run in the $3 and $4 million range. That is, if you can get your hands on one.

Realtors will list these properties for a few days, then "take offers" from bidders lined up around the block. Bidding wars often drive prices hundreds of thousands of dollars higher. In the Eastside community of Bellevue, a 3,440 square-foot home was listed at $1.5 million in November 2021 and sold a month later for $2.4 million. Many times, the winning bids are all-cash. Oh, and buyer contingencies like a post-acceptance home inspection? Forget about it. You don't win Seattle bidding wars by checking to see whether the century-old knob-and-tube wiring actually works, or risks catching fire, forcing you to sell your burned-out shell of a home at a profit before you're ready.

If you want to win that charming "antique" home, you'll likely need to pay $400 or $500 up-front to a home inspector who checks things out before you even bid and keeps the money regardless of whether your offer prevails.

It isn't unusual for the same home inspector to be hired multiple times at one property by bidders vying against one another. Some inspectors show up to jobs driving a Mercedes or Porsche. For homes in serious demand, the owner sometimes gets an inspection beforehand and leaves the results stacked on a hallway counter for buyers to draw conclusions from.

So, yeah, real estate is valuable in Seattle and growing ever more so. And that growth won't always go hand-in-hand with natural spurts seen in the region's surrounding tree canopy.

Some of these towering beauties, such as the aforementioned 90-foot tulip tree, will have the misfortune of sprouting right where somebody wants to build.

Or they might have leafy branches blocking what would otherwise be a perfect view of the city's skyline or Elliott Bay from an existing home. Seattle homeowners have been known to pay hundreds of thousands of dollars for "air rights" above properties in front of theirs. In other words, they literally buy the invisible air to keep their neighbors from building anything upward that might block their view.

But you can't buy air rights from trees to keep them from growing any taller. And when something gets in the way of making valuable Seattle land even more valuable, well, it has been known to end in murder.

Or, in this case, tree murder. That's what happened in a West Seattle neighborhood sometime around January 2016, when a group of neighbors pooled resources and contracted out the killings of 153 big leaf maple, Scouler's willow, and other deciduous species of trees. One day, the trees were where they'd always been for decades. The next? Nothing but dead stumps. At first, nobody fessed up to the mass arborcide, even though some obvious prime suspects were those living in adjacent hillside homes with newly improved water and mountain views.

The Seattle Police Department got involved, doors were knocked on, lawyers hired, and lawsuits filed. A year later, two couples settled a lawsuit brought by the city for $440,000. They had actually come forward on their own, apologizing for a contractor they said was supposed to prune the trees and instead chopped them down.

A separate lawsuit against nine other nearby neighbors was settled 10 months after that for $360,000. That second case was far more acrimonious in that one couple agreed to flip on their neighbors and name their alleged co-conspirators in exchange for immunity from possible felony criminal prosecution.

All told, the city collected $5,229 per tree from both groups of neighbors. It used the money to re-plant saplings on the site.

Now, trees aren't the only thing sometimes paying with their lives when tensions flare over Seattle real estate.

Some of these paper-millionaire homeowners experiencing double-digit yearly property value growth quickly come to realize they can't afford to cash out and use their proceeds on a new home. Not if they hope to keep living in the same, exponentially more expensive neighborhood.

Some can't even afford to stay in the city, county, or region. So, they instead eschew their sale plans, fire up HGTV for inspiration, and look to renovate their existing homes into something better.

And with thousands of homeowners doing this at the same time, there just aren't enough qualified contractors, plumbing specialists, electricians, painters, and drywallers to get jobs done when and how homeowners want them. There's a "take-it-or-leave-it" attitude among some contractors. And impatience among homeowners. It doesn't always end well.

Yoon Myong Bang was a 73-year-old retiree living in the Seattle suburb of Spanaway, a town of 35,000 or so inhabitants just south of Seattle. Now, Spanaway isn't exactly the safest place. In fact, FBI crime data will tell you there's a 1-in-43 chance of becoming the victim of a violent crime or property crime while living there. The crime rate in Spanaway is roughly 69 percent higher than in the rest of the state, so best to not go picking violent fights—especially over property.

Nonetheless, getting killed by a retiree used to rank rather low on the probability list.

Until the particular case involving retiree Bang, who hired an unfortunate 52-year-old contractor to remodel his bathroom. As is often the case in Seattle—and apparently Spanaway as well—the two disagreed over the quality of work being done.

All that's known from there is that on August 28, 2021, the contractor was found lying in a pool of blood inside the home, a fatal gunshot wound to his head. Police reports say a toilet the contractor was working on had been leaking and Bang threatened not to pay for the work.

The only thing worse than a leaky toilet in Seattle is not getting paid for home renovations. There's big money to be made by contractors in Seattle real estate and any time wasted working for free on somebody's toilet project can amount to hundreds of thousands of dollars lost in not sprucing up another homeowner's kitchen.

Police reports aren't always the most reliable, but the one in this toilet case claimed Bang had calmly handed over a handgun to officers at the scene. They say he recounted a tale of warning the contractor he'd best produce a non-leaky toilet if he wanted actual money. To this, the future dead man allegedly responded by going to his truck for a hammer and proceeding to swing away at the bathroom counter adjacent to Bang's commode.

What happened next is up to the courts to decide. But the contractor didn't leave the house alive.

Neither did the tulip tree in Queen Anne that day. But its legacy lives on by virtue of a viral YouTube video featuring a onetime Seattle punk rocker named Suzanne Grant. She'd gone to a land use committee hearing at Seattle City Hall two months after the tulip tree was toppled. After signing up for a public comment session, she approached the microphone and began belting out a song she'd written with a to-the-point title of "Tree Murder Song."

There's an unwelcome sight in the neighborhood, a developer is being greedy, she sang. *There's a hole in the sky where a tree once stood. Such a lack of light and sound, all that's left is bare muddy ground. A magnificent tree was murdered. The mighty dollar cut it down.*

And on and on it went. As she broke into the song's main chorus, four tree activists who'd stood behind her at the microphone joined in with backup vocals.

There's a hole in the sky where a tree once was, somebody's making money, they sang in unison.

The purpose of the visit was to push the city to toughen its tree ordinance. By mid-2022, a Twitter post of Grant's city hall performance has received more than 835,000 views.

It served as another reminder of the diverging forces within an ever-changing Seattle.

On the one hand, it's a city where every scrap of land is coveted and fought over by homeowners and developers who seemingly can't find enough of it. A place where you hold on to what you've got at all costs and try to somehow make it better. But Seattle, just as during its pioneer days when Chief Sealth was either rightly or wrongly credited with raising environmental issues amid the mill town's development, has also long been a place for those championing its surrounding beauty and craving non-material things. A place where bigger isn't always better unless it was created as one of God's natural wonders. And finding enough room for everybody to coexist in this emerging modern reality of Seattle was proving a challenge.

Chapter 10

HOCKEY HISTORY IN SEATTLE

An old line about the great Guyle Fielder is that he never stuck in the National Hockey League because he was as magnificent at shooting with a pool cue as he was a hockey stick. And back in the greedy NHL owner days of the 1950s and '60s, when players earned peanuts and their coaches terrorized them, being out after games swilling beer and pocketing eight balls wasn't viewed with a sympathetic eye by anyone deciding hockey futures.

So, Fielder would instead play 1,368 of his 1,496 professional games in the minor Western Hockey League, the level right below the NHL. And it was in those WHL games that Fielder logged 1,929 of his combined goals and assists to cement his contribution as the sport's fourth all-time leading pro point-getter. Only Wayne Gretzky, Mario Lemieux, and Jaromir Jagr could claim to have tallied more.

In fact, when Hall of Fame goalie Glenn Hall was once asked in an interview which player from his 1960s heyday Gretzky most reminded him of, he quickly mentioned boyhood chum Fielder.

But Gretzky and the others ahead of Fielder compiling most of their points in the NHL meant it was their names ingrained in the minds of hockey fans. Fielder was largely overlooked, even in the city of his biggest feats achieved on a championship level.

That city happened to be Seattle.

And from 1953 through 1969, with only a one-season interruption, Fielder dazzled the Emerald City's arenas like few players before or since. Certainly, no single player had enjoyed the enduring longevity of greatness Fielder did in Seattle. He played for the city's same WHL franchise under the names Bombers, Americans, and Totems, teaming with figures Fred Shero, Emile Francis, Keith Allen, and Pat Quinn, who would achieve legendary NHL status as players who became Hall of Fame coaches, general managers, and builders.

Certainly, the Idaho-born, Saskatchewan-raised Fielder knew a thing or two about building. Starting in 1958–59 and through the next decade, he captained the Seattle Totems to three WHL championships. Over 15 seasons with the Seattle franchise, he was league MVP six times, its top point-getter nine times, and its most gentlemanly player on three occasions.

Moreover, his awards spanned the life of his playing career. Fielder was 23 during his first MVP season with the Bombers in 1953–54 and 38 in his final 1968–69 Totems season. It was Fielder captaining the Totems the night they opened what later became KeyArena and then Climate Pledge Arena.

Back then, the venue, built for the 1962 World's Fair, was simply the Seattle Center Coliseum. And on opening night, September 30, 1964, the defending Stanley Cup champion Toronto Maple Leafs played an exhibition against Fielder and the Totems in front of a packed house of 8,601 fans. Naturally, the Maple Leafs throttled the home side 7–1. There were few fairy-tale endings for Fielder, or Seattle, that involved the NHL.

But a living legend Fielder was. Even if few sports fans in Seattle beyond true hockey diehards remembered him.

And by February 2022, he was still living. In fact, with the death that month of Hall of Famer Emile Francis at age 95, Fielder at 91 became the oldest living former Seattle pro hockey player. Fielder had made light of his age the first few times we'd spoken, hoping to stick around long enough to see the NHL make it to the city he'd put back on pro hockey's map. In fact, Fielder's performances through the 1960s grew the pro game so much in Seattle that the NHL eyed the city with expansion interest as the 1970s began.

Totems owner Vince Abbey was even awarded an NHL franchise in 1974. But Abbey's fortunes were sagging as Totems performance dropped off following Fielder's 1969–70 departure. Abbey struggled to make a required payment on the league's $6 million franchise fee. The NHL got skittish and pulled the franchise, and the Totems folded that same year.

Seattle had one more NHL sniff in late 1990, as a group headed by ex-Totems coach Bill MacFarland teamed on an expansion bid with Microsoft executive and future Seattle Mariners baseball owner Chris Larson. They later joined forces with a group led by Bill Ackerley, son of NBA Seattle SuperSonics owner Barry Ackerley, and headed for a presentation in front of the NHL's board of governors in Florida.

Right before the meeting, Ackerley asked his partners whether he could privately address the governors beforehand. Once inside, he formally withdrew the offer and slipped out the back door.

No one really knows what the true intent was. Theories abound that Ackerley sabotaged the group so his father's NBA team wouldn't face NHL competition. Indeed, a mid-1990s renovation of KeyArena by Barry Ackerley reduced the venue's hockey capacity and seemed to guarantee the NHL would never be interested in Seattle again. And the league didn't show much for another 20 years. By then, the feats of Fielder and all those before him were but fleeting memories. Seattle's long pro hockey legacy, launched with the Metropolitans a century prior by brothers Lester and Frank Patrick, was little more than mere rumor.

When I first caught up with Fielder in the fall of 2018, he was, of course, in a pool hall. The difference was, this one was in the Leisure World retirement community in Mesa, Arizona.

By then in his late eighties, Fielder could still shoot some stick. Did it three days a week, sometimes more. The 10 pool tables inside the community's recreation center are among its prime attractions. And Fielder could hustle just as well away from the pool table as on it. It was while playing one day that a woman nearly two decades his junior spotted him playing while she was with friends at the recreation center.

"Who's that?" she asked.

They told her he'd been a hockey player. But she didn't know the first thing about hockey.

Before long, Fielder was offering to teach her to play. Years later, he and companion Betty Johnson were still going strong. Fielder is notoriously fearful of flying, dating back to his playing days, so Johnson will take the wheel of her car and they'll head off on cross-country road trips.

Or shoot some pool.

"That's the only thing I've got left, is playing pool," Fielder told me. "That and hockey were something I loved equally but I'm sure it didn't do me any favors when it came to the NHL."

Fielder has no illusions about his off-ice reputation for late-night beer and shooting pool after games. It was a stress reliever. But for teams of the buttoned-down NHL, a stress inducer. He played just nine regular season contests for the Chicago Black Hawks and Detroit Red Wings, failing to register a point. Six additional playoff contests with Detroit and Boston also saw him held scoreless.

But while Fielder comprehends his own shunning by the NHL, he can't figure out why it took the league so long to consider Seattle a hockey town. As word of Seattle's NHL possibilities grew within the past decade, his legacy began experiencing a public resurgence.

And the sweater-vested Fielder, a few inches shorter than his listed 5'9" during his playing days, lapped it up. He can get emotional discussing the tributes to his former prowess, a new generation of Seattle hockey fans discovering the exploits of him and teammates such as Don Ward, Gordy Sinclair, Rudy Filion, Bill Dineen, and Val Fonteyne.

"It's better late than never," he told me with a smile.

And he felt the same way about the NHL finally giving Seattle a shot.

"I'd have thought they'd have been here decades ago, because this was a great place for hockey," he said. "I remember when I finished playing, there was all this talk about how a team was coming. That never happened, but at least they're finally coming now."

Indeed, the Metropolitans becoming the first U.S.–based team to win a Stanley Cup in 1917 made Seattle seem a natural NHL fit. The Metropolitans played in the old Pacific Coast Hockey Association back then, having been brought to town by the Patrick brothers two years prior.

The Patricks had raided the roster of the Cup champion Toronto Blueshirts, immediately supplying the Metropolitans with stars Frank Foyston, Harry (Hap) Holmes, Jack Walker, Eddie Carpenter, and Cully Wilson. The team was named after the Metropolitan Building Company and played its games downtown at the newly constructed Seattle Ice Arena.

In only their second season, coached by iconic Seattle sports figure Pete Muldoon, the Metropolitans captured the PCHA title by going 16–8 to finish first overall. Back then, that meant they would play the NHL precursor National Hockey Association champ for the Stanley Cup. As it was Seattle's turn to play host, the rights switching back and forth each season, the NHA champion Montreal Canadiens traveled west.

Montreal was heavily favored and showed why as Didier Pitre scored four goals in an opening 8–4 rout for the Canadiens. The game had even been played under seven-man PCHA rules that should have favored the home side, so by that point, the series appeared lost for the Metropolitans before it had ever truly begun. But little did anyone know it would be

Montreal's final victory and the last time the Canadiens would score more than a goal. The Metropolitans rebounded to win 6–1 in Game 2, then 4–1 in Game 3 to move within a victory of the Cup.

Game 4 featured NHA rules, but it didn't matter as Bernie Morris of the Metropolitans scored six goals in a 9–1 blowout. More than 3,500 fans had piled into the 2,500-capacity arena to witness the event, described thusly by the *Seattle Times* the following day: "The lexicon of sport does not contain language adequate to describe the fervor of the fans who saw Seattle triumph last night. The largest crowd that ever saw an ice game in The Arena stood on its feet and cheered until the iron girders of The Arena roof rattled as the Seattle team left the ice with the world's title safely won."

The teams would meet two years later for a title rematch in Seattle under far darker circumstances. The Spanish Influenza pandemic was still raging, unbeknownst to most as the series got underway in March 1919.

At first, the Metropolitans dominated and were within a goal of retaking the Cup. Game 4 had gone into double overtime but was called with players from both teams collapsing to the ice in exhaustion. Then, the Metropolitans led 3–0 heading to the third period of Game 5, but faded from fatigue, allowed the tying three goals, and lost in overtime to send the 2–2–1 series to a decisive sixth game.

By then, it was apparent that something more than valiant on-ice efforts were causing depleted players to be carried off the ice. Canadiens defenseman Joe Hall lay sick in his room at the Georgina Hotel along with teammates Newsy Lalonde, Billy Coutu, Jack McDonald, Louis Berlinguette, and coach George Kennedy.

The series was called off. Metropolitans coach Muldoon had been offered the chance to claim the Cup by forfeit but famously said he did not want to win that way. Hall checked into the Columbus Sanatorium and died two days later.

Kennedy would die two years later at age 39, having never fully recovered from his flu bout. Muldoon also was sickened that series and suffered a fatal heart attack a decade later at age 41 that many attributed to his vital organs being weakened by his prior illness.

To this date, that series was the only time a major pro sports league canceled a final due to a pandemic. And Hall's death remains the only one by a major pro sports athlete attributable to a pandemic illness contracted during competition.

The Metropolitans never again won a Cup, losing 3–2 to Ottawa in the 1920 final series. They folded in 1924, with the PCHA soon following suit. Their arena became a parking garage.

But the city's hockey tradition kept going, as Muldoon helped the Patrick brothers form a Seattle Eskimos squad within a new Pacific Coast Hockey League. A new Civic Ice Arena was built for $1.1 million and Muldoon began coaching the Eskimos in their 1928–29 debut season. But his fatal heart attack late in that campaign was the beginning of the end for the franchise.

A total of 15 former and future NHL players spent time with the Eskimos, but the league folded in 1931.

Former Metropolitans star Foyston then returned to coach the Seattle Sea Hawks in the five-team North West Hockey League in 1933. They won a championship in 1935–36 and routinely drew crowds of 4,000 or more that surpassed even Metropolitans numbers. But the league folded soon after and though the Sea Hawks tried their hand in another newly formed circuit, that ended by 1940–41.

Amateur hockey bridged the gap for seven years from there until Seattle entered a revived PCHL in 1948–49 with the Seattle Ironmen. That league became the WHL by 1951 when the Ironmen, who already had future Totems great Filion, took on young defenseman Fred Shero, who'd later coach the "Broad Street Bullies" Philadelphia Flyers to two Stanley Cups in the 1970s.

Two years later, the franchise was renamed the Seattle Bombers and Fielder came aboard.

Fielder had struggled to crack a Red Wings roster loaded with future Hall of Famers such as Howe, Ted Lindsay, Alex Delvecchio, and Red Kelly. He was ready to play hockey anywhere that would take him. "I just wanted to go someplace that would give me a chance," he said.

Seattle did just that. In 1961, the Totems threw a "Guyle Fielder Night" at a packed arena that remains his career highlight. Fielder remembers such nights well, when the Totems owned a town with no major pro sports, just as the Metropolitans had shared top billing with the University of Washington football Huskies and pro boxing in its heyday.

And as his eighties approached his nineties, Fielder hoped the sport could claim its former place in a city that could again love pro hockey the way it had once loved him.

Chapter 11

DRIVING OVER MISS DAISY

Understanding modern-day Seattle and some of the main arguments against reviving KeyArena and putting an NHL team there involves getting behind the wheel. Few things best underscore some of the city's psychology than navigating by car through its streets, thoroughfares, and highways.

The aggressive drivers quickly stand out. Remember the old Japanese expression prevalent within the city—a nail that sticks out gets hammered down. And nothing sticks out more on Seattle streets than drivers attempting to exceed the speed limit. For locals, these four-wheel scofflaws will almost always be designated as Californians or, perhaps, East Coasters attempting to import their lethal habits within a law-abiding automotive community.

Of course, these "outsiders" will have an entirely different outlook. They tend to see the native Seattleites puttering along in the left lane a mile or two under the posted limit as passive-aggressive ninnies afraid of their car's shadow. They will view the reluctance to risk a little danger by flooring the accelerator as another example of the city's aversion to risk or, more bluntly, refusal to adapt to what's around it.

Truthfully, it could just be bad driving. Seattle drivers are famous for the type of left lane "camping" that can get you shot in places farther east. They also famously refuse to use turn signals regardless of where they are or how many of their fellow drivers might be dangerously confused by their upcoming intentions. Some drivers, not certain whether they want to go left or right, have been known to stop dead in the middle of the street—an act known locally as "giving up"—while they gather themselves and make everyone behind them wait.

When a Seattle driver does signal, especially while going 60 mph—never a mile over—in the left lane of a highway, the move will usually be followed by an immediate merge into the adjacent lane to the right, regardless of whether a vehicle is actually occupying that space. A Seattle driver going through the exhausting effort of lifting a finger to flip the turn signal device figures everybody else must drop what they're doing and immediately accommodate the merge.

Now, of course, not every local agrees with this assessment. And their voices tend to be heard in news stories defending the city whenever some insurance association survey lists Seattle as one of America's worst driving places. But, regardless of those defensive opinions, the same survey results keep cropping up year after year.

Perhaps not so coincidentally, Seattle also keeps finding its way onto lists of the worst traffic cities in America. Now, a part of it is undoubtedly linked to the city's tremendous growth. With more people come additional cars and volume on often narrow streets that were built decades prior in anticipation of far less traffic. Throw in the lack of sophisticated regional public transit until very recently—pushing people to stick to their cars—and some of the gridlock is as understandable as it would be in any of the nation's bigger cities.

Alas, one of the questions that rarely gets asked, given the sensitivity of the topic, is whether some of America's worst drivers are also contributing to Seattle's abominable traffic. Beyond the propensity for left-lane hogging, non-signaling, and steadfast speed limit adherence regardless of traffic flow, Seattle drivers are known for some other habits akin to running sharp nails across a chalkboard.

The "zipper effect" of vehicles merging one at a time onto highways? Forget it. A foreign concept. One of the great pastimes when stuck in Seattle traffic, if it weren't so irritating, is watching the comical procession of drivers refusing to allow one another to merge from two lanes into one and thus preventing anybody from going anyplace fast.

It would seem to be an outgrowth of the "No, you go" fake politeness found at four-way intersections when not a single driver from the quartet of cars halted at each stop sign can seem to remember whose turn it is. The Seattle-based PEMCO insurance company in 2009 and 2010 ran television advertisements poking fun at this universally acknowledged local driving flaw. One ad depicted cars at a four-way stop each inching forward but refusing to advance farther as the drivers politely wave at one another to ride on through. It won a coveted SAMMY "Best of Show" award.

"PEMCO. We're just like you. A little different," the ad proclaimed. Locals smiled knowingly, but newcomers sneered. Or spat at their TVs, having just arrived home from an hour-long, 10-mile commute.

While some defend this extreme form of hesitancy as good old Pacific Northwest politeness, less patient types call it out as another form of prevailing passive aggressiveness. Are these drivers truly being friendly? Or are they actually cursing the words "No, you go!" under their breath from the safety of their cars, frustrated at having to partake in such a ridiculous ritual?

With everybody going so slowly, clogging up roads, and refusing to exercise their legally mandated right to advance at stops, the temptation to play a little "Seattle Slalom" is great. This involves hitting the accelerator pedal about 5 mph above the speed limit and zig-zagging calmly from lane to lane in order to bypass cars the way a skier navigates around the slalom flags in a World Cup race. The skiers are going much faster than the cars in many cases, but there you go.

Unfortunately, there's also the dreaded "Seattle Wedge," which can foil such plans before they ever get going. This phenomenon occurs on two-lane roads when the vehicle in front of yours in the left lane is going below the speed limit and the car to the right is also slightly ahead of you and going roughly the same speed. When that happens, there's no way to switch lanes and get around either vehicle. Sometimes, the car in the right lane will slow down just enough so you can pull up right alongside it and look over at its clueless driver staring straight ahead, both hands with a death grip on the steering wheel. But there will be no way to actually speed up and switch lanes in front of that vehicle. That's because the left-lane car directly in front of you is only going one or two miles an hour faster. It is, in fact, the perfect tag-team wedge guaranteed to prevent you from getting anyplace quickly. And chances are good that neither wedge-producing driver is aware they've choreographed something akin to what world-class synchronized swimmers are forever trying to accomplish through years of training.

And all of this can take place on perfectly sunny days. When it rains, well, that's why home offices were invented. For reasons not scientifically explainable, Seattle residents seem bizarrely yet unequivocally ill-equipped to show even minimal driving competency once a few drops of rain fall. When there's actually a steady rain, well, the city loses its mind entirely and the roadways become an exercise in chaos. It isn't much different from the usual chaos found seven days a week, just 10 mph slower.

You heard that correctly. In a city where it seemingly does little else but rain in all but a handful of weeks every summer, the drivers somehow act as if they've never seen liquid falling from the sky before.

So, yes, driving in Seattle can be a very frustrating experience the locals tend to blame the newcomers for while those from elsewhere gasp in astonishment at how any city's inhabitants can be so utterly hopeless behind the wheel.

It would all make for good spectator sport except for the road rage that occurs. And that isn't limited just to roadways, either. No, in Seattle, the road rage also found its way into debates about what to do about poor old KeyArena.

Census data shows the city's population grew by 128,000 people between 2010 and 2020, making Seattle one of only 14 American cities to have topped 100,000. Given it only had just more than 600,000 people to begin with, that's a 21 percent increase. It goes without saying that the city's aging road system was ill-equipped to handle that big a volume surge. One of the arteries most impacted was along Mercer Street, running from Elliott Avenue on the city's western tip all the way east past Lower Queen Anne, the Seattle Center campus, and the downtown South Lake Union area on through to Interstate 5. Some 80,000 people a day drove along this critical east-west transportation route. That area, known as the Mercer Corridor, also happened to be the primary way drivers got to and from KeyArena.

Traffic in and around the arena was already becoming nightmarish in the final years before the Sonics left for Oklahoma City in 2008. Locals even had a name for it—the "Mercer Mess." But by 2010, it was about to get a whole lot worse as the city finally began long-awaited roadway infra-structure upgrades. The Mercer Corridor Project opened the entirety of Mercer St. to two-way traffic, whereas beforehand, drivers needed to take a bypass route when going east to west.

Problem is, the project took five years to fully complete. And during the interim phases between 2010 and 2015, as traffic slowly opened back up to portions of the corridor, the clogged road often resembled a parking lot. It didn't help that Seattle had been slow to implement coordinated traffic signals as other municipalities had. So, instead of computers gauging the volume of traffic at specific times of the day and adjusting traffic lights accordingly, huge bottlenecks at intersections became routine.

All of this happened to coincide with the very moment city planners and would-be arena builders were arguing over where a new arena should go. For the city's drivers forced to navigate the Mercer Mess daily, the answer was: "Anyplace as far away from KeyArena as possible."

Even once Mercer St. had fully reopened by 2016, battle-scarred Seattle drivers had a visceral reaction to any notion that KeyArena might be renovated. The popular option instead seemed to be the brand-new arena in the city's SoDo District proposed by an entrepreneur and hedge fund manager named Chris Hansen. After all, proponents argued, the area had already been zoned as a "stadium district" by the city. So, why not put an 18,000-seat arena in there next to the NFL and MLB stadiums? On the surface, it made a whole lot of sense.

Behind the scenes, though, alarm bells were going off. First, the supposed "stadium district" had not been zoned that way because the city wanted developers to cram as many sports venues as possible within the land. In fact, the opposite was true. Local stakeholders such as the Port of Seattle had asked for the designation to limit expansion of any sports facilities beyond that stretch of land.

Just like the Mercer Corridor, the transportation routes within the industrialized SoDo neighborhood had become congested beyond their ability to function properly. With limited routes to the nearby interstate, freight vehicles heading to and from port ships became caught up in paralyzing traffic at certain points of the day. And one of those points happened to be whenever a game was played at one of the two stadiums. Sometimes, there would even be two games going on at both places at roughly the same time. The teams tried as best they could to coordinate with one another to prevent this from happening, but when it did the results were nightmarish.

So, the idea of a third sports venue being plunked down right next to the baseball stadium was not at all welcomed by the Port or the local teams playing in SoDo. The Seattle Mariners, in particular, were quick to go public with their objections, while the Seahawks and Sounders took a quieter, behind-the-scenes approach. All three teams joined the Port in writing letters to city officials clearly specifying their objections to Hansen's planned arena. As one might expect, the sports fans hoping for a new arena that could bring back a revived Sonics team were none too pleased with the opposition.

They promptly vilified the loudest opponents, those being the Mariners and the Port. At the same time, they scoffed at the idea of a KeyArena renovation. Why make horrendous Mercer Corridor traffic even worse, they argued. Especially when the city already had a zoned "stadium district" specifically geared to handling sports traffic, with nearby light rail stations and quick access to the city's interstate and highway systems?

No, the local Seattle traffic wasn't doing the sports venue debate any favors. And just like the Mercer Corridor Project, that debate was about to get worse before it got better.

PART TWO

Forcing the Arena Issue

Chapter 12

TIGHTENING THE PUBLIC MONEY SPIGOT

Chris Van Dyk knows he can be a pain in the ass. And for the better part of a decade, that's exactly what the onetime Seattle lobbyist and self-described "political campaign operative" became for any local sports team seeking public money.

Van Dyk's actions nearly torpedoed stadium bids for the Seattle Mariners in 1995 and the Seattle Seahawks in 1997, despite overwhelming financial resources deployed by both teams to secure public handouts. And it was Van Dyk, above all others, setting the stage for a rejection of similar demands by the Seattle SuperSonics that inevitably hastened the departure of that NBA team for Oklahoma City in 2008. By the time anybody in the following decade began talking about an NHL team for Seattle, the mere idea of public funds being used set off alarm bells locally. Ultimately, the debate surrounding an arena plan became framed by ideals first espoused by Van Dyk and his supporters some two decades prior.

And it all came about by accident. Van Dyk never set out to become an anti–sports subsidy crusader. Like so many men with grand ideas throughout history, he was merely trying to impress a woman.

Van Dyk by 1994 had left the political ring and was working as an investment adviser. Flipping through the newspaper, he happened to glance at the front page and saw an item about an old political acquaintance he'd worked for. It was King County Executive Gary Locke, soon to be Washington governor and then the highest elected official for the county's ruling body. Locke was proposing a public subsidy to get the Mariners a new stadium built so they wouldn't leave town as they'd threatened to many a time.

This really irked Van Dyk, who'd helped with Bill Clinton's presidential campaign in the state two years prior. Van Dyk viewed Clinton as a fiscally responsible Democrat and felt Locke was laying waste to that legacy. "It was like, 'Gary, what are you doing?' This was total bullshit," Van Dyk said. "It really stuck in my craw."

It so happened that Van Dyk a week later, as often was the case given his past political work, found himself invited to a Locke fundraiser. "I was single at the time, so I took a lady friend," Van Dyk recalled. "And being somewhat obnoxious, I took her up to introduce her to Gary."

To further impress the woman, Van Dyk decided to show he wasn't afraid of giving the guest of honor a hard time about the proposed Mariners subsidy. "I then proceeded to literally poke my finger in his chest," Van Dyk recalled, "and told him, 'This is obscene.'"

Van Dyk was playing up the drama, knowing he and Locke were old allies and his date was watching. But Locke kept calmly arguing back that a subsidy was best. As he did, Van Dyk grew even more peeved. The conversation ended with Van Dyk blurting something he hadn't thought through. "I said, 'OK, Gary, you do this, and I can guarantee you one thing. I'm going to push it to the ballot," Van Dyk said. "'We'll have an initiative—a referendum on it—and put it to the ballot.'"

Locke wouldn't budge, telling him he welcomed voters having a say. "And I told him, 'OK, we'll hold you to that.'"

They walked away cordially, but with Van Dyk now pumped up with bravado and figuring he'd put in an impressive showing. His date, however, sensing he was badly outgunned, was staring at him bemusedly. "Here I had this new lady friend who then turns to me and says, 'So, what the fuck are *you* going to do about it?'

"And I said, 'Well there, let me impress you.'"

But as night turned to cold mornings in the weeks ahead, the enormity of Van Dyk's threat suddenly dawned. The Mariners were owned by a Japanese billionaire with a cabal of local wannabe billionaire minority owners running the daily baseball operations. The team's massive financial resources were what had so annoyed Van Dyk about the subsidy to begin with. Now, he realized he'd be facing those very resources campaigning for the hearts and minds of King County voters.

Van Dyk admittedly did his best thinking in the shower. And it was there, he said, that he thought up the name of the nonprofit group he'd use to oppose Locke's measure—Citizens for More Important Things. Sure, it sounded whimsical and more than a little arrogant. But, well, Van Dyk was kind of that way to begin with. And the name resonated.

One thing he'd despised was politicians who always opposed but never stood for anything. It had been a struggle when Van Dyk realized he was doing just that: tearing down Locke's idea. But then, somewhere between the shampoo rinse and soap lathering, he realized he actually did support something after all. And that was just about anything other than giving money to the Mariners.

"It just hit me that there were more important things than stadiums to build with public money, since we already had one," he said. "And the real challenge was on the field. The reason that nobody went to the games was because the Mariners were such chronic losers. And I just didn't buy the song and dance that if you put them in a new stadium, all of a sudden they would become winners."

His conscience squared, Van Dyk recruited others. He'd soon be joined in his date-impressing crusade by city councilmember Nick Licata and a local businessman named Mark Baerwedt.

Together, they rallied support for their cause. And boy, did it rally. By the September 19, 1995, vote, it was clear they had a chance to topple the behemoth Mariners machine.

At first, the result was too close to call. It would take nine more days counting absentee ballots for a winner to be declared. Unfortunately for Van Dyk, the Mariners at that exact moment of ballot counting were in the midst of their first taste of serious on-field victory after nearly two decades of futility.

They'd kept winning all through September to overcome what had been a 13-game deficit the prior month to the California Angels in the American League West division race. They eventually retook a two-game lead with less than one week to go. The entire state was transfixed by a Mariners team that seemingly refused to lose. Not surprisingly, the "Refuse to Lose" slogan would later be trademarked and trotted out by the team's diehard supporters for decades to come whenever the Mariners found themselves in deficits too great to climb out of.

Pro sports teams thrive on this type of illogical belief by fans that the impossible is possible. It allows team owners to promote faith even when they balk at doing what it takes financially to best compete on the field. But this time, things were different. This time, the Mariners were pulling off the impossible in front of everybody's eyes.

By September 28 of that year, with the Mariners trying to hold on to win their first division title, the final referendum results were announced: voters had rejected the team's public funding push by a mere 1,082 votes out of nearly 500,000 cast. But it would be a short-lived victory for Van Dyk and his anti-subsidy group.

Mariners ownership was confident the team was going to complete the third-greatest standings comeback in MLB history that week. So confident that Mariners chairman John Ellis gave an ultimatum to King County chairman Locke the day after the final vote tally was announced: get them a stadium plan finalized within a month or the team was gone.

The Mariners would blow their two-game lead. But then, in a one-game playoff against the Angels at the Kingdome, Randy Johnson dominated with a three-hitter in a 9–1 victory that sent the Mariners into their first postseason.

Van Dyk knew then and there that a new stadium deal was coming, regardless of his group's ballot-box victory. His base of opposition, he remembered, "had gone to the other side." What sealed it was a talking-to from his mother, then 83, who was living with Van Dyk at his home in Bainbridge Island across the Puget Sound from downtown Seattle. She was one of those newly converted Mariners fans convinced the team was refusing to lose.

"I remember coming home after work one day and she looks up at me and says, 'Chris, why are you so opposed to what everybody wants?'

"And I said to her, 'Mom, when was the last time you watched a baseball game?'

"And she goes, 'Yesterday!'"

It was a hard lesson in realpolitik.

The Mariners overcame a 2–0 deficit in the AL Division Series against the New York Yankees to force a decisive Game 5 at the Kingdome. There, they tied the game in the eighth and sent things to the 11th inning, where, down a run, Edgar Martinez lined a two-run, walk-off double to left that changed Mariners history.

Though the Mariners lost the ensuing AL Championship Series to Cleveland, the stage was set for their owners to truly win where it mattered to them. Van Dyk and his group had been in conversations with state lawmakers and their representatives, hoping to at least salvage "the spirit" of the prior election victory against public funding.

Nobody in their group wanted to be known as the people who chased everybody's favorite baseball team out of town.

By October 14, the state finalized a deal to fund what became Safeco Field. It would be two-thirds funded with a 0.5 percent sales tax on restaurants and bars, 2 percent on rental cars, and a 10 percent admissions tax on events at the new ballpark.

Van Dyk wasn't thrilled. But he realized it was the best he'd get under the circumstances. Others weren't so happy and filed lawsuits, claiming the new measure thwarted the spirit of the county referendum. Cost overruns also hampered the project and the Mariners again threatened to leave if public money wasn't used to cover them. Eventually, the lawsuits were beaten back and public funding for the deal was boosted to $372 million out of the stadium's final $517 million cost.

It all left a lingering bad taste. So much so that two years later, a statewide referendum spearheaded by billionaire Paul Allen seeking public funds for a new stadium for the Seahawks was also nearly defeated. Again, Van Dyk's group was at the forefront of the opposition, spending what he estimated at $300,000 in the face of $11 million in campaigning by the football team.

Van Dyk accepted the narrow 30,000-vote defeat graciously.

"They beat us," he said. "And we were true to our word. We didn't raise any legal challenges."

But the repercussions would be felt eight years later. SuperSonics owner Howard Schultz, the billionaire who'd turned Starbucks into a global empire, wanted a new arena. It hadn't even been a decade since a public-funded overhaul of KeyArena. Now, Schultz either wanted a $200 million makeover or a new venue.

"To Schultz, it should have been loud and clear that the river of sentiment was not on the side of subsidized arenas," Van Dyk said. "And here, the Sonics arena had just been rebuilt 10 years earlier. And Schultz was saying it wasn't good enough? Well, they'd had enough with the Kingdome that only lasted 20 years. So, the environment with him was toxic."

And it was irreparable. Politicians told Schultz there was no money left for him. Schultz promptly sold the team in 2006 to an Oklahoma City group led by Clay Bennett. Within two years, the team would move.

But in the interim, the new owners kept seeking local money for an arena. That's where Van Dyk's group stepped in. They came up with a ballot initiative known as I-91 that prevented the City of Seattle from handing out any sports subsidies unless offered a fair market return from teams.

The initiative passed overwhelmingly in November 2006. Any chance of the Sonics sticking around ended that night, though many feel Bennett and his group were always going to move the team regardless.

As for Van Dyk, he doesn't lose sleep worrying whether his efforts hampering the Mariners and Seahawks eventually caused Seattle to lose the Sonics. But his fingerprints are all over what became the future dialogue about bringing an NHL franchise to Seattle.

"We did, to our credit, change the dialogue on stadium financing in the Pacific Northwest."

Chapter 13

THE ONE THAT GOT AWAY

Hedge fund manager Christopher R. Hansen came along at the perfect time for a Seattle sports community that had suffered through plenty of imperfection. Not to be confused with the broadcaster of *To Catch a Predator* fame, though he often was, this particular Hansen was out to snag an NBA team. His family had moved from his native San Francisco and ultimately settled in a house on Horton Street in Seattle's Rainier Valley when Hansen was in second grade. He'd grown up a high school wrestling star and an avid Sonics fan. By the time the team was sold and relocated to Oklahoma City, Hansen himself had relocated to San Francisco, where his Valiant Capital hedge fund, founded the same year the Sonics departed, was making quite the name for itself with investors.

Flush with cash, Hansen began buying up commercial land in the SoDo District of his former Seattle hometown. The street was soon buzzing—Hansen wanted to build a new arena, right next to where the Mariners played baseball. Actually, it would be right next to the parking garage the Mariners had built next to where they played baseball, but it was still close enough. Too close, in fact, for the baseball team, which would prove a formidable nemesis for years to come. But in those heady immediate days post-Sonics, Hansen would forge an alliance with the Save Our Sonics fan movement and create momentum to bring the NBA back in short order.

By 2011, just three years after the Sonics departed, Hansen began meetings with then Mayor Mike McGinn and King County Executive Dow Constantine. Hansen's group carried considerable partner clout: billionaire Microsoft CEO Steve Ballmer, brothers Peter and Erik Nordstrom from the city's retail shopping conglomerate, and former Sonics executive Wally Walker.

By early 2012, Hansen announced plans to build a $490 million, state-of-the-art arena. He had worked out a deal with McGinn and Constantine in which he'd put $290 million toward the cost of the arena as well as purchase an NBA franchise to play in it. The remaining $200 million for the arena would come from public bond funding by both the city and county, triggered only once the NBA team was acquired. Hansen's group pledged to repay that money over time, seemingly satisfying the I-91 requirement that had been put into place by Chris van Dyk's "Citizens for More Important Things" six years earlier. The city's council was somewhat blindsided by the agreement, having been unaware of the discussions between Hansen and the mayor. But after lengthy negotiations, in which the council hired a team of sports management consultants to advise it, the deal was tightened up and approved in September 2012. It seemed as good a deal as Seattle could hope for.

Hansen was given five years of arena exclusivity within the city. That's how long he had to find a team, trigger the $200 million in public bond funding, and build his arena. While that was happening, the city agreed it would not pursue any other arena offers.

At the time, the exclusivity arrangement seemed an afterthought. For one thing, it didn't appear he'd need anything close to the full five years to get something done. Hansen already had a team targeted for relocation— the Sacramento Kings. And that drama was already playing itself out. Also, the city and county at the time didn't feel as if they'd get a better offer from any group beyond Hansen's. It had barely been four years since the new Sonics owners had tried to leverage a sweetheart deal out of Seattle-area governments before moving to Oklahoma City.

Carl Hirsch, a New York sports consultant hired by McGinn's administration to gauge Hansen's offer, still refers to it as one of the better ones he'd seen. "The proposal was one that would have been pretty hard to turn down, to be honest with you," Hirsch told me. "And it was hard to turn down, which is why we pursued it. Because the city was getting away pretty scot-free."

Hirsch said the $200 million in public bond money in the deal amounted to little more than Hansen using the city's credit and paying it back with interest. To this day, he remains convinced that the bond funding "was never going to happen" anyway, as interest rates plunged so low that Hansen likely would have financed everything privately had actual construction begun.

But before any construction could happen, Hansen needed a team. And the NBA wasn't expanding. So, Hansen's group targeted the Kings. Their ownership group, the Maloof family, had been lobbying Sacramento for a public-financed arena to no avail. Now, they had Hansen offering to pay handsomely to take the Kings off their hands.

Still, there were early warning signs things wouldn't go smoothly. Besides the Mariners, the Port of Seattle was protesting that an arena in SoDo next to baseball and football stadiums would be disastrous for traffic and impact local freight transportation. And perhaps even more important, the NBA seemed to have reservations about Hansen as the group's leader.

Early on in courting the Kings, Hirsch and Mayor McGinn visited with NBA commissioner David Stern and future commissioner Adam Silver at the league's New York City head office on a Monday morning in June 2012. McGinn's preliminary deal with Hansen had been reached a few months earlier but was still being finalized by the city council.

McGinn had gone there to assure Stern that he was very open to the NBA returning and different from his mayoral predecessor, Greg Nickels, who'd presided over the failed arena negotiations that resulted in the Sonics leaving town four years prior. After they'd discussed Hansen's proposal, McGinn said Stern had a strange question for him. "He asked me whether I'd have offered the same deal to somebody else," McGinn said.

The question seemed odd to McGinn. He said he told Stern that Hansen had come to them offering money and land. And that, had anybody else done that, he supposed he'd have considered them as well, but there was nobody doing that.

"I don't know that they had somebody else in mind," McGinn said. "And I don't know what the motive was. But it does, in retrospect, looking at how everything played out, well, the NBA is a club. And who they admit matters. It matters to them."

The question of whether the NBA ever wanted Hansen as a partner would haunt the process.

By January 2013, the Maloof family had reached a deal to sell a 65 percent controlling interest in the Kings to Hansen at a valuation of $525 million. Hansen later increased his offer to $550 million, meaning his stake would cost $357 million. The following month, he filed for relocation with the league.

But Sacramento wasn't about to lose its team without a fight. Mayor Kevin Johnson, a former NBA player, pushed a plan for a $447 million arena through the city council and lined up an ownership group to buy the team.

By April 2013, McGinn was back at NBA headquarters with Hansen and Ballmer this time, helping make a pitch to team owners for why the Kings should be relocated. Ballmer gave an especially energetic performance that would be remembered by owners for years afterward. Hansen told the owners he'd rename the team SuperSonics and had been working behind the scenes with former Seattle general manager Walker.

McGinn said he didn't sense any outward hostility toward the group from team owners. But there was skepticism expressed about whether local governments were prepared to stand by their word and support the squad if relocation was approved.

And later that month, the NBA's relocation committee unanimously dealt Hansen a major setback by voting to recommend that owners oppose moving the Kings to Seattle. Chairing the committee was Clay Bennett, who'd bought the Sonics and moved them to Oklahoma City nearly five years prior.

A few weeks later in Dallas, the NBA board of governors voted 22–8 against letting Hansen buy the Kings. McGinn today remains philosophical about the outcome.

"I just had a feeling they didn't want to do to Sacramento what they did to Seattle," he said.

Hansen vowed to keep trying to land a team. In fact, Hansen tried too hard to regain some lost momentum. A few months later, it came out he'd violated California elections law by secretly donating $100,000 toward funding efforts to block a bid to build Sacramento's proposed new arena. Without the arena, he'd figured, the Kings would again be forced to relocate. But Hansen got caught and was fined $50,000. Far more damaging, though, was the fact that the NBA, by all accounts, was not pleased.

Years later, in my one and only face-to-face meeting with Hansen, I asked him whether he thought the league harbored a grudge. After all, messing with the NBA's preferred arena and team location was, in effect, messing with the money. Doing that to any cabal in any business, legal or otherwise, is typically a fatal mistake.

"We were in this very competitive process, some mistakes were made, we apologized," Hansen said. "People get caught up in the heat of battle, people make mistakes. I've made very few mistakes in my life, and that's one of them. And I would take Adam [Silver's] acceptance of my apology at face value."

In April 2014, eight months after Hansen's illegal donation surfaced, I had the first of many brief chances to chat with new commissioner Silver, who'd replaced the outgoing Stern two months prior. We were standing in a hallway at the NBA offices in New York after partaking in the Associated Press Sports Editors commissioners meetings, a small gathering of about 20 newspaper editors in a conference room with Silver and select NBA executives, including Mike Bass and Kiki VanDeWeghe. I'd asked Silver several times about Hansen's group and Seattle's chances of landing an NBA team. Now, we were briefly continuing the conversation alone outside.

Silver assured me NBA owners harbored no ill will toward Hansen's group, despite the illegal funding fiasco. But he also told me they particularly liked Ballmer. "There's a guy any league would love to have as an owner," Silver said.

Silver likely had no idea exactly what he was foreshadowing. But the timing of his comment proved uncanny.

Just a few weeks later, Los Angeles Clippers owner Donald Sterling did about as good a job of destroying his legacy as humanly possible when he was caught on tape making racist remarks. Though he tried to talk his way out of it, he was done. Silver banned him for life and forced a sale of the team. It was the opening that Ballmer, spurned only a year earlier in his joint bid with Hansen for the Kings, had been looking for. This time, though, he wouldn't be moving any teams to Seattle. The Clippers buy was all about Ballmer, not his city of residence.

Ballmer knew the NBA wouldn't let a team leave Los Angeles for Seattle. He also sensed it would take years before another opportunity for Hansen's group came around again, if ever. The NBA clearly had no problems with Ballmer, as Silver had indicated to me.

So, this was personal. Ballmer had grown up in Michigan an avid basketball fan. He was taught the game's finer points later in life as a rising Microsoft honcho by onetime Sonics trainer Steve Gordon. They'd had a chance meeting at a local racquet club outside Seattle frequented by

Microsoft executives and immediately hit it off. The men became friends after Ballmer started paying Gordon for lessons.

This time, though, with the Clippers, Ballmer would be reaching far deeper into his wallet than he ever had for Gordon. At age 58, he wasn't getting any younger and didn't want to blow this bid. So, he overbid— shocking the sports world by offering $2 billion, which was $500 million more than a runner-up group headed by music mogul David Geffen.

Ballmer got his NBA team. But he also caused untold headaches for Hansen back in Seattle. For one, he wound up leaving Hansen's group. As the group's only asset anyone in the NBA appeared to be paying serious attention to, that left Hansen in a precarious position.

Not to mention, the optics of Ballmer making what many sports analysts considered a $500 million "overpay" on the Clippers wasn't a great look for Hansen back in Seattle. After all, his group had been seeking $200 million in public bond funding even while Ballmer was still a partner with $2 billion apparently burning a hole in his pocket.

So, Hansen had his work cut out for him if he wanted to keep his SoDo arena project alive. The clock was ticking on his five-year deal with the city, and he had little time to waste.

Chapter 14

SEATTLE "GAMESMANSHIP" IN ARIZONA

It was a scorching June 2013 afternoon—not that there are many other kinds in Glendale, Arizona—when I met for lunch there with local city council member Gary Sherwood. We strolled through the Westgate entertainment district, a collection of shops and restaurants adjacent to what was then known as Jobing.com Arena and that served as home to what was then called the Phoenix Coyotes.

Yes, there are quite a few "then known as" and "then called" references to hockey in the desert. The Coyotes had been an off-ice mess pretty much since the franchise up and relocated from Winnipeg in 1996. Their Coyotes name stuck, but that's about all. When it comes to the team's ownership, you never know who's going to be the next "former" version, as everybody from Wayne Gretzky to the National Hockey League has taken a stab at running the franchise to no avail.

On this particular afternoon, as Sherwood and I settled in at a Gordon Biersch brewpub, it was the NHL running the Coyotes. Their prior owner, Jerry Moyes, had declared bankruptcy and turned operations over to the league in 2009. In the four years since, a never-ending search for new owners had continuously met with headaches and headlines. But now, the league had new owners from Canada ready to step in and buy the team.

Only trouble was, Anthony Leblanc and his partners at Renaissance Sports and Entertainment wanted a better lease negotiated for the Coyotes at the city-owned arena. In fact, Leblanc's group wanted one of the best lease deals ever negotiated by a team in the history of professional sport.

Under the terms, the city would pay the Coyotes $15 million annually for the next 15 years to stay at the arena. The city had budgeted for only $6 million annually.

That's right, the city was effectively paying the Coyotes to play in its own arena. And for 15 more years at that, the rationale being that Westgate and its various businesses risked being rendered an economic wasteland if the main anchor arena was suddenly without a feature hockey attraction.

Every so often, the Coyotes threatened to move someplace else in greater Phoenix that wasn't out in desert suburbia, upon which Glendale promptly coughed up new cash. Under NHL stewardship, the Coyotes had been given $25 million over four years even as Glendale pared back its parks, police, and fire services.

Naturally, some on Glendale's council were skeptical of the sheer amount of money involved in the proposed new lease. In fact, they hated it. Their ability to keep providing essential services was mentioned repeatedly. After all, there was only so much money any city had and the Coyotes, well, would see a lot more of it directed their way if this deal passed. The job of cities was to provide such services to the community, they argued, not be extorted by wealthy hockey team owners.

"I just do what's right," councilmember Norma Alvarez, one of those opposing the lease, had told some of us standing outside a closed-door council meeting the morning of my lunch with Sherwood.

Sherwood didn't agree. In fact, he'd grown up a Detroit Red Wings fan in Michigan and couldn't stand the idea of the Coyotes leaving his adopted Arizona burb. That put him directly at odds with Alvarez, as well as with Glendale's new, tough-talking, hard-on-sports Mayor Jerry Weiers. He was sick and tired of Glendale being used as a piggy bank by sports teams and, truth be told, growing more than fatigued with the sight of Sherwood's face.

It shouldn't surprise that talk back then had the pair gearing to oppose one another in the next mayoral election. But for the time being, well, there was a lease to either approve or quash.

And it just so happened a gentleman from New York by the name of Ray Bartoszek had shown up in town and was turning up the heat even balmier than a 3 PM afternoon stroll through Westgate. Bartoszek was an investment banker who made his residence in the posh New York bedroom community of Greenwich, Connecticut. He'd appeared out of the blue with a partner named Anthony Lanza and the NHL's apparent blessing.

Just as the Canadian group had done, Bartoszek and Lanza were offering to buy the Coyotes.

Only thing is, they had no interest in Glendale leases or even Glendale at all. No, Bartoszek seemed to be spearheading the whole thing and wanted to buy the Coyotes just so he could move them to Seattle. It turns out his wife had family there and, well, he could read the papers and sensed an opportunity.

Or so he claimed.

Just weeks before, the NBA had rejected a plan to move the Sacramento Kings to Seattle to play in KeyArena and then a new SoDo District arena proposed by entrepreneur Chris Hansen. So, sure, it's plausible Bartoszek sensed an opportunity to make a PR splash, soothe a spurned city's hurt feelings somewhat, and fill a winter sports void there. But his Coyotes play was causing quite a few scratched heads among bankers and consultants who made their living off gauging team sales. Namely, they wondered, if the wealthier NBA wasn't prepared to let a team relocate to Seattle, how was the NHL going to go there first without a major arena to play in?

Hansen had long stated he had no intention of building any new arena without the guarantee of an NBA franchise coming his way. Hockey was an entirely different entity, largely dependent on gate revenue as opposed to the additional billions the NBA, NFL, and MLB generated from national television deals.

But Bartoszek was unfazed. He was prepared to play a few seasons at KeyArena and see what happened. Bartoszek was definitely a sports junkie, owning a small piece of the New York Yankees and routinely flying on his private jet to ski the slopes at Big Sky, take in the French Open in Paris, or visit his 48-meter yacht docked in the Bahamas. He wasn't a billionaire, but he wasn't broke either. In NHL owner context, that had typically been good enough.

Owning an NHL team as the big cheese seemed a logical next step, given Bartoszek's resume. NHL commissioner Gary Bettman certainly wasn't doing anything to rule out the notion of the Coyotes relocating to Seattle.

A vote was upcoming on whether Glendale's council would approve or quash the massively lopsided Coyotes lease. The afternoon of my lunch with Sherwood was 10 days before a deadline to either approve the lease or risk having the NHL sell to Bartoszek instead of the Canadians.

Sherwood was all-in on the new lease and the sudden insertion of Bartoszek into the conversation clearly irked him as we dined on chicken wings and beer. Sherwood wanted the lease deal passed on its merits, not because of some proverbial gun in the form of Bartoszek being pointed at the council's head by Bettman and the NHL.

"It's just gamesmanship," he assured me. "That's all it is."

Former Seattle Mayor Mike McGinn, who held office from 2010 through 2014, isn't so sure. Nearly a decade after those events of 2013, he remains convinced today there was a chance of the Coyotes relocating to his city. McGinn told me of a phone call he'd received from NHL commissioner Bettman in the weeks before the Glendale lease showdown advising him of Bartoszek's interest in moving the Coyotes.

"It was a check-in," McGinn said. "If the council didn't vote for this lease, they were going to move the team up here to Seattle. And they wanted to make sure we were ready. I told him, 'We're ready.'"

Later, McGinn recalled meeting with representatives from Bartoszek's group in his office. He wasn't certain Bartoszek himself attended but remembered the details.

"I remember the discussion was that if the team was acquired, then the team was going to move up and they were going to use KeyArena as is," McGinn said. "It wasn't relevant to them whether a new arena was going to be built. It was relevant to the future, as Chris Hansen was describing, but that was not essential to them moving up and having the team occupy KeyArena here."

McGinn said Bartoszek's group "definitely didn't put a hard timeline" on needing to have a new arena. "I kind of got a sense that they were parking the team there. It's like, 'You're not going to give us a lease in Glendale? Then, we're moving.' I think it was kind of implicit—it certainly wasn't explicit—that if it didn't work out in Seattle, then they'd move on."

It wouldn't be the last time Bartoszek inserted himself into an arena issue that involved Seattle. He seemed to have an uncanny knack for showing up exactly when the NHL needed some kind of lever to pull to get local governments to do exactly what it needed.

Bartoszek and I would meet, speak, and text one another numerous times over the years that followed, though not initially during the Coyotes saga. Later, he would tell me he had moving trucks at the ready to load up Coyotes equipment, furniture, and files and start moving them to Seattle the day after the vote if the lease deal was quashed. And that he'd watched the vote itself on a livestreamed feed from his laptop back on the East Coast.

I've heard from people working closely with the NHL that Bartoszek is not a league-mandated stalking horse, just a guy who really wants to own a team. And that NHL commissioner Bettman and his deputy, Bill Daly, play that to their advantage as any good businessmen would. Still, Bartoszek for years to come, starting in Glendale and later in Seattle itself and Long Island, New York, would keep showing up with alternative arena plans whenever a local government dithered on ruling the NHL's preferred way. In essence, he remained the gift that just couldn't stop giving to the league.

And it all began in Glendale. On the eve of the Coyotes lease vote, a councilmember named Samuel Chavira suddenly had a change of heart. Chavira had opposed the Coyotes lease deal, but then, at the last minute, decided it really wasn't so bad for the city after all.

Chavira cast his vote for the lease alongside my lunch companion Sherwood, swinging a 4–3 decision in favor of the Coyotes staying put for years to come and sending Bartoszek home empty-handed.

Coincidentally, or maybe not, about a year later, Sherwood would have a similar epiphany. He decided that a casino project planned for directly across the street from a local high school probably wasn't the blight on the community he'd long argued it was.

It just so happened that Chavira was a staunch proponent of the casino. And wouldn't you know it, the day of a vote on that project, Sherwood cast his alongside Chavira and swung things 4–3 in favor of letting the roulette wheels spin while recess bells rang in the background.

Much grumbling ensued, little of it favorable to either politician. Phrases like "horse trading" were thrown around. When I caught up again with Sherwood at his office soon after the casino vote, in August 2014, he looked as if he'd aged exponentially.

When I asked him about his casino vote, he told me, "I changed my mind after further exploration of the facts."

At the time, Sherwood was fending off the first of multiple petitions to have him recalled from his council seat, claiming he'd gone against too many of the positions he'd campaigned on. That initial attempt to remove him failed. But things were about to get worse. Two additional petitions with more than 15,000 signatures apiece had been submitted to the council attempting to get it to nullify the Coyotes vote.

Nine months later, in June 2015, the Glendale council voted 5–2 to terminate the Coyotes lease after just two years of the agreed-to 15. Sherwood and Chavira were the two councilmembers opposing the termination. By then, the city had become a nationwide laughingstock and a cautionary tale. But Glendale had found a way out—namely, that Sherwood and others had violated the state's Open Meetings Law before the 2013 lease vote when they'd met secretly with a lawyer for the team's future Canadian-based owners to discuss confidential items from one of the council's private executive sessions.

So, the Coyotes' lease was terminated. And a few months later, in November 2015, Sherwood was voted out of office in a recall election. Chavira was voted out a year later.

From there, the Coyotes and Glendale undertook a series of year-to-year leases. The Coyotes ever since had let it be known they were seeking a new Arizona arena location. Yet they continued to renew their yearly Glendale leases for ensuing seasons. And they kept burning through owners: first the Leblanc-led Canadian group, then Philadelphia investment banker Andrew Barroway, and finally, Alex Meruelo in August 2019. By mid-2022, the Meruello-led Coyotes had been evicted by the City of Glendale from what's now called the Gila River Arena. They plan to indefinitely play at a 5,000-seat venue being built in Tempe for the Arizona State University hockey team until a new NHL facility is approved nearby.

In November of 2021, I met with Glendale city manager Kevin Phelps in the same arena-adjacent Westgate plaza as where I'd lunched with former councilmember Sherwood years earlier. Phelps had just served the team the eviction notice and told me there was no going back. The city, he said, pointing all around at new development within Westgate, had found more lucrative uses for the complex than a hockey team that kept threatening to leave.

As for Bartoszek, his efforts to buy the Coyotes had ended with him hunched over his laptop watching the lease initially approved on the strength of Chavira's swung ballot. He and partner Lanza soon parted ways. But it was only the beginning of some of Bartoszek's rather wacky involvements with the NHL as it pertained to Seattle.

Chapter 15

OVERHAULING KEYARENA FOR NBA AND NHL

Michigan native Ryan Sickman always imagined his biggest contribution to the sports world would be blocking things. A standout high school soccer goalie in Ohio, he'd made the United States under-17 men's squad. Later, he accepted a Division I scholarship to play at Penn State University.

But Sickman earned something else from Penn State as well: his degree in architecture. And once he was done blocking shots on the soccer field, it would be Sickman applying his expertise to Seattle's arena discussions in a way few before had tried. Rather than blocking things this time, it would be Sickman arguing that new ideas should be allowed through the preventive mind-set that had dominated all Seattle thinking regarding KeyArena's possibilities.

Namely, it was a Sickman-led team from the AECOM architectural firm that suggested KeyArena could be overhauled to again stage major professional sports events. His critics had scoffed at the notion, especially legions of Seattle basketball fans angling for Chris Hansen's proposed new arena in the SoDo district. For years, prevailing Seattle wisdom had been that KeyArena's footprint was too small. And that knocking it down and starting over was impossible because of its 44-million-pound roof, designed by iconic Pacific Northwest architect Paul Thiry for the 1962 World's Fair. That roof had passed the half-century mark in age and qualified for historical preservation status. In other words, anybody wanting to redesign the building had to do so without touching the roof.

Naturally, most agreed this was impossible. Also, no one was about to try. The City of Seattle in late 2012 had signed a five-year deal with Hansen to explore building his SoDo arena. As part of that deal, Hansen received arena exclusivity, meaning the city could not entertain offers to build a rival venue. And that included reviving KeyArena.

Hansen planned to use KeyArena as a temporary home for an NBA team while his new arena in SoDo got built. As for what would become of KeyArena after that, well, that part was anyone's guess. It seemed like a minor detail at the time, but a growing sense of worry began popping up behind the scenes at city hall. After all, KeyArena had been built with public money. Then, in 1994, when the NBA Sonics embarked on a slapdash $95 million renovation of the facility, an additional $75 million in public funds was used.

As of early 2014, with the Sonics long gone to Oklahoma City, KeyArena was now playing host to the WNBA Seattle Storm. And to whatever major concerts the city could attract. Though the acoustics were terrible, KeyArena still was the region's only major indoor concert venue. It was expected that Hansen's new SoDo arena would become the city's prime concert draw. Which did little to quell the question of what to do about KeyArena. For one thing, it still carried the name of its former Key Bank naming rights sponsor. Those naming rights had lapsed back in 2010. But a city analysis had shown the cost of removing signage would likely be more than any new rightsholder would be willing to pay—especially with the venue's future in doubt. So, Key Bank got several years' worth of continued free advertising while city officials fretted about what would become of the venue bearing its name.

Well, it just so happened that Hansen had agreed to help the city answer the question making them fret. Another often-overlooked part of his deal with the city was his pledge to pay for a study exploring KeyArena's potential future uses.

And by early 2014, an alert city councilmember named Jean Godden, a onetime local journalist, realized this part of the deal had gone ignored. So, she decided to take Hansen up on his offer. She spearheaded a council move to pay an outside expert $150,000 to study KeyArena's potential future uses. That expert would be the AECOM firm that Sickman had just joined as its lead sports architect.

A contract was agreed to and the scope of work outlined, and for the next several months, AECOM officials led by Sickman dug into the issue. They explored transforming KeyArena into a parking garage. Looked at continuing to stage only smaller sports events and concerts there. And at downsizing the arena for even smaller events still. At building a theme park inside. Even at turning the arena into affordable housing. But those options required significant city investments and did not guarantee much of a financial return. In some cases, AECOM found the arena would start losing money even after the new city investments. Doing nothing similarly wasn't an option since the venue was badly in need of an overhaul. It would cease attracting events if investments weren't made.

Of course, there was also the idea NBA and NHL teams might invest in redoing the arena. But prevailing Seattle wisdom, as usual, had already discounted that. At 17,000 seats and just under 400,000 square feet of space, they argued, it would be the smallest arena in either league. No team owners or developers in their right mind would play there, knowing the protected roof made expanding the site impossible.

But Sickman was an idealist, impassioned by the idea of repurposing older buildings into new ones rather than leveling them and starting over. And he wondered whether, regardless of the roof situation, the city wasn't giving up on KeyArena as a major pro sports venue just a little too quickly.

"I think we have a responsibility to really take a look at our infrastructure and our existing facilities and see what's feasible—without pulling a plug and building a new arena every single time," he told me in an extensive conversation not long after his work for the city.

During our talk, Sickman described in detail how he'd made it a personal mission to present such remodel solutions. He'd quietly looked at KeyArena's expansion dilemma and quickly discovered its big problem wasn't the roof. It was that the arena floor was not properly centered. Running further calculations, he'd figured out by mid-summer 2014 that tilting the venue floor diagonally would help better maximize the arena's space.

Encouraged, he kept exploring the matter in greater detail. By then, word began leaking out in city council circles that a potential KeyArena solution was emerging. In November 2014, a preliminary 103-page interim report was delivered to select council members by Sickman and AECOM.

The report stated that additional KeyArena floor space could be created by tilting the arena floor diagonally and changing the seating sections to make them steeper. It concluded that the changes would be enough to potentially expand seating and back-of-house space to attract major pro teams again.

Eyebrows were raised. Skepticism was expressed. This was KeyArena, they reminded Sickman. Everyone had concluded it was impossible to fix. The fact that nobody had ever seriously explored "fixing" it this way wasn't really a concern. Everyone knew what they already knew. They peppered the AECOM team with questions. All of which were answered. So, they threw different questions at the AECOM team. Who was going to pay for this fix? Again, all of Seattle, it seemed, knew that nobody sane would ever pay for a KeyArena overhaul with private money.

AECOM hadn't really done a cost analysis. After all, it was an architectural firm and its scope had merely been to find alternative solutions for KeyArena once Hansen had moved the NBA team into his SoDo venue. Still, councilmembers pressed for more—some out of keen interest, others to confirm their resolve that nothing could be done.

The city, they knew, was knee-deep in Hansen's plans for a SoDo arena. By then, it was only two years into the five-year exclusivity arrangement Hansen had been granted to find a team and start building. Talk of reviving KeyArena? Well, not only did it sound crazy on some levels, but it was probably illegal. Or, at least, probably something that could get them sued by Hansen if they began seriously entertaining it before his deal was up.

Sure, Hansen hadn't broken any records getting his SoDo arena off the ground. Or out of the ground, to be more precise. The NBA had rejected his bid for the Sacramento Kings two years prior. Steve Ballmer had just left his group months earlier to purchase the Los Angeles Clippers and wasn't moving them to Seattle. And an environmental impact study of Hansen's project had been delayed for months because of his reluctance to turn over requested documents. Though the study was now again underway and expected to be released by spring 2015, he still didn't have the NBA team he needed before construction could begin. Hansen had made clear he wasn't going to build without such a team, lest he be stuck with an empty arena.

Whenever an NHL team was mentioned, Hansen would politely remind folks he'd grown up loving basketball, not hockey. Pucks weren't his passion. If some hockey-crazed billionaire wanted to show him a plan where the NHL could be profitable at his arena, he was all ears. But he wasn't building anything without an NBA team.

Quietly, many within city hall had started to doubt Hansen's ability to land that team. Especially with Ballmer gone and after the illegal election funding fiasco in which Hansen had secretly tried to block the NBA-backed new Sacramento arena from getting built. The NBA sure didn't seem to be rushing to give Hansen anything. Some wondered whether the NBA secretly had it in for Hansen.

But the city was stuck with him for three more years. So, all this KeyArena talk was best kept quiet until more could be figured out.

By early 2015, though, AECOM had run some numbers and drilled down more on the KeyArena fix. It was estimating that $285 million might be enough to carry out the diagonal-floor version first conceived by Sickman. That number got attention. Hansen's arena plan in SoDo was for a $490 million arena paid for with $200 million in public bond funding. Sure, Hansen had pledged to eventually repay that money over time with interest. But that didn't solve the problem of what would happen to KeyArena. In fact, it appeared that the city's arena would be rendered obsolete by Hansen's project. In effect, the city would be supplying tens of millions of dollars in bond money for Hansen to destroy its own, still-profitable KeyArena asset.

No matter how they tried to twist it, the logic of green-lighting Hansen's project was seeming less palatable. AECOM, a global firm, was confirming that no solution out there would allow KeyArena to survive intact without oozing taxpayer money.

And the only solution AECOM was suggesting was this crazy diagonal rink idea. Now they were hearing it could be done for $285 million? That wasn't exactly a pittance. Then again, they were willing to give Hansen the bulk of the $200 million in bond funding. It wasn't too far off to spend $285 million to fix their own arena and cut him out of the equation entirely.

Sure, getting somebody else to pay the cost was an easier option to swallow. In fact, AECOM was suggesting that route. That way, the city could immediately turn small profits off a split in revenues with private partners without construction costs eating up all of it and more.

Still, the question lingered: Who was possibly going to pay private money to expand KeyArena beneath a roof that couldn't be touched? Up until then, nobody had bothered to try to find out. They technically weren't allowed to because of the city's exclusivity deal with Hansen.

But as winter evolved into spring of what would be a tumultuous 2015 year on the city's arena front, some answers slowly began to emerge.

Chapter 16

DON'T CALL HIM "ED"

Of all things Seattle Mayor Ed Murray was equipped to do upon taking office, resolving a festering arena situation wasn't one of them. Campaign as a state senator for a $2.4 billion tunnel project that bored for years beneath the city's former Alaskan Way Viaduct? Murray was the guy. Champion gay rights, spurred on by his mentor, former state lawmaker Cal Anderson? Perfectly suited. Push for police reforms and a $15 an hour minimum wage? That's where Murray excelled.

But a sports expert he was not. That became apparent in the rare times Murray took to the airwaves and rolled the dice with sports radio talk show hosts eager to carve him a new one. Murray just didn't know what he didn't know. But he did sense upon taking office in January 2014 that the arena question wasn't going away.

Murray knew that Chris Hansen wanted to build an arena in the city's SoDo district, despite being rejected by the NBA in his 2013 bid to acquire the Sacramento Kings. He'd been introduced to Hansen his first weeks in office while attending a Seattle Seahawks playoff game in owner Paul Allen's suite during their early 2014 run to a Super Bowl championship.

Murray said he and Hansen "had a great chat" and that a follow-up dinner was arranged. They met not long after at El Gaucho, an Argentinian expense-account steakhouse in the city's Belltown neighborhood. After dining on prime beef, they retired to the restaurant's fabled cigar lounge to talk business.

By all accounts, it was a disaster of epic proportions. For years, folks whispered about it being Hansen's undoing. And when I met for lunch with Murray years after he'd resigned from office in disgrace, he was all too willing to share details.

"He managed to hit every one of my working-class chips on my shoulder," Murray said. "I was fairly irritated. I walked out at one point. I just had to go to the bathroom and wanted to visit a friend of mine—she was a server there—just to cool off and then go back in. Because there was arrogance, and it wasn't going well."

Murray said he'd made it clear to Hansen the SoDo site wasn't his first choice, but he'd campaigned in favor of it and would honor it even though it hadn't been his deal. But Murray said things went sideways when he told Hansen he'd have "a significant hole in the ground" with KeyArena being rendered obsolete if the SoDo arena got built. Murray also had a broader vision for reviving Seattle Center, site of the 1962 World's Fair and where KeyArena was an anchor. Hansen, he said, brushed off those concerns.

"He was just incredibly condescending," Murray said. "Incredibly entitled. There was a lot of talk about the money he had, how he made it.... Which, of course, really irritated me. It wasn't a great dinner."

Others attending that night said Murray was thrown off from the preliminary handshake. "I think one of the things that may have triggered him is when Chris called the mayor 'Ed' rather than 'Mr. Mayor,'" said Rollin Fatland, a longtime Seattle lobbyist and Hansen's local spokesperson. "He called him 'Ed'. He sat at the table, had a good discussion with him. I was sitting right next to him. I would not say he didn't pay him deference other than his informally calling him 'Ed' rather than 'Mayor.'"

Two others at the dinner that night confirmed this version of events.

Then, in May of that year, Murray was paid a visit by NHL commissioner Gary Bettman and his deputy, Bill Daly. They were on their way to California for a Los Angeles Kings–Anaheim Ducks playoff game and decided to make a Seattle stopover. And they brought a guest with them. His name was Victor Coleman, a British Columbia native who'd grown up a Vancouver Canucks fan. Coleman also headed Husdon Pacific Properties, a growing West Coast commercial real estate conglomerate based in California.

Coleman had money, the desire to own a hockey team, and Murray's ear. Actually, it was the other way around. It seems Coleman had already held preliminary discussions with SoDo arena pitchman Hansen. But Coleman wanted to know the state of play in Seattle from Murray.

Murray said he reiterated that Hansen had a five-year exclusivity deal to get his SoDo arena built, and it had some three and a half years remaining. Murray described Coleman as "fairly agnostic" about where the arena should be. "He just wanted to play hockey in Seattle," Murray said.

City records show Coleman the following year held conversations with the Anschutz Entertainment Group about the AECOM report and reviving KeyArena for the NHL. AEG was managing KeyArena's marketing on the city's behalf at the time.

But during that May 2014 meeting with Murray, the would-be NHL owner and Hansen were still in discussions. The AECOM report hadn't gotten off the ground and the general assumption was KeyArena was a waste of time. Hansen was still the only game in town. Murray had to tell the NHL, Coleman, and anyone else asking that the city's exclusivity deal with Hansen running through November 2017 prevented discussions about putting an arena anywhere but the SoDo site.

And Hansen, Murray informed them, wasn't going to even start his $490 million arena project until the NBA awarded him a team. Murray reiterated how Hansen's deal with the city and King County required the basketball team before he'd receive up to $200 million in public bond funding.

It was old news to Bettman and Daly. A month before their meeting with Murray, I'd gone to New York, met both, and asked their opinions about putting an NHL team in Seattle.

"Chris Hansen controls the rights to what may be a building in downtown Seattle, and I think he controls those rights for a number of years," Bettman said. "And so, unless somebody comes in and says, 'OK, we have an understanding with Chris and we've got this and we've got that and we've got that' at that point, we may say, 'Let's listen to this more seriously.'"

They'd gone to meet Murray a month later hoping Coleman's presence might jump-start something. But Coleman, Bettman, and Daly left somewhat frustrated. By then, word was out that billionaire Steve Ballmer was making overtures to buy the Los Angeles Clippers from the wife of disgraced former owner Donald Sterling. It was evident Hansen's group was about to lose its "whale" and would be further away than ever from an NBA team.

Later that year, once Ballmer had indeed left Hansen's group, Murray arranged to meet in New York with NBA commissioner Adam Silver in January 2015. By then, Hansen had supplied missing documents needed to revive an environmental impact study being undertaken by the city at his planned SoDo site. As Murray watched the laborious process unfold, he wanted clarity from the NBA on Hansen's chances of actually landing a franchise.

So, as Murray's predecessor, Mike McGinn, had done years earlier with former NBA commissioner David Stern, the latest Seattle mayor wanted a face-to-face with new league head honcho Silver. It was both a get-to-know-you and temperature-taking mission at the same time. And what

Murray heard at the January 2015 meeting was a game-changer for Seattle's arena discussions.

"The meeting was a huge eye-opener," Murray said. "And the eye-opener was that we weren't getting a basketball team anytime soon. And that all of this talk among sports people in Seattle was pretty much not based on anything."

That was a serious problem. Hansen's five-year exclusivity deal with the city still had just under three years to run and now Silver was telling Murray that no team was coming. More than that, he said, Silver made clear that NBA owners did indeed hold a grudge toward Hansen for secretly funding a 2013 petition to stop a new Sacramento arena the league wanted for the Kings. Hansen had been rebuffed in trying to buy the Kings franchise, but had funded the anti-arena effort hoping that if it blocked the venue, he'd get another shot at moving the team to Seattle.

"There was animosity toward us," Murray said of what Silver relayed to him. "And they were really harsh in their clarity that if there was any more trying to steal a team, Seattle would never get a team."

Murray said Silver didn't see NBA owners being willing to change how they split revenue. The league had just entered a nine-year, $24 billion national television deal in 2014 with ESPN and Turner Sports.

"So, there was that and that was really clear," Murray said. "But there was the added Seattle problem. And they did not state it publicly, but it became very clear to me that they weren't in love with Chris. They did not believe that Chris Hansen had a viable path forward. Because of [Steve] Ballmer buying the L.A. [Clippers] team and leaving his group. And so, it was an eye-opening meeting."

Murray from there returned to Seattle and tried to spread the word that the NBA wasn't coming. And that a new path toward an arena needed to be found by Hansen or somebody else. He never mentioned in public that he'd felt the league wasn't enamored with Hansen. Nonetheless, Murray's warnings met with considerable resistance within his city.

"It seemed to upset both the fans and actually some of the sports reporters that I was saying no team was coming. And that even if I was the mayor for eight years, I don't see it."

But what Murray was saying about Silver's views was apparently the truth. I know because I had the chance to ask Silver about it directly a few months later during an April 2015 meetup with him at the NBA's offices.

I asked Silver about his meeting with Murray and what the mayor concluded from it. We'd already met at those same offices a year earlier, so there was some familiarity. Silver confirmed Murray's assessment that the league was a good two or three years from expanding, which would likely extend beyond the November 2017 deadline of Hansen's arena exclusivity deal in Seattle.

"I very much enjoyed being in Seattle when we had a team there," Silver told me. "They had fantastic fans there. But what I said was, unrelated to any specific market, there didn't seem to be much interest in expansion at the time from our owners."

Silver also told me the league's new $24 billion national TV deal was indeed fueling the NBA team owners' reluctance to expand. "We've seen, maybe for the first time in the history of this league, what seems to me to be a true 30-team league," Silver told me. "Where fans in every community… can believe that their team is well-managed, that their team can compete for a championship."

Silver then added: "My sense right now is that, from a competitive standpoint, we have a 30-team league that can be competitive. But the talent is such that it shouldn't necessarily be the case that we should be adding additional roster slots."

Those words, though not overly aggressive, should have sounded the death knell for Hansen's project in Seattle. At least, if Hansen had any hope of first bringing in an NBA team to trigger the $200 million in public bond funding. The NBA commissioner was, in fact, saying that Hansen would likely not get a team before his deal with the city expired.

But Murray felt he'd discovered a possible path forward. The same January 2015 day he'd met with Silver and NBA executives, he also headed a few additional blocks over to NHL headquarters for a meetup with commissioner Bettman and deputy Daly. As opposed to the NBA, Murray said the hockey executives he'd first met with at his offices the previous spring "were incredibly excited" about putting a team in Seattle. They offered up several possible paths to attaining one. But all depended on resolving the arena issue.

It's hardly a coincidence Murray's public statements thereafter on Hansen's arena plan throughout 2015 always mentioned "NHL first" being the plausible way forward. He implored Hansen to consider building the arena for an NHL team, then seeking an NBA franchise later. But Hansen continued to resist.

In the meantime, the NHL was about to go on the power play.

Chapter 17

NHL PUSHES FOR SEATTLE EXPANSION

It was in the weeks before the Seahawks lost their February 1, 2015, Super Bowl to the Patriots in Glendale, Arizona, that a businessman named Mason Cave popped on to my radar. The date sticks out because I happened to own a second home in Glendale at the time, directly across the street from the University of Phoenix Stadium, where the Seahawks would fail to hand the ball off to Marshawn Lynch in the big game's dying seconds.

Truth be told, I'd eventually wind up walking from my condo to that Super Bowl in about five minutes to help the *Seattle Times* cover it. Not many people can say that out loud. Anyway, I'd bought the place back while covering the Mariners baseball team and their two months of annual Arizona spring training in neighboring Peoria. Later, I'd kept it as a sunny refuge from Seattle's rain after moving on to cover other subjects of sporting interest. Often, I'd pop down for a few weeks and work on investigative stories from there.

So, down in Glendale in the weeks leading up to the big game, I'd gotten a call from a trusted, well-connected tipster who prodded me to look deeper into Cave with regard to Seattle's arena situation. In an interesting twist, it turned out Cave owned an Arizona-based real estate company, IntraVest Development, that had its corporate office near the Mariners' spring training site in Peoria just 10 miles away from where I was sitting. That alone was enough to prompt me into action that day. I figured I could literally go knock on IntraVest's door if I couldn't reach Cave by phone.

I quickly discovered Cave and his partners had an option to purchase a 4.4-acre parcel of land in Bellevue, a fast-growing, high-end suburb with its own downtown core directly across Lake Washington from Seattle.

Piquing my interest, the land in the city's Wilburton district sat adjacent Highway 405 connecting downtown Bellevue to the rest of the region. And it was also, if you built a footbridge over a small ravine, only a short walk from a downtown Bellevue light rail station expected within a decade. In other words, it made for a strong arena site.

IntraVest was hoping to eventually buy and flip the land if the right investor came along to develop it. I phoned IntraVest's offices in Peoria, but no one answered. Then, after acquiring Cave's cell phone number through public records, I got hold of him. It turned out he wasn't in Arizona that day, but up in Bellevue leasing a much nicer condo than mine in a fancy building called The Bravern.

Cave was chatty. And in our conversation, I learned of the existence of a man known in NHL and NBA circles as the "Deal Whisperer." Cave told me multiple investor groups had interest in the Bellevue land but the "Deal Whisperer" was interested in building a sports arena.

So, who was this "Deal Whisperer" guy? Turns out, he was worthy of his name. Jac Sperling wasn't on any reporter's dial-a-quote list because, as with any good whisperer, he could keep things quiet.

But when Sperling spoke, people with power in the sports world listened.

He'd helped the NBA in 2010 by temporarily running the Hornets franchise in his native New Orleans when the league assumed control of the team. Sperling then brokered the 2012 sale of the Hornets, since renamed the Pelicans, to Tom Benson.

In 2005, he'd brokered Disney's sale of the NHL's Mighty Ducks of Anaheim to his clients Henry and Susan Samueli.

And from 1997 to 2004, Sperling had served as CEO of the NHL's expansion Minnesota Wild, overlapping a period when a young executive named Tod Leiweke was that team's first president. When I phoned up the "Deal Whisperer," he was then a 63-year-old vice chairman for the Wild's ownership group. And he'd been reunited with Leiweke on a project in Tampa Bay, helping Lightning owner Jeff Vinik redevelop the waterfront surrounding his NHL arena.

Leiweke was by then the Lightning's CEO and a minority team owner. Cave told me it was Leiweke who'd introduced Sperling to him about getting an arena built on the Bellevue land and putting a hockey team there. Leiweke had even introduced Sperling around Seattle to various sports figures, including his good friend Adrian Hanauer and Hollywood producer Joe Roth, co-owners of the Sounders soccer team.

This sounded too good to be true. Leiweke five years earlier had left the Seahawks as an extremely popular NFL team president, who, with help from his brother, Tim, had hired coach Pete Carroll to eventually lead the franchise to Super Bowl glory. Now, Leiweke had spent half a decade reviving the Lightning's business operations to the point where that year would see the franchise reach the Stanley Cup Final.

Leiweke's pal, Sperling, was never about leading the deal-seeking groups he represented. As his nickname suggested, he was all about brokering the deal, collecting a handsome commission, then moving on. Our phone conversation was brief, and Sperling used words sparingly, allowing me only to quote him saying, "Seattle would be a very strong market for an NBA or NHL team."

But words didn't matter. Connections did. And Tod Leiweke was the biggest one. We'd never met in person during Leiweke's time in Seattle, with me covering the Mariners and him running the Seahawks. But a mutual friend arranged drinks for us in March 2015 at The Roanoke, a local watering hole on Mercer Island, a suburban Seattle locale for wealthy sports figures that Leiweke had called home before moving to Tampa Bay.

Leiweke had once lived in a Mercer Island waterfront property purchased from former Seahawks coach Mike Holmgren. It had a boat slip, and Leiweke liked his boats. Of course, his latest home, in an exclusive island community in the Tampa area, also had a boat. And during our sips of red wine, he assured me Sperling's presence scouting out a Bellevue arena location had nothing to do with him.

We had a good time chatting. But I didn't believe a word of Leiweke's guarantees he and his wife had mentally left Seattle behind and adjusted to Tampa Bay living. My wife a few years prior had worked for a Tampa-based company. We'd loved heading to Bern's steakhouse, tasting the finer wines on their list of thousands, and lounging on nearby beaches. But trying to picture where a sports executive enjoying the good life would rather be, well, you could always fly down to Florida from Seattle for a few weeks to escape the rain. Besides, Leiweke's son still lived in Seattle, working for his dad's good friend Hanauer and the Sounders. Blood is much thicker than Florida's Gulf Coast water. And the wine we were drinking wasn't thick enough for any of Leiweke's assurances of distance from Sperling's group to sound believable.

But I let it go and we parted ways promising to keep in touch. We even texted back and forth as his Lightning advanced through multiple playoff rounds. I resisted making a quip as Leiweke's team lost to Chicago in the Cup Final. You don't joke about a man's team losing, be he an owner, an executive, or just a fan. Leiweke was all three, traveling to Chicago for the series road games and sitting in the United Center stands rather than a private suite.

By then, I had little doubt Leiweke would be involved in a Seattle NHL franchise if Sperling's efforts paid off.

Right after the Cup Final, the NHL announced a process in which it would take expansion bids from cities. It was widely assumed the league wanted to go to Las Vegas, but a twin pairing was needed. And Seattle fit the type of wealthy U.S. market the league wanted, far more than reviving a team in Quebec City or adding a second one in Toronto. Today's NHL is about U.S. money. And Seattle had that. It just needed an arena.

But Sperling's group was now seeking its own NHL home right across the water in Bellevue. That would be in direct competition with Chris Hansen's arena project in Seattle's SoDo district and his potential partnership with would-be NHL owner Victor Coleman.

And finally, there was Ray Bartoszek, the NHL's reliable old friend from the aborted 2013 attempt to move the Arizona Coyotes to Seattle. Just as he'd shown up in Arizona as the NHL was pressuring Glendale's city council into a Coyotes arena lease, Bartoszek by early 2015 had popped up in Seattle just as the frustrated league was trying to get Hansen to move on his dragging SoDo project.

Bartoszek this time was touting an all-private arena plan in the humble and somewhat far-flung Seattle suburb of Tukwila. By then, I'd met with him a handful of times, including once in his Greenwich, Connecticut, neighborhood in April 2014 roughly nine months after his failed Coyotes effort. Over lunch, he'd told me he was still interested in Seattle as an NHL city. He'd even looked into renovating KeyArena but eventually passed. Too many issues with the historic roof, he told me. Interestingly, almost right after and unbeknownst to Bartoszek, the AECOM architectural team discovered KeyArena could work for the NHL and NBA by tilting its rink floor without the roof being disturbed.

As usual, Bartoszek's timing again seemed a little off when it came to getting anything done. But when it came to pressuring those the NHL wanted to lean in a certain direction, Bartoszek had the uncanny ability to appear out of nowhere with some project. An all-private arena in Tukwila initially seemed like lunacy.

First, it was in the wrong location. Everybody who knew Tukwila figured Bartoszek would go for the United Grocers lot owned by local businessman David Sabey adjacent to an existing light rail line. Instead, Bartoszek picked up land options at a more remote location. Though that land was close to connecting highways, it also had Union Pacific Railway tracks running through it.

Bartoszek did have local partners, including Downtown Freddie Brown, a former longtime Sonics player. He'd also had multiple meetings with Tukwila's mayor and council and was expediting an environmental review of the site. It all seemed legitimate. And it sure was moving faster than Hansen's project in SoDo. Or was it?

Bartoszek had dangled investor names for me, including Thomas Tull, a Hollywood producer and Pittsburgh Steelers minority owner. But when I contacted Tull's people, they told me they'd passed on the project. Bartoszek assured me he was meeting with other potential investors.

Whatever Bartoszek was doing, NHL commissioner Gary Bettman was loving it. He went on a Vancouver, B.C., sports radio station touting the Tukwila and Bellevue projects. Bettman was no "Deal Whisperer" like the league's friend Sperling. He wanted everybody to know there were competing projects for the Hansen group in SoDo to watch out for. And now, as the NHL's July 20, 2015, expansion application deadline loomed, everyone was waiting to see whether one, two, or even three Seattle-area bids might materialize.

The bidding wasn't for bluffers. A $10 million application fee was required, $2 million of it non-refundable. I'd kept in touch with Bartoszek by text in May and June of 2015, asking about his financing. He was friendly, as always, but kept dodging. Then, on June 24, less than a month before the NHL's expansion deadline, I got tired of waiting. "Will you do it?" I asked him by text.

It took 24 hours for Bartoszek to respond. I was sitting with my newspaper boss, Don Shelton, at a journalism dinner in San Diego when Bartoszek's text came in. "Do what?" Bartoszek asked. "Apply I assume? We are way ahead of that."

I showed the texts to Shelton. We both agreed, as would any normal person, that it meant Bartoszek had applied for NHL expansion. I sent further texts to Bartoszek every few days, but he went dark.

Then, just three days before the NHL's application deadline, the city got a double whammy. Victor Coleman announced he'd informed the NHL he'd delay applying. Hansen at the time did not have his SoDo arena plans lined up to accommodate the NHL before an NBA team. Coleman stated he still felt the NHL could work in Seattle but needed to see a clear arena path.

I'd also been tipped off that very week that a venture capitalist financing the Bellevue arena project "Deal Whisperer" Sperling had been working on had pulled out. Sperling had been in town the previous week pushing Bellevue officials to expedite a memorandum of understanding to build a future arena. The expedited deal had needed to be in place before the league's July 20 application deadline and that was already a dicey proposition. Without the VC money, the Bellevue project died immediately. Sperling and his team packed up and went home.

Years later, I found myself in a private cigar lounge in an exclusive Sea Island, Georgia, hotel with some hockey executives, including a gentleman seated directly to my right. We were introduced. It was the "Deal Whisperer" himself, whom I'd never met in person. Sperling seemed to flinch just for a millisecond upon realizing who I was, but quickly reverted to a calm, smiling demeanor that probably made him so successful in relationships and deals to begin with.

Over the next hour, we all chatted about anything but the Bellevue arena effort from years prior. But at one point, while others were engaged in discussions, I leaned over and asked Sperling how close he'd come.

"Oh, I wouldn't say close," he told me. "There was an awful lot that had to happen and just not enough time."

There are some who believe Sperling was just a plant used by the NHL to pressure Hansen and his SoDo project. I go back and forth. A few months after Sperling pulled out, I was introduced to Seahawks president Peter McLoughlin. The first thing he told me was that he knew I'd been speaking to the right people when I'd mentioned Sperling and the Bellevue arena group in newspaper stories.

"If anybody was going to get it done, it would be those guys," McLoughlin told me. "Those were serious people."

Once Sperling and the Bellevue hopes vanished, that left Bartoszek and Tukwila. He'd still not responded to my texts for nearly a month. Then, on the day of the NHL's expansion application deadline, he finally sent a brief message. "We could not meet the NHL timeline," Bartoszek wrote. "We continue to have an arena first discipline."

Seattle had begun the week with three prospective NHL bidders. And Bartoszek had sealed an 0-for-3 showing.

We texted more that day, Bartoszek telling me multiple wealthy investors had wasted his time "verbally committing but then bailing" on his project. The project drifted along stalled for the remainder of that year before he, too, faded into obscurity.

I doubt the NHL ever imagined Bartoszek would complete his arena. The league wanted to be in Seattle. Or possibly the money hotbed of Bellevue. Not in Tukwila. Bartoszek served a purpose for Bettman in pressuring the Hansen group to get moving on its SoDo plans. And the NHL's brass had gladly availed itself of Bartoszek's presence, playing it up whenever they could. For years, I wondered whether the NHL had put Bartoszek up to it. But too many folks I've spoken to say Bartoszek is just a well-intentioned lover of sports with big ambitions—just not enough of his own money to make those dreams a reality without help.

Sort of like the NHL and its ambitions for Seattle that summer of 2015. It had gotten Las Vegas and eventual Golden Knights owner Bill Foley to apply and pay a record $500 million expansion fee. But the 32nd franchise slot, which it hoped would go to Seattle, was again back on hold.

Chapter 18

TWO REPORTS, TWO DIFFERENT KEYARENA CONCLUSIONS

The failure of Seattle's three competing arena projects to bid for NHL expansion in July 2015 was outwardly met with frustration by the league. But behind the scenes, plenty was going on to bring major professional hockey to the Emerald City.

It would be months before any of it was made public. And nearly two years before the full implications of these secretive machinations on the city's dual arena and NHL fronts became clear. For the first five months of 2015, the story put out for public consumption was that the city was finalizing an environmental impact study of Chris Hansen's proposed arena in the city's SoDo district. And that part was true. After months of delays, Hansen's group had submitted needed documentation to jump-start the city's review and it had ticked toward a May 7, 2015, completion date.

Much of the city's sports fans and media remained fixated on the review's completion. They hoped it would be enough to persuade the NBA to award a team to replace the departed Sonics. They continued to ignore warnings from Mayor Ed Murray about his meeting the prior January in which NBA commissioner Adam Silver had told him no such team would be imminent for years.

But what those fans and media members were unaware of was that a completely separate KeyArena study had been underway since the previous summer. Commissioned by the city's nine-member council and spearheaded by councilmember Jean Godden, the AECOM architectural firm concluded by late 2014 that it would be possible to renovate KeyArena for major winter sports despite its historically protected roof.

That conclusion had been presented to select councilmembers in November 2014. Tim Burgess was on the council at the time and said Godden updated him.

"She came to me and said, 'We're going to get this report and we need to make sure that they go further than their original scope of work and go deeper into whether it's really possible to change KeyArena into an acceptable facility,'" Burgess recalled. "And I totally agreed with her that we should do that."

AECOM was sent back with orders to further investigate whether turning the arena's rink floor would expand available space inside. Also, to estimate a price tag for such a massive undertaking. And to further study potential alternative KeyArena uses.

AECOM did just that and by spring 2015 was striving toward a final report of its own. And that was problematic. First, there would be two reports coming out—one on the SoDo project, another on KeyArena. Making things worse, they'd be released just three days apart. There was the SoDo environmental impact study everybody knew about. But now, also the more secretive one on KeyArena that nobody knew about aside from a handful of political insiders.

The city was bound contractually to Hansen's SoDo project. Now, this KeyArena study the general public had never heard about was suddenly to be published. Once that happened, it risked sparking public confusion over what it all meant.

Adding to that confusion, the environmental impact study on Hansen's project was supposed to consider the merits of potential alternative sites to the SoDo location. It had concluded that KeyArena was not a reasonable option because the historically protected roof made the venue impossible to expand for modern NBA and NHL play.

Now, a contrary report was about to be released stating the exact opposite.

Mudding things up even further, the two individuals preparing the actual reports were also technically working for the same company. URS Corporation was handling the environmental impact review on the SoDo project and had just been bought in October 2014 by AECOM, the firm handling the KeyArena study. Also, Mayor Murray's office was overseeing the SoDo project review while the city council had paid for the KeyArena study. It didn't look great that two arm's length branches of government were effectively using the same company for arena analysis that was supposed to safeguard their respective interests.

Public document disclosures would later show there were early concerns expressed about a conflict of interest. But as both entities were already well down the line in their work, it was decided they'd keep going as long as they limited communication with one another.

But in March 2015, URS vice president Kathy Chaney received a phone call from AECOM counterpart Ryan Sickman. They discussed the fact they had separate reports coming out with very different conclusions on KeyArena. And that it would probably cause confusion.

Chaney later emailed Sickman seeking suggestions on how to modify the reports so the contradiction wasn't so glaring. Two weeks later, Sickman suggested a 221-word revision to Chaney's environmental impact study on the SoDo project. Sickman wanted her report to address the new KeyArena discoveries by AECOM. His suggested wording stated, "There are now studies in front of the city that show how the KeyArena could be reconfigured and redesigned within the building's existing structure to accommodate both NBA and NHL franchises based upon the now accepted Sacramento Kings design model for NBA seating distribution."

But none of that got added. Instead, as often happens in politics, too many hands and fingers poked their way into the decision-making. More concerns were expressed about a conflict of interest between the two companies now under AECOM's umbrella. And by the time watered-down versions of Sickman's initial request had been pored over, the final calculation was to do…nothing at all.

Instead, the council on May 4 postponed the AECOM report's May 10 release. And on May 7, the mayor's office released the 627-page SoDo arena environmental review with the unaltered conclusion that a KeyArena overhaul wasn't possible.

None of it was true. But the myth that KeyArena was beyond repair remained intact. And the SoDo project, in the eyes of the public, remained the city's only viable arena option.

It wasn't until late May that a draft of the final AECOM report was submitted to councilmember Godden, who'd spearheaded commissioning the study. AECOM was estimating KeyArena could be expanded for NBA and NHL teams for a minimum $285 million. That amount was a fraction of the $490 million Hansen was proposing for his SoDo venue, of which $200 million would comprise city and country bond money.

"I was pleased when I saw the final report," Burgess said. "Because it said, 'Well, maybe there is an option here that might work.'"

But Hansen still had a deal with the city running through 2017 that guaranteed exclusivity for his project, meaning a KeyArena overhaul could not be undertaken. So, no matter what the AECOM report said about KeyArena, there was no way of even pressure-testing it.

"When Jean Godden had the study done, there was really a sense of, 'Well, what can we do with this?'" said former city councilmember Sally Bagshaw, who at the time represented the district KeyArena was situated in.

So, while nobody hid the AECOM report, its existence wasn't publicized either. Technically, it was a public document. But if nobody knew it existed, there was little chance a media member might ask for it via a public records request.

And none did. All through the summer of 2015, the AECOM report remained a secret. Still, even though the public was kept in the dark, the study was gaining traction behind the scenes.

"It was helpful because it said, 'Yes, it could be done,'" Bagshaw said of overhauling KeyArena for the NBA and NHL. "And that kind of opened the door for me."

From then on, Bagshaw emerged as the council's most visible skeptic toward Hansen's SoDo venue. She was reluctant to approve it before the city exhausted attempts to salvage KeyArena.

"I remember just sitting down and writing out five principles that, until they were addressed, my answer would not be enthusiastic to support them," Bagshaw recalled of the SoDo deal. "And one of the first was, 'What are we going to do with KeyArena?' Because if that was not used, the city would be left with this very ancient aging arena that nobody was going to want to do concerts in. Anybody who played there would be feeling like a second-class citizen."

Meanwhile, on a different front, Mayor Murray wasn't making life easy for the SoDo project. On the day the May 2015 environmental impact study was released, Murray made clear he believed Hansen needed to revise his deal so an NHL franchise could be acquired ahead of an NBA team. As written, Hansen's deal with the city and county provided up to $200 million in public bond money only if he acquired an NBA franchise.

And Murray already knew from NBA commissioner Silver that wasn't happening. In fact, Murray was now screaming that from the rooftops.

One person who listened was Victor Coleman, the Hudson Pacific Properties mogul who wanted to own an NHL team in Seattle. The moment the AECOM report on KeyArena's marketing was quietly finalized, his representatives were shown a copy. So was Bob Newman, the local Anschutz Entertainment Group executive helping manage KeyArena's marketing on the city's behalf.

Coleman's efforts to get Hansen to switch to an "NHL first" model for his SoDo Arena were getting nowhere. And by early June of 2015, right before the NHL launched its expansion bidding process, Coleman was asking the city about the AECOM report and renovating KeyArena.

The report's suggestion that an overhaul could be done for $285 million had caught Coleman and Newman's attention. Both were skeptical about that figure. And that the NHL would be interested in a renovation of that scope. But they wanted to find out.

Yet, the city still had a binding deal with Hansen for another two-plus years. If Hansen ever acquired an NBA team during that time, no matter how increasingly unlikely that seemed, the deal allowed him to use KeyArena as a temporary home while he built his SoDo venue. In other words, the city couldn't start tearing KeyArena apart for its own renovation when it was still possible Hansen's project might be green-lighted.

On July 17, 2015, the city's finance director, Glen Lee, confirmed this very quandary to his budget director counterpart Ben Noble. The news was relayed to Murray and quickly to Coleman—a KeyArena overhaul was out of the question for now.

It was three days before the NHL's expansion deadline. Coleman immediately went public stating that he'd told the NHL he was delaying any expansion application until a clear arena path materialized.

Only a select few people knew about the secretive AECOM report. Everybody else listening to Coleman that day assumed he was talking about eventually playing at a SoDo venue built by Hansen. In fact, Coleman was referencing KeyArena. He wanted to see whether it would be possible.

So did the NHL. But the city was handcuffed by its exclusivity deal with Hansen.

By late September 2015, word of the AECOM report began leaking out in response to broad-ranging public-records requests by media outlets. None had expected to be given the report, nor did they know what to make of it. If it was truly possible to renovate KeyArena, why hadn't the city publicized the opportunity? And why hadn't private groups come forward offering to pay for a renovation?

The reality was that groups had come forward. But they'd been shut down by the city.

It wasn't until early 2016 that the back-room maneuvering to keep the AECOM report quiet began to materialize. Murray by November 2015, following increased questions about KeyArena from potential third-party bidders, obtained a legal opinion confirming that any KeyArena renovation discussions would violate the spirit of the exclusivity deal with Hansen and the SoDo project.

From there, Murray decided to force the issue.

One major problem with Hansen's project was that the land he'd assembled in SoDo was a very thin strip. And there was a one-block stretch of a street called Occidental Avenue South running right through it. Hansen would eventually need to purchase the street through a process known as a "street vacation" for an arena to get built.

The process required city council approval. But the council had been putting off calling a vote on it, as Hansen had yet to acquire an NBA team to actually launch his project. The council had tentatively scheduled a vote for spring 2016. And Murray by January of that year had every intention of the council seeing it through. He didn't think Hansen had any chance of landing an NBA team. And Hansen had shown zero interest in building an arena for an NHL franchise.

Murray didn't want to wait two more years to figure out whether Hansen was for real. He wanted the street vote to take place, leaving the arena in a "shovel-ready" position to start building the minute Hansen landed an NBA squad. And if having a shovel-ready arena plan still didn't attract an NBA team, Murray planned to go to Hansen ahead of schedule the following year to ask him to waive his exclusivity so a KeyArena overhaul could be explored further.

"I needed to honor my commitment to Hansen and those folks," Murray said. "But we also had opportunities for a hockey team. And while everyone was obsessed about basketball, hockey was not a bad thing either. And if we could have an arena that was bringing other events, well, Seattle's arena was already decrepit and outdated. But if we had hockey and could eventually bring basketball, I felt like that was a huge win, that could incrementally create a path for an eventual basketball team. But if we sat on this, then it wouldn't happen for years."

And force the vote Murray did. It was set for May 2, 2016. An overwhelming number of councilmembers seemed set to approve it. But a seismic shift was about to occur that would change the course of Seattle's arena and NHL fortunes.

Chapter 19

A VOTE FORCED ON SODO ARENA'S FUTURE

Seattle city councilmember Sally Bagshaw had a lot on her mind the evening of April 30, 2016. She was heading into an educational symposium at Garfield High School, but her thoughts were on an upcoming council vote two afternoons later.

Bagshaw back then was having a tough time flipping on the radio without hearing some host or their basketball-loving call-in followers taking a shot at her. The past year, she'd become the leading council opponent of Chris Hansen's proposed arena in the city's SoDo district. It cast her in a primary villain's role among the deal's staunch supporters, right up alongside the Mariners baseball team and Port of Seattle. It wasn't a fun place. Not for any politician that valued popularity, as most did. In two days, the nine-member council would vote on selling Hansen a part of Occidental Avenue South so he'd have enough usable land to build his arena.

Of course, Hansen still needed an NBA team to get his project off the ground. And Bagshaw knew NBA commissioner Adam Silver was telling everybody Hansen wasn't getting a team. Just more than a week prior, I'd again caught up with Silver at his New York offices and asked whether the league might approve a team if the council voted to sell Hansen the street and make his arena plan become shovel ready to begin construction.

"Whether or not the arena in Seattle is shovel ready is not a factor that we are considering in terms of whether or not we expand at this point," Silver told me.

I'd asked the question at yet another Associated Press Sports Editors annual commissioner's meeting. It's where a group of roughly 20 sports editors would venture around New York for personalized chats with those running various sports leagues. A few years back, they'd started inviting reporters to the annual meetings and I was one of only a handful to accept the invite. The sessions were usually in boardrooms and on the record. Silver by this point recognized me from prior meetings. As I approached him at a hallway water fountain beforehand, he'd chuckled and told me he wasn't going to say anything different about the SoDo arena this year. We chatted a bit. Then, as we headed into the room, he said, "You can still ask me the question. Ask me the question and I'll answer it."

I'd found that a bit odd. But I'd come all the way to New York planning to ask. And Silver didn't disappoint. After his initial answer about not being ready to provide Hansen a team, he'd continued, "We're going through a collective-bargaining cycle right now, it's no secret. So, certainly, it's not something that we would be thinking about as we're focusing on ensuring that we're going to have labor peace for the foreseeable future.

"I think that after we complete the extension of our collective bargaining agreement, I think that would be the natural time, at least, for owners to consider whether or not they would like to expand.... Right now, we are not hearing it coming from within the league. We are hearing from some groups outside the league. But from within the league, there's no strong push to expand at the moment."

Silver didn't rule out eventually expanding.

"Organizations do tend to grow over time, and I think that we're no different," he told me. "There are some great communities out there that I know would be wonderful NBA homes. Seattle of course is one of those and we've had a great experience there. But at least right now, it's not something we're even discussing internally."

It was about as strong an answer as Silver could have possibly given. An emphatic "no" to the idea the NBA would award Hansen a team to play at a SoDo arena no matter what happened with the upcoming council vote. Hansen by then had only 19 months remaining on his arena deal with the city. So, the NBA putting off even discussing expansion indefinitely meant it was likely at least a year or two from deciding anything. It was hugely problematic for Hansen's deadline. Clearly, if Silver had any intention of putting a team in a SoDo arena before December 2017, he'd have chosen his words far more carefully, given the looming vote.

About a half hour after giving me his answer, Silver let it be known to the room that he and his executive team had a flight to catch to San Antonio, Texas, for a playoff game that night. Silver glanced around the boardroom table, asking whether anyone had any last questions. Then, he looked directly at me. "Geoff, is there anything more you'd like to ask?"

I'd toyed with the idea of asking Silver about KeyArena. Even with the AECOM report now public knowledge in Seattle, the idea that any private group would want to pay $285 million to overhaul KeyArena was still being greeted with derision. At least in public. Nobody had ever tested the theory. And behind the scenes, as we'd later learn, there was huge interest from people willing to spend far more than $285 million. Still, the prevailing consensus in Seattle was the question wasn't even worth asking. After all, the party line went, no sports league in its right mind would play in KeyArena, renovated or not.

Well, I figured, I'd come all the way to New York and here was Silver practically daring me to ask him more. If he ruled out an NBA team ever playing at KeyArena right then and there, as a journalist I'd have one fewer angle to worry about chasing down. It would then be time for me to focus exclusively on Hansen's project and no alternatives.

So, I asked Silver as directly as possible whether the NBA had ruled out ever playing at a renovated KeyArena. And his answer floored me.

"For me, it's a fresh start. Nothing's a closed deal," Silver said of a KeyArena renovation. "Especially with what an arena renovation looks like these days compared to the old days. It's very different. And so, when somebody talks about renovating KeyArena—depending on how much was invested—it could look just like a new arena, frankly.

"And so, the devil is in the details there."

Silver added that he'd read media coverage of the AECOM report on KeyArena, but not the study itself.

"Ultimately, I'm not even sure what the Seattle community would want in terms of either a new arena or KeyArena," Silver said. "So, while we're not actively looking at expansion anywhere, it's far from me to say that one site or one arena is preferable. I just don't know."

From there, he asked me, "You all good?"

I nodded. Silver stood up, excused himself, and left the room. *Washington Post* sports editor Matthew Vita, seated to my right, looked at me. "I don't know anything about this vote," Vita said. "But it sounds like he sure isn't doing that [SoDo] group any favors."

No, he was not. The subsequent story got quite a bit of play in Seattle. After all, the NBA's commissioner had just undercut the entire line of reasoning for why the council should approve selling Hansen the street. If no NBA team was coming before his deal with the city expired, there didn't seem much sense finalizing plans for an arena that would never be built. Not only that, but approve the street sale and the fate of that Occidental Ave. block and the entire SoDo neighborhood surrounding the arena site would remain in limbo another 19 months.

Still, logic hadn't always prevailed in Seattle's arena debates. And the story quoting Silver, though widely read, didn't seem destined to change much. Mayor Ed Murray had been saying the same thing about Silver not offering up a team for the past year and a half. Silver had merely repeated it anew to me, albeit only days before the vote itself. Supporters of the SoDo project and legions of Sonics fans continued to insist the NBA would change its tune once plans were shovel ready and Hansen had the street.

And that seemed a foregone conclusion to Bagshaw the weekend before the Monday vote. The public speculation was the council would award Hansen the street by a 7–2 margin. Possibly by a 6–3 count if some councilmember, sensing Hansen's victory was already sealed, voted the other way for purely political reasons. Seattle was still a left-of-center town and quite a few labor unions opposed the SoDo project.

And as she headed into her high school symposium that night, Bagshaw was feeling quite alone. She knew she'd be voting against selling Hansen the street. And that councilmember Lisa Herbold was likely joining her and had said so publicly. But she had doubts about the rest. Even ultra-progressive councilmember Kshama Sawant seemed likely to vote in favor of the corporate arena-builder despite the opposition from some labor unions doing port-related work. A group of highly organized Sonics fans had boasted for more than two years about having propelled Sawant to victory in her narrow November 2013 election defeat of district incumbent Richard Conlin.

It had been an odd alliance, the socialist firebrand Sawant and the basketball-loving sports fans. But Conlin had refused to back the SoDo arena plan. And with Sawant's margin of victory a mere 3,151 votes, any particularly sizeable group could legitimately claim to have swung the ballot. And one group certainly was claiming it—Sonicsgate, a collection of politically active filmmakers with a hard-core following of basketball fans. They'd made a same-titled short film on the somewhat duplicitous way the Sonics had been relocated to Oklahoma City in 2008. The film was so well received, it won a Webby Award for internet achievement in the sports-video category, as voted on by the International Academy of Digital Arts and Sciences. Now, the filmmakers had taken things a step further and dabbled in sports politics beyond the screen, endorsing Sawant over Conlin.

"Councilman Conlin has alienated many local constituencies including Sonics fans," filmmakers Jason Reid and Adam Brown wrote online in their Sawant endorsement. "He was Seattle City Council President when its members unanimously approved the $45 million settlement agreement that let the Sonics out of the team's lease at KeyArena in 2008, officially sending Seattle's iconic NBA franchise off to Oklahoma City. Conlin missed a shot at redemption last year when he vocally opposed the SoDo arena deal and wrote an editorial letter attempting to justify his anti-arena position."

So, it seemed highly unlikely Sawant would now upset their applecart and undermine some of the slim support that helped put her in office.

Bagshaw was pretty good at political calculation. And she had a sense that the coming Monday would be a long one. She was mentally bracing for a victory dance by her opponents and another round of playing a piñata on radio airwaves.

Feeling somewhat tired and depressed, she walked into the high school symposium. And she'll never forget what she saw when she ducked into a backstage hallway behind the curtain before speaking.

"I walked into the hall and saw a giant sign there that said, 'Honesty is standing up for what's right, even if you must stand alone.'"

The words resonated. Bagshaw absolutely felt she was doing the right thing looking out for the interests of KeyArena. That the right questions weren't being asked. She didn't like how hamstrung the city was by Hansen's deal and that it prevented a truthful public debate about what the KeyArena options were. She felt to her core she was in the right, even if almost nobody else really seemed willing to acknowledge it. Now, there was a sign telling her it was OK to feel that way.

"It absolutely made me stand up straight as I was walking down the hall and saw that," Bagshaw said. "At that point I seriously had no idea how the vote was going to come out."

Three of the nine councilmembers, future Seattle mayors Tim Burgess and Bruce Harrell as well as Rob Johnson, had all but announced they'd vote in favor of Hansen's request.

"I think my mind-set was that we needed to signal we were willing to continue the discussions," Burgess recalled. "And that vote had a very important escape for the city in that we would never execute the street vacation until there was an assurance that we would have a team."

Mike O'Brien was leaning that way as well, even though he didn't initially want to even have the vote at all. He'd tried four months earlier to enlist support of other councilmembers to delay the May vote until Hansen had first secured a master use permit for the site. Such a move might have delayed Hansen well into 2017, bumping up against his deadline to secure an NBA squad before his deal with the city expired.

But Murray got wind of O'Brien's plans and forcefully prodded him to back down. The last thing Murray needed was Hansen's efforts to drag on an additional year-plus without resolution when there were groups interested in bringing the NHL to Seattle right away. He wanted to force a SoDo vote and see whether Hansen could secure an NBA team once the street sale was approved. And if Hansen's by then shovel-ready plan still failed to quickly draw NBA attention, well, Murray would then ask him to relinquish his arena exclusivity earlier than expected. And he'd move on to exploring a KeyArena overhaul.

Burgess said, "I do remember Murray was working beforehand to try to persuade council members to keep moving forward and to have the vote."

Murray, known for a quick temper and admitting to "a bit of a direct, non-Northwest edge" attributed to his New York–born mother, insisted he was calm but abrupt with O'Brien. "I said, 'I'll force this vote. I'll go to the media and tell them you tried to stop this vote.'"

O'Brien relented, agreeing not to delay things. Murray absolutely needed the vote to happen, no matter how it went. Indefinite delays were not an option.

"We wouldn't have an arena today if that had happened," Murray said.

Chapter 20

ALWAYS COUNT YOUR VOTES

Tension filled the air the afternoon of May 2, 2016, as the Seattle City Council gathered to determine the fate of Chris Hansen's proposal for an arena in the SoDo district. The nine-member council was technically deciding whether to sell Hansen a block of Occidental Avenue South running directly through his projected arena site.

Such "street vacation" votes were not unusual and rarely garnered public attention. But without acquiring the street, Hansen's plan had no way of proceeding. Quash the street request and the SoDo arena was effectively dead. Hansen was offering to pay fair market value of anywhere from $18 million to $20 million for the street. He'd also offered additional incentives, such as building a pedestrian overpass, a public park, and increased sidewalk space.

It seemed like a good deal for the city. But this vote had little to do with a lone street. It was about the fate of Hansen's project, already clinging to life with the NBA refusing to grant him a franchise and time running out on his deal with the city set to expire in 19 months. Nonetheless, SoDo project backers insisted the street sale would make the plan "shovel ready" to begin construction at any time and more likely to attract NBA interest. And those supporters had shown up in their usual green-and-gold Sonics colors in the packed council chamber for the 2 PM vote expecting to celebrate a major project milestone.

But this time, for once, they weren't the ones actually filling the chamber. This time, they were far outnumbered by unionized longshoremen and warehouse workers demanding the council not allow Hansen's project to continue. Senior executives from the Port of Seattle were also there. They were threatening a lawsuit by the very next day if the city allowed the street to be sold without a guarantee from Hansen that he'd ever build his SoDo arena.

The vote was still expected to overwhelmingly go Hansen's way. But the large crowd of opponents brought additional electricity to an already emotion-charged process.

Mayor Ed Murray wasn't in the council chambers. But he monitored the closed-circuit television feed as councilmembers debated proposed amendments to the street purchase request. He'd worked the council on Hansen's behalf, trying to solidify votes. Despite Hansen outwardly seeming to have things well in hand, Murray was uncertain how the vote would go. He'd encountered instances throughout his career of politicians publicly saying they'd vote one way and then doing the exact opposite.

"I was reading them behind the scenes," Murray said of the council. "It was clear their thinking was all over the place and that this could go anywhere. It was clear this was going to be a one-vote win either way."

Leading up to the vote, he'd seen "the far left" becoming agitated at the impact an arena might have on traffic and unionized workers in SoDo. He worried avowed socialist Sawant's support for the arena was becoming shaky and figured Lorena Gonzalez would follow suit.

First-time councilmember Gonzalez, a civil rights lawyer, had been in office only four months. She'd been hired by Murray in May 2014 to serve as his legal counsel, doing that for just more than a year before running and winning election to council in November 2015.

"Lorena wants to be the left-est person in Seattle," Murray said. "She wants to out-left everybody else and she wants the support of those people. I knew that as soon as this thing started to turn, we didn't know what she would do."

Murray's seeming contempt for Gonzalez didn't surprise me. He'd ignored her calls to resign his final year in office as the sexual abuse allegations mounted. Then, during her own losing mayoral bid against Bruce Harrell in November 2021, she'd feverishly worked to distance herself from Murray as much as possible.

Personal feelings aside, Murray was accurate in Gonzalez's vote not being locked down.

Murray said he shared his concerns that "the votes weren't there" with Hansen in a phone call and his strategists in person in the days beforehand. "They weren't happy with me."

And they chose to ignore him. After all, pundits had been predicting a 7–2, or, at worst, a 6–3 landslide in Hansen's favor. But Murray figured it would go 5–4 either way.

"I thought everyone was squirrelly," he said of the councilmembers. "Everyone was coming in and acting squirrelly for one reason or another. You know, as soon as one of them gets squirrelly down there, every one of them gets squirrelly."

But Tim Burgess, then one of the councilmembers planning to vote in Hanson's favor, saw no reason to doubt it would pass. Burgess had been part of the council that in 2012 had finalized the five-year arena deal with Hansen initially negotiated by then Mayor Mike McGinn.

"We renegotiated it with Chris [Hansen] and we brought in some experts that had done these types of municipal arena deals before," Burgess said. "And I was supportive of the deal. I mean, I want to see something like the Sonics come back."

But Burgess was under no illusions giving Hansen the street would automatically lead to a team coming. He knew the NBA was balking and that Hansen's five-year deal with the city would expire by December 2017. It was coming down to the wire. Still, Burgess preferred keeping all options open. He also knew the KeyArena option presented by the AECOM report was still there if Hansen couldn't get across the finish line. So, he'd vote to sell Hansen the street to "just keep the ball rolling" and see what came of it.

Sally Bagshaw that afternoon took her seat and glanced out at the audience of 250 or so people seated and standing in the council chamber. As she and her colleagues sifted through the pre-vote machinations, she thought about two nights prior at Garfield High School and the sign she'd seen in the hallway. The comforting message about doing what's right had helped her sleep, though the city had gone through a rough Sunday evening of May Day protests. Fireworks had been lit. Molotov cocktails thrown at police. One police officer had been injured. Arrests made. Bagshaw knew there'd be work ahead for the council figuring out preventive steps to avoid a future repeat.

But now, she was focused squarely on the arena vote. She'd be the first councilmember to speak. Finally, the time for the vote arrived.

Bagshaw stood up and reiterated her doubts about the SoDo project's impact on neighborhood traffic and Port of Seattle operations. She noted NBA commissioner Adam Silver had mentioned that Hansen was unlikely to get a team before his five-year deal with the city expired.

And she also mentioned wanting to further explore whether KeyArena could be overhauled. Finally, she concluded by saying, "Honesty is standing up, even if you must stand alone."

It was the phrase from the sign she'd seen at Garfield High School. Before speaking the words, she'd noted that council president Harrell, seated directly to her right, was a former all-Metro Garfield linebacker. He'd later gone on to star with the University of Washington Huskies. "So,

I may be an 8–1 vote here," Bagshaw concluded. "But I really believe that taking care of our Port and taking care of our Sonics in the future is the right thing to do."

And with that, she voted no.

That had been expected. But perhaps the biggest sign things might go off-script came next. Councilmember Debora Juarez spoke and was not immediately supportive of the arena. She touched on the "intrinsic value" of Seattle's deep water port. "Once we relinquish the street, we take away another piece of our maritime history," Juarez said.

She added that the street vacation guidelines were too simplistic. And that a more holistic approach was needed to gauge the impact of selling the street. That a future arena risked hampering the entire SoDo neighborhood and its port-related freight operations.

"For me, this decision weighs a non-existent NBA franchise against the city's 160-year legacy as a maritime powerhouse along the Salish Sea," Juarez said.

She also voted no. The majority of the room burst into applause, louder than it had been for Bagshaw. They'd seen Bagshaw coming. Juarez's vote was a surprise.

The anti-arena faction was now ahead 2–0 and needed three more votes of the remaining seven to pull off a stunning upset. It was obvious Hansen would get a chunk of support from those remaining. But the room was now hot with anticipation. No one in the audience budged from their seats.

O'Brien spoke next and supported the SoDo plan as expected. Though he'd initially opposed having the vote, he'd long backed the arena deal when previous Mayor Mike McGinn, his longtime ally, had crafted it. O'Brien termed Hansen's offer package for the street "an excellent public benefit across the board."

He voted yes to smaller, though vigorous applause from Sonics fans. That left the no side still ahead 2–1. But possibly the most telling of the votes was to be decided next with Kshama Sawant. It was widely assumed councilmembers Burgess, Harrell, and Johnson would support selling Hansen the street. That meant, if Lisa Herbold was indeed solidly in the no camp, that both Sawant and Lorena Gonzalez would need to also vote no to defeat the SoDo plan.

If Sawant now voted yes, then Hansen and the SoDo project almost certainly would prevail. And for the longest time, it had been a foregone conclusion she'd support the street sale. Sawant had been backed by Sonics fans in her narrow 2012 election victory. She'd supported the SoDo arena plan during her campaign.

But of all the councilmembers, Sawant was also the least predictable. Her socialist, labor-rooted base ran deep and there were an awful lot of unionized workers in the room waiting to scrutinize her every word. The speech Sawant gave that day would go down as one of the more memorable in Seattle's council history. Not for any unifying or inspirational message. More for how she skewered almost everybody in sight.

It began innocently enough, with Sawant commending the "genuineness and sincerity" of Sonics fans. But it was all downhill from there. Many of her intended targets in a seven-minute diatribe were sitting in the audience. People were squirming and wincing as Sawant spoke. But nobody could avert their eyes at the spectacle.

"I want to be very clear: I would never make a decision based on the claims of the bureaucracy that is the Port of Seattle," Sawant said, claiming—erroneously, it turned out—that a former United States Attorney had described the Port's leadership as "a cesspool of corruption."

Sawant skewered the Port for "disgracefully" fighting SeaTac Airport workers in their bid for a $15-an-hour minimum wage. She lampooned the Port's "super exploitation" of independent truckers. Blasted it for eschewing climate-change concerns "for a quick buck" by permitting the Shell oil company to lease space at one of its terminals to service an Alaskan oil-drilling rig.

Port executives and lobbyists in the audience sat stone-faced. They sensed their opposition to the SoDo arena crumbling before their eyes. But then, like a ping-pong ball, Sawant's attacks reversed course.

She accused Hansen and his arena backers of "slowly squeezing out our working waterfront." Took a shot at former Sonics owners for "screwing over Sonics fans" and lamented "the greed of billionaire sports owners" and their "monopoly control" over entertainment. And she reiterated that her support was not for the Port, but the unionized workers "who are trying to stand up against these forces of gentrification."

No one dared breathe. It was impossible to tell who Sawant would side with. Her next words proved telling.

"I recognize that Sonics fans will not like my no vote on this matter," she said, drawing gasps from the crowd. She continued ranting for several minutes, her verbal assaults on both sides not letting up.

She thanked *Sonicsgate* filmmakers Adam Brown and Jason Reid for helping her understand the issues. But, finally, having torched almost everyone else to a crisp, she ended things with a no vote. Once again, the crowd erupted. This was no longer a cakewalk vote. If Herbold stuck to her public no stance, it was looking like a deadlocked council with Lorena Gonzalez deciding things.

Burgess and Johnson were up next, voting to sell Hansen the street. And Herbold, as expected, rejected the proposal. This time, the applause was subdued. There was too much tension in the room.

What had been expected to be a shoo-in approval for the SoDo arena plan had come down to a lone vote. All eyes were on Gonzalez.

She'd been a tough read ahead of time. Murray that morning had sent one of his staffers to gauge her support. The staffer reported back that she was still on board with the SoDo proposal.

Gonzalez would later tell me she'd been worn out by all the lobbying from both sides. "Certainly, toward the tail end, I'd heard about every angle

I could possibly hear related to those who were in favor and those who were opposed," Gonzalez said.

She told me she'd been undecided about her vote as of that morning.

Burgess, seated to Gonzalez's left that day, admits now that he and others had pinpointed her beforehand as a wild card in Hansen's victory push. "She was the key," Burgess said. "We knew that she would be the key vote to get to at least five, if not more."

Gonzalez seemingly didn't have much of a speech planned. It's possible she'd never envisioned the vote being this close, let alone winding up as the councilmember deciding it. She opened with a preamble mentioning all the varied interests and constituents she'd met with and considered. Then, rapidly, she tipped her hand: "I believe it's in our city's best interest to protect the jobs we know we currently have than to sell the street for hypothetical jobs contingent on a hypothetical team," she said.

The audience sat deathly still, as if too stunned to believe what was happening. Few in the room that day had envisioned the SoDo bid being defeated. But here was Gonzalez sounding as if she'd be sealing its fate. Gonzalez continued a few more seconds, mentioning how she'd already suffered daily driving through SoDo traffic. "I don't believe that the traffic issues have been well dealt with," she said. "And today, I am going to vote 'no' on the street vacation."

Cheers and gasps erupted before she'd finished her sentence. A Sonics fan in the crowd shouted "noooo!" while union members roared their approval.

Some Sonics fans burst into tears. The SoDo arena plan, for all intents and purposes, was dead.

Burgess couldn't believe it. "I was very surprised," he said. "I sat right next to her. And I've watched that video. And I think you can see the surprise on my face when she announces she was going to vote no. A lot of people were surprised."

Her former boss, Murray, claimed he wasn't. He'd felt Gonzalez was "a very unpredictable human being" and had proved it.

"Whoever got to her between the time my staff talked to her and the vote changed her mind."

The reasons didn't really matter. To tearful Sonics supporters trudging from the council chamber in defeat, Seattle's arena hopes appeared dashed for good. And along with them, the chance of landing new winter teams.

Little did they know what was to come.

PART THREE

Starting Fresh

Chapter 21

FURY UNLEASHED

Emotion guided much of Seattle's arena debate right up to the May 2016 council vote that stopped Chris Hansen and his SoDo project dead. Sonics fans, understandably reeling from their team being snatched away by Oklahoma City eight years prior, wanted a new arena as soon as possible. And Hansen had shown up with a seemingly reasonable plan. In fact, it was an enticing offer compared to other U.S. cities—Glendale, Arizona, for example—which had typically been coerced into laughable agreements by teams and developers.

So, with a grand offer from Hansen to build a palatial arena in SoDo—in a neighborhood zoned as a "Stadium District" for heaven's sake—Sonics fans didn't want to hear anything else. They knew, or thought they did, that a SoDo arena was their ticket to an NBA team.

It didn't matter that NBA commissioner Adam Silver kept saying no team was coming. They didn't care that the "Stadium District" had actually been created to protect neighborhood industry by restricting the baseball and football venues within geographical borders. That it was never envisioned as an invitation to cram an arena in alongside them.

The AECOM report stating a KeyArena remodel was possible? Didn't want to hear it. That a revamped KeyArena might be better for taxpayers than discarding it for the SoDo plan? Weren't listening.

There was a lot of messaging being pushed. Lobbyists paid big money on both sides. Some messaging got intense and personal ahead of the vote. It was playing out on social media and the public airwaves. And the message Sonics fans seemed to keep hearing was: a SoDo arena was the only way to get an NBA team back. Anyone believing otherwise was clearly paid off by the Port of Seattle and others opposing Hansen's project.

That the message might not have been totally accurate never crossed anyone's mind. Opinions amplified and solidified as the vote neared, becoming entrenched. There would later be ample research into how social media activity, confirmation bias, and echo chambers could dangerously inflame public sentiment.

But back then, in May 2016, the nation hadn't yet gone through two of the most divisive federal elections in its history. Back then, Twitter, Facebook, and other social media sites were seen merely as ways for friends to communicate on common likes. Recipes and favorite TV shows. A nice vacation spot, or cute dog or cat. And sometimes, maybe sports arenas and NBA teams.

It was all rather harmless. Until it wasn't. Seattle's arena debate was nothing like what eventually happened nationally with federal politics and attempted insurrections.

But in Seattle's tiny little corner of a much vaster universe, some folks allowed themselves to get too emotionally wrapped up in an impassioned civic debate decided by the council's vote. A debate that, silly as it sounds today, wasn't deciding the fate of democracy or some life-and-death issue. It was merely about where a multimillionaire put a sports arena.

And when Seattle's City Council voted 5–4 against selling a street to Chris Hansen, effectively killing his SoDo project, all hell broke loose.

"It was probably the most unhealthy, sorrowful time that I saw in the public," then councilmember Sally Bagshaw recalled when I last spoke to her in December 2021.

The four votes in favor of selling the street had been from male councilmembers. All five opposing and defeating the proposal were women. It didn't take long for some disappointed by the outcome and apparent demise of the SoDo project to pinpoint blame—the women on council.

Within an hour, phone calls and emails began pouring in. Some were typical words of constituents politely disappointed and upset. But others were angry, vile, and full of misogynistic hatred.

"As women, I understand that you spend a lot of your time trying to please others (mostly on your knees) but I can only hope that you each find ways to quickly and painfully end yourselves," read one email sent each of the five female councilmembers.

Turns out, it came from an actual lawyer hailing from the Seattle suburb of Lynnwood. His email also suggested the women were "whoring" themselves to the highest bidder. He later issued a media statement through his own lawyer apologizing for his "abusive" missive and adding he was seeking mental health counseling.

Things weren't any calmer on Twitter.

One tweet from a sports-themed fan account targeted councilmember Lorena Gonzalez, whose vote broke the 4–4 deadlock. "Your [sic] a Disgraceful HAG…lining your pockets with port Money…! A disease in all aspects is what you are…!"

Another read: "Port has money. Now she does. Bitch."

Still another read: "I think someone should smash Kshama Sawant's head into a brick wall."

The next day, with the onslaught still raging, mayor Ed Murray and other politicians rallied to the councilmembers' defense. So did Chris Hansen, whose SoDo project had been derailed.

"While we may not agree with the council's vote," he wrote in a statement, "misogynistic insults, vile comments and threats are unacceptable and need to stop. We should all show respect for our elected officials and the legislative process, even if we disagree with their decision."

Bagshaw today remembers watching in dismay as calls and emails kept coming.

"There were many times before when people were claiming bad intentions, but that was the saddest because it was so loud and so long," Bagshaw said.

"And it really impacted my legislative staff. I had to tell them that week, 'Please don't take this personally.' And also, I told them, 'Don't answer the phone after three in the afternoon' because that's when one of the [FM] radio shows would come on. It just got really heated."

Within days, the vote fallout garnered national attention in the *New York Times*, *Los Angeles Times*, and *Washington Post*. It also caught the eye of Samantha Bee, a comedian with a late-night *Full Frontal* talk show and news satire program on TBS. Bee's crew flew to Seattle, devoting a four-minute segment to the controversy two weeks after the vote.

"They wanted to fly us all out to New York," Bagshaw said. "And we said, 'We're not going to New York. If you want to come here, then fine. But we've got better things to do than fly to New York for a taping.'"

Instead, Bagshaw, Gonzalez, Sawant, Lisa Herbold, and Debora Juarez individually struck sports-like poses for the TV cameras and were announced basketball-style on the show as a team called the Seattle Seawards (pronounced "C-words"). The name built on their reasoning that Hansen's arena might threaten maritime-related jobs. "Ports before sports," Bee proclaimed on the show.

The councilmembers were also given sports nicknames: Lorena "The Gavel" Gonzalez, Debora "Slam Dunk" Juarez, Lisa "Lay-up" Herbold, Kshama "The Socialist Slasher" Sawant, and "Supersonic" Sally Bagshaw.

Their political accomplishments were highlighted, as were some nastier tweets sent their way.

Bagshaw feels the taping blunted the tensions. If anything, it served as a mocking portrayal of how out of hand things had gotten.

"There were many fewer phone calls," she said. "Although there were some nasty things that continued, it sort of evolved to just a few people."

But repercussions were far ranging. The toxic aftermath had a chilling effect on open discussions about trying again on any Seattle arena plan. Despite how quickly Hansen urged SoDo arena supporters against reacting emotionally, the damage was done. Sonics fans were lumped together as perpetrators of the worst behavior.

"It was not helpful at all—all of the misogynistic bullshit that people were throwing at members," said Rollin Fatland, a longtime Seattle lobbyist and Hansen's main Seattle spokesman. "Chris [Hansen] was really upset about that, as was his whole team. We met with Lorena [Gonzalez] a month or so after the vote. And she said, 'That wasn't helpful that it happened, Chris. And anything you can do to keep fans from that kind of vitriol would be really helpful.'"

In the months that followed, I filed public-records requests and received hundreds of pages of emails sent to the councilmembers. I'd wanted to see who exactly was sending them and their tone. I scoured for names of known Sonics fan group leaders. While I found several, their emails were firm, yet respectfully worded.

Offhand, it appeared less than 10 percent of all emails and letters had ventured into risky language that might be deemed overtly misogynistic. But they poisoned the well. As somebody on the receiving end of many Twitter and email barrages, I know firsthand how you quickly stop measuring who said what as it starts to all register as one.

To the councilmembers under constant attack, it was tough not to see green-and-gold Sonics colors lashing out in waves. And it left a mark. There was no appetite at City Hall for the SoDo project. Or any arena project at all, it seemed.

But appearances weren't everything. As usual, there was much more going on.

Mayor Murray had prepared the next step well before the vote. Had Hansen won, Murray planned to force the issue of whether Hansen's "shovel ready" SoDo project would quickly attract an NBA team. Murray wasn't prepared to wait another 19 months until Hansen's deal with the city expired. He had the NHL anxious to come to Seattle once an arena plan was finalized and was tired of waiting for Hansen to deliver. Now that Hansen had actually lost the vote in stunning fashion, Murray wasn't waiting another minute.

Even before the vote, he'd re-obtained the services of New York consultant Carl Hirsh of Stafford Sports to see where the city should go next if the SoDo project fell through. And the first thing Hirsh told him was, rather than seeking alternative sites, the city should exhaust all efforts to salvage KeyArena and not render it a white elephant.

"They knew based on their intelligence and based on my intelligence that the NBA was never going to give Chris Hansen a team," Hirsh said. "They knew it as fact, or they felt it. That Chris funding whatever amount of opposition in Sacramento tarnished him with the NBA forever."

Murray told Hirsh to quietly gauge back-channel interest in a KeyArena renovation. "This whole second concept of me talking to these people was me suggesting to the city that we start with KeyArena and see where it goes," Hirsh said. "The city people thought I was crazy."

But right away, Hirsh found three companies interested in further exploration of the idea—the Anschutz Entertainment Group, Spectra, and Tim Leiweke's newly formed Oak View Group. Hirsh said those unofficial discussions were never framed as the city demanding a new arena. Only him suggesting the city had an issue at the broader Seattle Center campus that needed solving: the potential loss of its KeyArena anchor tenant and what could be done about it.

"We had conversations," Hirsh said. "We talked to Spectra, we talked to AEG, and we talked to the Oak View Group. And we said, 'Let's see what happens.'"

It's highly possible NBA commissioner Adam Silver knew of those discussions when he made his comments to me just days before the SoDo vote. I've always found it strange Silver seemingly went out of his way to suggest a KeyArena renovation could be akin to building a brand-new venue. But it now made sense. Silver had contacts within all three interested arena-building companies. They'd likely have quietly gauged with Silver the possibility of landing an NBA team before committing bigger money to any KeyArena overhaul.

Hirsh said the Seattle City Council was unaware ahead of the SoDo vote of these preliminary third-party talks he'd undertaken with potential KeyArena suitors.

Once the SoDo street sale was quashed, Hirsh and Murray moved on KeyArena. They were excited. These three companies weren't everyday entrepreneurs. These were three of the world's biggest players in the arena management business. Suddenly, talk of a $285 million renovation as the AECOM report suggested seemed merely an appetizer. Murray, Hirsh, and others realized they had suitors capable of building an entirely new venue at the KeyArena site.

"If we'd looked at it and said, 'We're renovating KeyArena,' nobody would have been interested," Hirsh said. "That's not what we asked for. What we asked for was for them to build an arena."

Chapter 22

THE UNSHACKLING OF KEYARENA

Back when the Seattle SuperSonics were losing and then winning the NBA title in back-to-back championship series with the Washington Bullets in 1978 and 1979, Robert Nellams was forging his own basketball legacy.

As a Seattle native and local Bellevue Community College standout, he'd averaged 14.4 points a game those two seasons under coach Ernie Woods, helping lead the Helmsmen to a fourth-place finish at the 1978 state tournament. Nellams would later be named to the Northwest Athletic Conference Hall of Fame for his efforts while also earning an associate degree in business.

He transferred to Central Washington University, helping the team win the district title in 1981 and advance to the NAIA championship tournament. More importantly, he picked up an accounting degree and used it to land his first job in 1982 as a City of Seattle accountant.

By November 2006, after a quarter-century of Nellams diligently working his way up the city's ladder, then mayor Greg Nickels appointed him director of the 74-acre Seattle Center public park from the 1962 World's Fair. And, by default, he was now in charge of KeyArena, the park's anchor.

Unfortunately, the appointment coincided with the Sonics' purchase by Clay Bennett and eventual exodus of the NBA team Nellams had grown up cheering for in his favorite sport. Nellams had a front-row seat to that saga, culminating with the Sonics' departure for Oklahoma City in 2008.

Ever a pragmatist, Nellams knew the pros and cons of the arena he'd been tasked with overseeing. Lately, following a patchwork mid-1990s renovation attempt, it leaned toward the cons. There wasn't a rat licking grease off the cardboard french-fry containers in the arena's garbage bins he wasn't on a first-name basis with. If a water droplet from the arena's ventilation system plunked into the coffee cup of a WNBA Seattle Storm fan, transforming said brew from regular to partial decaf, Nellams heard about it.

And he'd heard it all by 2012, when Chris Hansen began making noise about building a rival arena in the city's SoDo district. Nellams was smart enough to realize proposals as good as Hansen's didn't come around often. But he also knew it meant the likely demise of his beloved KeyArena. And by extension, perhaps the gradual end of the Seattle Center park he'd been entrusted with.

"After dealing with all the nonsense of the Sonics leaving and Hansen coming in and saying he wants to build an arena somewhere else, I mean, there was no interest in KeyArena at that time," Nellams said. "And I had to kind of suck things up when I went through the things with Hansen and tell our staff, 'Look, this is bigger than Seattle Center. This is about the City of Seattle. We're going to have an arena and someone's willing to come in and help build one and we're going to have to support that.' Even though that might have meant that Seattle Center might have been crushed."

But then, something unexpected happened. Hansen lost the Seattle City Council vote in May 2016. Suddenly, city sports consultant Carl Hirsh was describing big companies being interested in renovating KeyArena. Nellams had admittedly scoffed at Hirsch's prior suggestions the city solicit KeyArena interest. Now, he didn't know what to make of some of the biggest arena groups on the planet supposedly lining up for a crack at his french-fry cartons and dripping ventilation system.

And so it came to pass that, in a city where common wisdom had declared no sane company would ever undertake a KeyArena renovation, Mayor Ed Murray, consultant Hirsh, Nellams, and others secretly met with Tim Leiweke's newly formed Oak View Group company in early summer of 2016.

It was just weeks after the SoDo project had been defeated. OVG co-founder Leiweke flew into Seattle with a key associate, Peter Luukko, in tow. Luukko was a well-connected, likeable former amateur hockey player from Worcester, Massachusetts. With his Boston-accented, beer-at-the-bar affability, Luukko could walk the walk and talk the talk. Besides holding a senior position with OVG, he was a former Philadelphia Flyers president and then a current executive chairman of the Florida Panthers. He also served as the Panthers' acting representative on the NHL's board of governors. So, when it came to knowing how NHL owners would vote on awarding a Seattle franchise, Luukko had more than just an opinion. He typically sat in the room casting votes right alongside them.

"We came in and had our first real conversation after that SoDo vote," Leiweke said. "Because that's when you knew they needed to find a solution. And they didn't have one."

Nellams had tried to keep an open mind during the meeting. The city already knew AEG was somewhat interested in a KeyArena renovation, given the company and its Seattle-based representative, Bob Newman, had for years handled marketing for the venue. But Leiweke sounded as if he wanted to build an entirely new arena akin to what Hansen had proposed in SoDo. Nellams couldn't believe it.

"He came in and he said, 'Look, I believe that I can build an arena,'" Nellams said. "He said, 'We can do it at KeyArena and I want to give it a shot.' He was saying all these grandiose things and everything and I was kind of rolling my eyes. I was saying, 'I just don't buy into this.' I just didn't see it happening. I thought it was going to be too expensive to do."

Murray had also brought in Brian Surratt to help him with the city's arena efforts. Surratt had joined the mayor's policy office early in his term, becoming the primary staffer working with business and labor groups to get a $15-an-hour minimum wage law passed. The weekend of November 6, 2016, Surratt had gone to watch the then No. 5–ranked University of Washington football team destroy Cal at Berkeley. He was hanging out in Oakland with his buddies the night before the game when a call from the mayor came through on his cell phone.

"It was pretty clear he needed help," Surratt recalled.

Surratt had grown up a rabid sports fan in Tulsa, Oklahoma. He later wound up moving to Seattle, which would have its NBA team snatched away by Bennett's group from his home state.

The coincidence wasn't lost on Surrat that he'd now be helping facilitate an arena and new NBA team for Seattle to replace the one his home state had taken. "I've told everybody since that there's no mixed loyalty here," Surratt said, chuckling. "But the funny thing is, my younger brother, David, he's the dean of students at the University of Oklahoma and he knows Clay Bennett."

Surratt knew a revived Sonics or NHL franchise was a long way from happening. But now, a game-changing opportunity had materialized. And some of the world's biggest arena builders were knocking at the city's door about KeyArena.

And they didn't just want a renovation. Tim Leiweke, one of the planet's foremost arena builders, was pledging the equivalent of an entirely new venue. And unlike Hansen's venture in SoDo, this would be all privately financed.

Between Leiweke, AEG and Spectra, they could open a bid process and play those companies off against one another for bigger concessions. And best of all, the problem of what to do about KeyArena as a secondary venue would be eliminated.

Problem was, Hansen still had a year and a half to go on exclusivity for his SoDo deal. So, they needed to do something about that before KeyArena offers could be considered. Hirsh said nobody in the mayor's office or various city departments wanted to wait around until December 2017 to see whether Hansen could get his SoDo project launched.

After all, even if Hansen somehow persuaded a now increasingly resistant city council to grant him a new vote, he'd still have to win it. And even if that happened, he'd still need the NBA to grant him a team before construction could begin.

"Everybody knew that wasn't going to happen," Hirsh said.

And so, Mayor Murray and the city's budget director, Ben Noble, got on the phone with Hansen. Others were listening in as well. Murray began by apologizing to Hansen for failing to deliver the council vote. But soon, he switched topics.

"I explained to Hansen that I needed to proceed with KeyArena," Murray told me. "And that I had a liability, and the city had a liability. I said that if he felt I couldn't [proceed], then I needed to know that. And he said that he wouldn't stand in our way."

Others listening in recalled Hansen advising the mayor that he and his SoDo team had already studied KeyArena and felt it too expensive to upgrade. Hansen, they say, added that traffic and parking congestion around KeyArena only compounded those difficulties.

From there, he basically wished the mayor "good luck" and the call ended. It would be the final time Murray and Hansen ever spoke.

Rollin Fatland, a SoDo area lobbyist and spokesperson, said Hansen phoned him after speaking with Murray and relayed the same story. "He called me after that and told me Ed [Murray] had wanted to take a look at

KeyArena. And Chris said, 'Sure. All I ask is that you keep me posted. Let me know where it's going.'"

Just like that, Hansen had waived arena exclusivity. KeyArena would be open to renovation offers. In years to come, those familiar with the city's arena efforts would describe it as a fatal miscalculation by Hansen and his advisers.

"First of all, he was convinced he was going to get the [SoDo] arena and KeyArena wouldn't happen, so he wasn't worried," Murray said. "And he was, I think, understanding of us in realizing that whatever happened with him, I was going to have a problem with KeyArena. But he really thought he was going to get the votes."

Surratt said Murray had excellent political instincts and gambled that Hansen believed any KeyArena bid process would fail. That prior studies had deemed the challenge too foreboding, and Hansen believed the city would go crawling back to the SoDo project once bidders passed on their RFP. Foremost on his mind was the 44-million-pound elephant in the room. KeyArena's roof was destined for historic preservation status. And that meant nobody could damage it while attempting any type of renovation beneath.

Leiweke was aware of the challenge. The question was whether he'd resolve it.

Surratt said Murray asked him to immediately plan a Request for Proposals (RFP) process so KeyArena renovation contract requirements could be outlined for interested companies.

"He said, 'We have a very, very small window after that [SoDo] vote to really push on this RFP,'" Surrat said. "And he was banking on the fact that Hansen and those guys wouldn't drop their name in there. And he bet right."

Chapter 23

BIG BERTHA BITES THE DUST

One of the bigger obstacles to a public buy-in on the great KeyArena overhaul plan wasn't Chris Hansen or the still-flickering SoDo project. No, a much bigger impediment to attaining credibility among local taxpayers was the aptly named Bertha. As her name implied, she was mighty big. And she bored through underground tunnels for a living.

Bertha wasn't a taxpayer. More of a tax money eater. She was the world's largest tunnel-boring machine, an $80 million, 6,700-ton, 57-foot-diameter beauty built by a Japanese firm specifically for the Washington State Department of Transportation's project to rid the city of its Alaskan Way viaduct. For six decades, the two-tiered, elevated section of Highway 99 shuttled what became 110,000 motorists a day through the city, offering a spectacular view of Elliott Bay on one side and downtown skyscrapers on the other.

Unfortunately, besides blocking seaside views for low-lying condos and office buildings, the elevated highway cut the city off from its waterfront. Oh, and it was an earthquake hazard, as were many of the region's surrounding bridges left poorly maintained by various governing branches.

The Nisqually earthquake of 2001 had caused $14.5 million in damage to the viaduct and prompted studies suggesting its imminent demise. As with the region's poor transportation infrastructure, various governments kept passing the buck on fixing anything that wasn't actually falling down. Then, in 2007, a group of University of Washington researchers warned the viaduct had to be replaced within four years or politicians might have blood on their hands. Finally, Governor Christine Gregoire decided the viaduct should be taken down and replaced by a 1.7-mile underground tunnel.

It sounded straightforward. After all, the city of Boston had just done something similar in replacing aging roadways with underground tunnels and...oh, wait a minute.

Boston's so-called "Big Dig"? Re-routing I-93? That became the most expensive highway project in U.S. history, a boondoggle of epic proportions rife with cost overruns and allegations of corruption and incompetence. It was supposed to finish by 1998 at a cost of $2.8 billion. Instead, it ended on New Year's Eve of 2007 for more than $8 billion. Dustin Pedroia had just helped the Red Sox celebrate a World Series victory over Colorado right before the project ended. He'd been eight years old when it began.

Not to worry, Seattle and Washington state civic leaders assured everyone. Projects like the "Big Dig" went astray on the evil East Coast, not the enlightened West Coast. Seattle did things differently, after all. With astute management and responsible regulation, there was no way the Alaskan Way viaduct couldn't be razed and the tunnel completed within a few years.

In January 2009, Governor Gregoire chose the $2.8 billion tunnel bore option, leading to Bertha's creation. Interestingly, the legislation was sponsored by then state Senator Ed Murray, who four years later became the city's mayor. The tunnel dig was also to begin in the SoDo district, not far from the future arena site proposed by Chris Hansen that Murray would reluctantly try to help. And the tunnel would finish in South Lake Union, barely a quarter mile from KeyArena.

Bertha was shipped to Seattle in separate parts and assembled to start her dig by July 2013. The machine had been named after Bertha Knight Landes, the first female mayor of Seattle from 1926 to 1928. Unlike many of her more modern counterparts, Landes actually got things done. One of her crowning achievements was the Seattle Civic Auditorium, later refurbished as the Seattle Opera House.

It was hoped that Bertha the tunnel boring machine would plow full speed ahead as Bertha the mayor once had. The digging was to take 14 months. Instead, just five months in, the machine overheated and shut down after striking a steel pipe. It would take two more years and millions of dollars replacing the machine's cutterhead to get Bertha up and running again.

Seattle Tunnel Partners, the contractor carrying out the dig, blamed the state for the pipe and wanted taxpayers to pay for repairs. The state countered that the pipe was put in to study groundwater and was included in plans the contractor had received prior to the bid process. Much litigation ensued.

Meantime, the machine sat dormant. It had tunneled only 1,019 of a planned 9,270 feet. And it was making Seattle a laughingstock both at home and abroad as national and international media lampooned the story of the behemoth underground drill nobody could reach. Finally, in December 2014, workers began digging a 120-foot-deep trench to pull up the machine's nose for repairs. That caused groundwater to spurt up and damage a neighboring street and buildings.

It wasn't until March 2015 that workers retrieved the machine's nose. By then, the damage was more severe than anticipated. That further delayed the tunnel-digging restart until December 2015. Two weeks later, a sinkhole appeared, and the project halted again as new governor Jay Inslee ordered the contractor to determine what caused it.

Finally, in April 2017, the boring was complete. The tunnel took two more years to finish, opening to traffic on February 4, 2019. But the two-year delay, right in the middle of Seattle's ongoing arena debate, fueled the perception local politicians lacked competence on major projects. After all, it wasn't just the Bertha fiasco still ongoing as the city prepared a bid process for developers wanting to overhaul KeyArena.

There were other factors. The Mercer Street Corridor project in and around KeyArena had literally torn up the neighborhood throughout much the same period. That wasn't a state-run project like Bertha. The attempt to modernize the "Mercer Mess" had caused years of traffic paralysis all at the City of Seattle's doing. Now, that same city was proposing a major arena overhaul disruption in and around the same neighborhood. Just as Mercer St. and the surrounding roadways were finally reopening. And with Bertha still boring away beneath the ground.

It wasn't a great selling point.

Amplifying doubts was the fact that the city had been duped on the cost overruns part of the state's Bertha project gone awry. The city in 2009 had agreed to pay $937 million for surrounding infrastructure, such as a seawall to make the underground tunnel possible. The state was supposed to cover the actual dig and all cost overruns.

But one month after agreeing to those conditions, the state legislature passed a law capping its spending at the agreed-to $2.8 billion. Under the law, the city would then theoretically have to cover cost overruns. But the city had already passed its own tunnel law committing to spend only the $937 million previously agreed to.

It seems nobody clarified the fine print before the project began. But they sure did once Bertha got stuck.

All of this was still playing out as Mayor Ed Murray was seeking to get a KeyArena deal done. The same Murray who'd sponsored the tunnel dig law as a state senator and now was on the opposite side of this Bertha squabble while running the city.

Fortunately, Bertha sped up her digging throughout 2016 and cut into those overruns significantly. But they still came out at some $223 million.

And the contractor wound up suing the state for an additional $642 million in costs for delays and repairs to the machine. The case would drag out through various courts and appeals, all while a skeptical citizenry wondered about the capacity of local government to pull off any project of formidable size.

Too many vocal Sonics supporters already weren't viewing the arena question through the lens of the best taxpayer deal. Naturally, restoring a civic arena previously built with tax dollars would be preferable to a new facility constructed with additional subsidies. That part was a no-brainer. Or, it should have been. But this wasn't how the debate was framed. Instead, restoring KeyArena was greeted with suspicion. There had to be a catch. Some backroom deal. The prevailing wisdom had been that no private developer would touch KeyArena. Now, developers were suddenly lining up to do it? That didn't fit the local narrative spun for years within a closed arena market contractually limited only to the SoDo project.

Who were these "outsiders" coming in to tell Seattle its arena business? And how could they be given precedence over a locally raised entrepreneur in Hansen, touting a spanking new arena?

It didn't help public perception that Hansen threw a curve ball at the city just as it was preparing to announce its Request for Proposals process. Up to that point, the general public had been kept unaware there even was interest in KeyArena. Then, out of the blue, on October 26, 2016, Hansen emerged after nearly six months in seeming exile following his lost city council vote.

His message was designed for maximum impact—he announced he'd make his stalled SoDo arena project an all-private venture. No more $200 million in public bond funding. And his projected cost for the SoDo project would jump from $490 million to $600 million.

Hansen's followers celebrated. "At last!" they shouted in unison. A plan the city could not possibly reject. Something the NBA would recognize as a serious step toward awarding Hansen a basketball franchise before the December 2017 expiry of his deal with the city. A basketball franchise Hansen needed for any construction on his project to begin.

But to those in the know, Hansen's offer wasn't good enough. Behind the scenes, Tim Leiweke and OVG were already offering the same type of all-private, brand-new arena. Sure, it was a new venue under the same KeyArena roof. But new nonetheless. And the kicker? KeyArena and the surrounding Seattle Center park would not risk being rendered obsolete, as would be the case if a SoDo arena were built.

The city now saw KeyArena as the only option that made sense. And if somebody repurposed it into a world-class venue, the future of the entire Seattle Center park could be transformed along with it. Naturally, city officials were fuming at Hansen's announcement.

"That's why he did it," Hirsh said, suggesting Hansen wanted to blunt the KeyArena bid process in the public's eyes.

Less than 24 hours later, with news of Hansen's offer still reverberating around Seattle, I took a call from a contact at city hall spelling out what was really going on. He threw the names AEG and OVG my way. I'd never heard of OVG. But I knew who Tim Leiweke was. His reputation preceded him and besides, his younger brother, Tod, had been a very popular Seahawks and Sounders president before leaving in 2010. I'd met with him for drinks the previous year, right before his pal Jac Sperling had seen an arena effort in Bellevue collapse right before the NHL's expansion process deadline.

A few hours later, Tim Leiweke phoned back and told me what his group planned to do. That he hoped to bring NHL and NBA franchises to Seattle, with hockey coming first. That he was ready to build with all-private funding.

"We understand that the private sector is going to have to do the heavy lifting here," Leiweke told me. "The private sector is going to have to take the risk here. The private sector is going to have to operate it here. We get that."

But then Leiweke took things further. At this point, it became clear to me that Hansen's proposed SoDo project was finished if Leiweke's plan ever became reality. Leiweke told me, pending whatever the city laid out in its coming bid process, that he planned to rebuild KeyArena "on spec"—meaning regardless of whether any teams committed beforehand to playing there.

"I learned a long time ago that you don't dictate to commissioners; you follow their lead," Leiweke said. "We would never get ahead of the commissioners. You follow their lead. Our belief is, you've got to have a real building and a real vision. And it has to be coming up and out of the ground and a reality. And then, and only then, would we have their attention."

It was a step further than Hansen had ever gone and ever would. Hansen seemingly lacked the money in his group to gamble $600 million on an arena with no guarantees of teams.

It was all coming into focus now.

That afternoon, it was clear as day that Tim Leiweke would rebuild KeyArena and Tod Leiweke would almost certainly return to his adopted hometown to run an NHL franchise and maybe a future NBA organization.

Sure, AEG was also in the equation. They'd built so many arenas worldwide that if they beat Leiweke in a bid process, it wouldn't be a problem getting teams or people to run them.

This was a game-changer. From the outside looking in, the city appeared on the verge of getting everything it wanted.

Brian Surratt (left), the City of Seattle's point man on the Request for Proposals process to overhaul KeyArena, accepts the official bid from Anschutz Entertainment Group (AEG) local president Bob Newman on April 12, 2017. AEG and Hudson Pacific Properties did a joint bid under the Seattle Partners umbrella, but it quickly became a no-go when it suggested up to $250 million in public bond funding would be needed.

The Lenin statue in Seattle's Fremont neighborhood is frequently vandalized and decorated. It now features blue and yellow paint meant to symbolize the Ukrainian flag and modern Russia's invasion of its neighbor.

Oak View Group CEO Tim Leiweke and his daughter, OVG executive Francesca Bodie, look on during December 4, 2017, Seattle City Council vote approving an interim development deal to overhaul KeyArena for major professional sports. Two days after the council's approval, the NHL granted a Seattle ownership group headed by David Bonderman and Jerry Bruckheimer permission to apply for NHL expansion to the city.

Oak View Group cofounder and CEO Tim Leiweke, seen here speaking at a community meeting in Seattle in July 2018, is often viewed as more of a showman than his younger brother, Kraken CEO Tod Leiweke (left).

Kraken majority owner David Bonderman, left, and Seattle mayor Jenny Durkan speak to media outside NHL headquarters in Manhattan on October 2, 2018, after pitching league's executive committee on awarding Seattle a franchise. CEO Tod Leiweke and minority owner David Wright in background along with book's author Geoff Baker (far right holding recorder). *(AP Photo/Mark Lennihan)*

Kraken CEO Tod Leiweke and author chat outside NHL headquarters in Manhattan after NHL Seattle contingent's meeting with league executive committee in October 2018. Executive committee would decide unanimously that day to recommend a December vote on whether to award a Seattle franchise.

Kraken minority owners Jerry Bruckheimer and David Wright, then chair of the future team's executive committee, enter the room ahead of the announcement awarding Seattle a franchise.

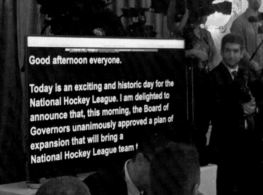

While the hockey world waited in suspense for an announcement in Georgia on whether Seattle had been awarded an NHL franchise, a teleprompter inside the room gave away the secret several minutes early.

The NHL Seattle group up on stage with commissioner Gary Bettman in Sea Island, Georgia, after Seattle was awarded an NHL franchise on December 4, 2018. From left: minority owners Adrian Hanuaer, David Wright, Jay Deutsch, Jerry Bruckheimer, and Gary Bettman; majority owner David Bonderman; senior Bonderman adviser Len Potter; and CEO Tod Leiweke.

NHL Seattle opened its season ticket preview center in April 2019, with a projection wall and full-scale model of what an overhauled KeyArena would look like. The group began selling club-level season tickets later that year before the COVID-19 pandemic forced everything to go virtual.

Author Geoff Baker with longtime Seattle Totems great Guyle Fielder in April 2019 at NHL Seattle's season ticket preview center. In 2022, Fielder at age 91 became the oldest living former Seattle pro hockey player.

Kraken CEO Tod Leiweke, head of analytics Alexandra Mandrycky, and minority owner Jerry Bruckheimer at a June 2019 breakfast meeting with the author to introduce him to the newly hired Mandrycky as the NHL Seattle contingent prepared to depart the NHL entry draft in Vancouver, BC.

The 44-million-pound KeyArena roof in January 2020 being held up by dozens of orange support posts so venue below can be completely gutted and rebuilt. Later, the original cement columns holding up the roof were reattached to it.

The interior of Climate Pledge Arena racing toward completion in June 2021. The new arena floor is now 53 feet below ground.

(left) The future Kraken dressing room nears completion. (above) Author Geoff Baker in Climate Pledge Arena's future press box.

ESPN's live telecast of the NHL expansion draft event at Gas Works Park on July 21, 2021.

Hundreds of boaters and kayakers pulled up alongside the park's shore to watch the televised draft event.

(left) Kraken coach Dave Hakstol addresses media at NHL expansion draft on July 21, 2021.
(above) Kraken defenseman Jamie Oleksiak, the team's pick from the Dallas Stars, was onsite at the expansion draft event at Gas Works Park.

Kraken open training camp at the new $80 million Kraken Community Iceplex training facility at Northgate Mall site in Seattle in late September 2021.

Kraken fans among those arriving at T-Mobile Arena in Las Vegas for the team's franchise opener against the Golden Knights on October 12, 2021.

The Kraken take the ice for the first time in an NHL game at T-Mobile Arena in Las Vegas against the Golden Knights.

Fans begin arriving prior to the Kraken's first home game at Climate Pledge Arena on October 23, 2021.

The Kraken take the ice for the first time at home on October 23, 2021, ahead of that night's game against Vancouver Canucks.

Pregame warm-ups as seen from the Kraken bench at Climate Pledge Arena before a March 2022 game.

Chapter 24

TIM LEIWEKE PARTS WAYS WITH AEG

Every welcome eventually gets worn out. What happens next depends on one's affinity for the other person and whether that's strong enough to override perceived shortcomings. With Tim Leiweke and the Anschutz Entertainment Group, it took 15 years. Then another two tacked on at the end where said welcome was overstayed beyond all affinity.

Either way, the end of the Leiweke–AEG marriage wasn't a happy event. A press release barely scratched the surface, with multibillionaire AEG patriarch Philip Anschutz stating Leiweke was departing by "mutual consent" and that "we appreciate the role Tim has played in the development of AEG, and thank him for the many contributions he has made to the Company. We wish him well in his new endeavors."

But you don't just walk away from a legacy of jointly building arenas and stadiums worldwide. Leiweke and Anschutz weren't quite Butch Cassidy and the Sundance Kid. More like Batman and Robin. Maybe Han Solo and Luke Skywalker. It was never a union of equals, owing partly to age difference but also to financial status. Anschutz had the serious money and therefore the power. Leiweke had the savvy and drive to get things done. They didn't always agree. But they didn't have to. This was business. To both men, it was probably a little more than that, stubborn as they might be about it. And it ended badly.

They'd met in Denver, where Leiweke had been directed in 1991 by then NBA commissioner David Stern to take over the presidency of the Nuggets basketball franchise and get a new arena built. Anschutz grew up in Colorado, using family money to build an empire in oil and gas, real estate, telecommunications, and eventually—thanks in no small part to Leiweke—sports and entertainment.

When Leiweke was finalizing plans in Denver for the Pepsi Center, a multisport venue to replace the McNichols Sports Arena, Anschutz was one of several investors he courted. Ultimately, Leiweke would bail on the president's role, citing professional burnout, within days of lining up Pepsi as the future venue's naming rights sponsor. But not before he'd helped Charlie Lyons, president of the the Nuggets' parent company, do a deal with Marcel Aubut to move the Quebec Nordiques to Denver, where they became the Colorado Avalanche to start the 1995–96 season. Anschutz reportedly wanted a piece of the incoming NHL franchise and, when he didn't get it, removed himself from any affiliation with the future arena and headed west to buy the Los Angeles Kings along with partner Ed Roski.

Not long after, Leiweke, who'd taken up running the U.S. Ski Team program, was summoned to L.A. by Anschutz in 1996 to serve as Kings president and head what later became AEG. From there, the duo launched an ambitious partnership, highlighted by the creation of Staples Center and surrounding L.A. Live entertainment district. The privately financed $375 million venue—today known as Crypto.com Arena—was built as a new downtown home for the Kings, who'd outgrown their old digs at The Forum in the Inglewood neighborhood out by the city's international airport.

Staples Center construction broke ground on March 31, 1997, and the venue opened on October 17, 1999. Initially, the main tenants were the Kings and the NBA's L.A. Lakers and Clippers. But that was only a part of AEG's efforts to develop the surrounding 5.6 million-square-foot neighborhood for $2.5 billion over the next decade.

By 2001, Leiweke was named president and CEO of AEG and began planning the three-phase L.A. Live venture along with Wachovia Group and Azteca Corp. Phase 1 opened in October 2007 with the 7,100-seat Nokia Theater and its surrounding Xbox Plaza, which became home to red carpet events, movie premieres, and corporate outings.

A year later, ESPN studios and ESPN Zone were added in Phase 2, while a Ritz-Carlton/JW Marriott hotel and a multiplex theater completed Phase 3 by late 2009. It was a crowning real estate achievement for AEG, credited with revitalizing downtown L.A.

From there, future planning for the neighborhood included a mid-2010 pitch for a potential 72,000-seat NFL stadium adjacent to the L.A. Live location of the city's convention center. The retractable-roof stadium was to be called Farmers Field—owing to a 2011 naming rights agreement with Farmers Insurance Group—and used to lure an NFL team back to the city. The Rams had departed for St. Louis the same year Leiweke arrived in L.A. in 1996, and reviving a franchise became something of an obsession for him. A non-binding memorandum of understanding was agreed to by the Los Angeles City Council with AEG in September 2012, with Leiweke spearheading the venture. But on one condition—construction could only begin once a team committed to playing there.

Teams could begin applying to relocate on January 1, 2013. But that 2013 year would spell the end of the Leiweke–Anschutz relationship and ultimately doom the stadium project. In hindsight, Farmers Field was merely the catalyst that sent a deteriorating relationship between them spiraling off a cliff. Leiweke, for all his successes at AEG, began to be seen by some within the company as too grandiose in his vision. Sure, he'd partnered in

AEG's name with the NBA and future commissioner Adam Silver to open basketball arenas in China. But he'd also built an arena in Kansas City, all but promising NBA and NHL teams that never came.

With Farmers Field, the doubts grew. The NFL seemed lukewarm to its existing teams relocating to Los Angeles. Anschutz was also the one footing the bill for a stadium initially projected at $750 million, but that industry analysts and later Leiweke himself suggested would require at least $1 billion. Anschutz also wanted to buy a discounted portion of any team playing at a stadium he was paying for, yet no NFL squads seemed interested in that.

Word inside AEG was that Leiweke was forgetting who his boss was. And there were others, including Leiweke's No. 2, Dan Beckerman, said to be angling for his job. Anschutz hadn't helped matters with the NFL or the city council by putting AEG up for sale in late 2012, hoping to generate a $10 billion haul. Leiweke was in an uncomfortable spot, having to reassure the NFL and local politicians that AEG remained committed to the stadium even as Anschutz was looking to bail.

Somehow, he persuaded the council to approve his stadium plan despite no guarantees of who would own the company proposing to build the venue. But the writing was on the wall for Leiweke.

Tensions had been brewing for years. Leiweke was a global visionary feeling somewhat constrained by his boss. And Anschutz was the guy writing checks for a rock-star employee not always showing proper deference.

In a 2013 wrongful death suit filed by Michael Jackson's mother and children against AEG, a 2009 email surfaced in which Leiweke spoke of Anschutz in less-than-flattering terms.

"Phil can be such a paranoid scrooge," Leiweke wrote to AEG Live CEO Randy Phillips, head of the company's concert wing. "He wants to know why I am so certain that none of our key folks are taking Michael Jackson tickets and scalping them."

So, the Farmers Field dustup didn't just happen overnight. And if not over a football stadium, it likely would have resulted from a disagreement over some other venue.

Six months after putting his company up for sale, Anschutz abruptly terminated those plans. But in the same breath, he announced that Leiweke's position within the company was also being terminated. Or severed by "mutual consent," as the press release indicated. The Farmers Field project officially died two years later, but it truly ended that day along with the Leiweke–Anschutz bond.

Beckerman took over Leiweke's role within AEG. That dynamic would come back into play in a not-so-friendly way four years later when Leiweke and AEG battled it out in Seattle for the right to overhaul KeyArena.

For now, Leiweke was an empire builder without an empire. His AEG departure came with a three-year non-compete clause attached. That gave him time to plot his future career move—building a company to rival AEG on the global stage. He'd no longer feel shackled answering to a boss whose vision wasn't always mutually aligned.

But that would be a textbook violation of any non-compete deal. So, Leiweke left Los Angeles and headed north, across the border to Canada, where the parent company of the NHL Maple Leafs, NBA Raptors, and MLS Toronto FC franchises needed tending to by a new company president.

Realizing his stay would be short, something he communicated to those hiring him, Leiweke wasted no time reimagining how Maple Leaf Sports and Entertainment should run. The buttoned-down Maple Leafs got a front-office overhaul with former NHL player Brendan Shanahan brought in as team president. The Raptors saw ex-NBA player Masai Ujiri imported as president, while Toronto FC saw Tim Bezbatchenko hired as general manager and given a pile of cash to upgrade the roster.

The moves paid off rather quickly.

Toronto FC became an MLS powerhouse with the signings of Jozy Altidore, Michael Bradley, Sebastian Giovinco, and others, losing the MLS

Cup final to Adrian Hanauer's Seattle Sounders in 2016 and then winning it all against them in 2017. The Raptors in 2019 under Ujiri won the NBA championship, while the Maple Leafs became a top regular season squad despite a tendency to bow out early in playoff quests for their first title since 1967.

Leiweke was no longer around once those championships began materializing. But he'd been on hand to witness them firsthand from the stands. By early 2015, he and his music mogul partner were ready to launch what became the Oak View Group. They began doing marketing deals with various NHL teams even though Leiweke was still running the Maple Leafs as MLSE president through June 30, 2015.

He'd announced that as his departure date months earlier. It was time to give his new company full attention. And prepare for the inevitable battle to come with AEG. Today, with years of additional hindsight, Leiweke insists he holds no grudge against Anschutz.

"I have great respect for Phil to this day," Leiweke told me. "I still do. We got along just fine and built a hell of a company. I made some mistakes. He made some mistakes. It was just 20 years' worth of wear and tear. But to this day, I'm grateful for the opportunity and respectful for who he is."

But that respect wouldn't prevent Leiweke from going to war with Anschutz over KeyArena in Seattle. And far from a fight to overhaul just the arena itself, the showdown between challenger OVG and reigning heavyweight champ AEG would largely determine the future of who controlled sports and entertainment in one of America's fastest-growing cities.

Chapter 25

COURTING THE
SKEPTICAL FANS

Brian Robinson had an unfulfilled dream of becoming a writer. And like many putting pen to paper, he'd found the dreaming part easier than the actual writing. But while no books yet bear his name, Robinson's quiet passion did lead to his unlikely role heading up a nonprofit group dedicated to keeping his beloved NBA Sonics in his native Seattle. Save Our Sonics and Storm was co-founded by Robinson and Steven Pyeatt on July 19, 2006. It was the day after Howard Schultz had announced his sale of the Sonics and WNBA Storm to the Oklahoma City group headed by Clay Bennett.

Robinson's group had a stated goal of "uniting sports fans throughout the region, working with elected officials, and motivating them to find a solution which will keep the teams in the region."

Later, once Bennett moved the Sonics in 2008 but left the Storm behind, the group's name would switch to "Save Our Sonics" alone and devote itself to landing a replacement NBA team.

Robinson's involvement had begun, innocently enough, by writing a freelance basketball article for a Sonics Central website run by future ESPN writer Kevin Pelton. Later, when Pelton left, Robinson took over the website, later renamed Sonics Rising. Once the team relocated to Oklahoma City, the Save our Sonics movement and Sonics Rising would become one and the same. Sonics Rising emerged as the written voice of the movement and the go-to place for the effort to land a replacement NBA team.

It would later become the unofficial voice of entrepreneur Chris Hansen's efforts to build an NBA arena in the city's SoDo district. When Hansen announced his arena plans in 2012, it would be Robinson, the Save Our Sonics members, and readers of Sonics Rising helping to organize and participate in rallies to get the venue built.

Robinson runs a small real estate company, and the Sonics quest was quickly rivaling his day job for time. But he did it out of a passion for the sport and a feeling he was helping, in a small way, to make a difference. One thing he'd spent "hundreds of hours" trying to do with Sonics Rising was "remove the bitterness from the equation." He wanted disenfranchised NBA fans to have a constructive, productive voice in galvanizing efforts to land a new Sonics team and make political alliances. Robinson realized no politicians or community leaders would attach their name to a movement of bitching, griping sports fans. So, he'd urged followers to adopt a strategic, professional approach to acquiring what they wanted.

"I think Seattle fans always have an 'expect the worst' mentality," Robinson said. "And they have a survivor's mentality where they think things are going to go wrong. And that's part of what brings us together and from where we get our strength that we're going to survive.

"That's kind of dominant throughout the city's culture. But where you look at the Sonics issue in particular, the lack of trust and the lack of confidence in the process that was created by the team's departure, it had taken years and years to mitigate."

Now, a decade later, Robinson was at a crossroads. He'd just lived through the May 2016 city council vote that denied entrepreneur Hansen a shot at acquiring the street needed to build his SoDo arena. As with most Sonics fans, Robinson had felt "crushed" by the 5–4 vote. And then, increasingly alarmed at being lumped in with the misogynistic backlash brought against the female city councilmembers who voted down the proposal.

We'd gotten to know each other in the years prior to and since that tumultuous vote. And by early 2022, when we spoke for this book, Robinson had come to see that 2016 period as one in which he made a significant shift in his thinking.

Robinson admitted the post-vote aftermath, in which Sonics fans were being criticized for the venom aimed at council members, caused enormous harm to those pushing for a SoDo arena.

"We felt very betrayed that they had painted us with one brush," Robinson said. "It was a real, open reminder that when you put yourself out there in the public, you can get hurt. And it happened there. I had to explain to my 13-year-old daughter why Dad was involved in accusations of misogyny. And it was horrible."

Nonetheless, even before the vote, Robinson sensed the resentment some local fans felt toward politicians and worried a few might get out of hand if the vote did not go in their favor.

And though Sonics fans felt they'd become a greater political force in the interim, taking credit for councilmember Kshama Sawant's upset victory a couple of years prior, Robinson realized it was tenuous. Leading up to the vote, he'd worried the SoDo effort hadn't spent enough time lobbying councilmembers the way the Port of Seattle had been doing in opposition of Hansen's arena plan. He didn't see Hansen himself making enough appearances locally. Three days before the vote, Robinson said he sent out a warning to Hansen's organizers saying, "People are really hot" and asking them about talking points in the event the vote failed.

Robinson said he told them, "I am issuing talking points to all of my supporters urging them not to say anything bad. What are you going to do if this doesn't pass?"

But he was told not to worry, that the vote was in the bag. Then, in the aftermath, when the vote went 5–4 against the SoDo proposal and the vitriol directed at the female councilmembers erupted, Robinson remembered being overwhelmed by personal bitterness. Not at the women on council, though he didn't appreciate that they seemed to be lumping him in with the worst offenders. His resentment, he realized, was more directed at the SoDo group he'd long supported.

"I'm like, 'Wait a minute. Why are the volunteers facing all the heat and the professionals aren't doing their job? And like, is there any accountability?'"

Robinson sensed the SoDo movement being cast adrift in the months that followed. Hansen, it seemed, had vanished from public view, during which time Sonics supporters often felt leaderless. But Robinson during that time began hearing from contacts in NBA and local government circles that arena plans were indeed still underway.

Robinson was told to be patient and that he'd soon find out more. When Tim Leiweke and the Oak View Group showed up six months later in late October 2016 touting a plan to bid to overhaul KeyArena, Robinson knew this was what he'd been hearing about. He was well aware of Leiweke's reputation in NBA circles and felt if anyone could get a Seattle arena built, it would be him.

But he also knew Leiweke was walking into a hornet's nest. That he was the outsider coming in to replace the local guy. And that KeyArena, of all places, was not what local sports fans were going to want to hear discussed as the solution to their venue problem.

"I think that Tim Leiweke walked into a minefield of distrust where everything they said was taken with skepticism," Robinson said. "And the sports fans that would normally be their allies in many ways became the opposition. And it was a very, very hard-earned battle for trust that Tim had to fight when he first arrived here."

Robinson said he was impressed when Leiweke first reached out to him through OVG's local legal counsel, Lance Lopes. He sensed that Leiweke truly understood the predicament he was in and wanted the support not only of Sonics Rising, but of sports fans in general.

"It was a horribly fractured fan base," Robinson said. "People were bitter and people were angry and people were emotional. From our perspective, we knew who Tim Leiweke was. And we had a good understanding that some of the [arena] challenges were not about good intentions. But they were about capabilities. And Tim Leiweke was a guy who brought the capability to get it done."

Robinson quickly realized Leiweke's group, if it prevailed in landing the KeyArena bid, likely represented Seattle's best hope of getting an NBA franchise. But much like Leiweke, he faced an avalanche of distrust from amongst his own supporters that anything other than the SoDo project offered a solution.

"I had been a leader of that fan movement for well over a decade," Robinson said. "And the support of OVG and of Tim Leiweke earned me a large amount of animosity. I had death threats. I had people calling me a traitor. The anger that boiled over and seized out was really difficult. Really difficult to deal with."

Robinson also sensed he was dealing with more than just an arena debate. The Sonics movement, he said, had become deeply ingrained within the city's "progressive activist movement" and adopted some of its mantras. It became what Robinson termed a "truth to power" and a "small guy versus big guy" movement that largely believed past arena debates had been about "a rich white guy saying opera's important, but basketball is not."

Not to mention, Seattle had always been a somewhat provincial place.

"I think there's also a lot of distrust in big versus small, local versus non-local," Robinson said. "And the thing that was so magical about Chris Hansen that I don't think people understood was that he was this kid from Horton Street. So, when he showed up in town, we knew the same people. And people vouched for him. And he came out and had beers with us and people got to know him. And it was personal.

"So, the idea that you had to set aside this guy from Horton Street who you knew wanted it—and no one ever doubted how bad he wanted it—in exchange for somebody who was kind of part of the team that screwed us previously…it was just a hard sell emotionally from that regard. It showed just where people were in the process. We'd had five straight years of heavy battles. You look at the initial [memorandum of understanding] battles with [Mayor] Mike McGinn in 2012, and the battle for the Sacramento Kings, then the battle during the street vacation vote. We had been beaten down and beaten down and lost and lost. And I just think that became very visceral and very emotional for a lot of people."

But the courting of Robinson's group would pay dividends for Leiweke, if anything strictly by easing at least some of the distrust. Robinson said he was never promised an NBA team was coming. He knew better than to expect such guarantees. But he'd been told an NHL team was likely as soon as an arena deal was struck with the city. And that the arena plans would contain provisions for an NBA team to come in at any time.

"I did hear from a lot of people affiliated with the league and owners' groups within the league, that are friends of mine," Robinson said. "And they told me that Tim Leiweke was a person that had the capability to get it done. That he was a person who was a member of the league's inner family."

And Robinson believed Leiweke when he said he was committed to trying to bring the NBA back to town. Robinson had never been much of a hockey fan. But he immediately immersed himself in the NHL, hoping to support the new team any way he could. If the NHL was successful in Seattle, he believed, the NBA would not be far behind.

"I've never been a believer that the NBA isn't an aspirational goal of this," Robinson said. "Because if you're going to build this building and you're going to make this move and put all of this into it, of course you want the NBA. So, they made logical sense. They said that and I believed them."

Chapter 26

THE BATTLE FOR SEATTLE

Seattle wasn't exactly rippling with excitement over news that AEG or Tim Leiweke's new Oak View Group might be interested in overhauling KeyArena. The general reaction of sports fans was akin to how they'd cheer an empty-net goal that clinches a hockey game with the opposing goalie pulled for an extra attacker.

Sure, it was nice and all. But in their minds, Chris Hansen had already scored the go-ahead breakaway winner with his announcement 24 hours prior that he'd go all-private on a $600 million SoDo project instead of the previous $490 million. Breakaway winners come out of the blue and lift frenzied fans from their seats. Empty netters? They get smaller cheers, then everyone scrambles for the parking lot early.

And that was still how a KeyArena remodel was viewed. As a nice add-on, but not the game-changer a SoDo arena represented. Fans had been conditioned for years to believe the SoDo option was the only way the NBA would award Seattle a franchise. This KeyArena thing, to them, was redoing something they felt the NBA wouldn't care about. Also, it seemed about bringing the NHL to Seattle first. That was nice, but it wasn't basketball.

Once again, prevailing wisdom was trumping common sense. The major differentiator between the plans was that Tim Leiweke had come out and said he'd rebuild KeyArena before even having teams to play there. Once approved, construction could start right away. It was vastly different from the more popular SoDo option requiring an NBA team before anything got started.

In fairness, none of those fans downplaying the KeyArena option were privy to what had been happening behind the scenes for months. To them, it appeared as if the KeyArena plan was simply piggybacking on Hansen's proposal rather than the other way around.

Leiweke took it in stride. In one of our later conversations for this book, he told me he was aware Seattle fans were "pissed about the Sonics" and looking to the SoDo project as their salvation. And that he, as a late arrival to the arena debate, would be viewed with suspicion and even resentment. But it ultimately didn't matter.

"We knew SoDo was not going to happen," Leiweke said. "I mean, it was amazing to us how many people had opinions about how it should be down there. And I'm like, 'Great, let's go build it in the middle of a lake because wouldn't that be the greatest arena ever built? And by the way, it ain't ever going to happen.'

"So, have any vision you want. But I live in reality. And I knew what was going on politically."

And what was happening politically was city bureaucrats and elected politicians alike were salivating over a potential showdown between Leiweke's current company and his former one. By this point, Spectra had balked at participating in what was shaping up as a two-company clash of titans.

A backlash had also been forming nationwide against municipalities and states handing over public money to sports leagues and teams. The debacle in Glendale over the Coyotes was cited as a low point in taxpayers getting fleeced. In Seattle, the opposite was happening. Now, private companies were offering to take a diminishing KeyArena asset and revive it on their own dime.

"It was such an interesting contrast," said Brian Surratt, the man Mayor Ed Murray brought in to help spearhead the Request for Proposals bid process. "You've got AEG, the big dog in the industry. We had a previous relationship with them, and they were still under contract at Seattle Center. And then you had Tim [Leiweke] and he was putting all of his chips into his company. And we were seeing this unfold and began telling ourselves, 'We've got something here.'"

Surratt would be part of a three-man group tasked with creating the RFP and running it. With Surratt serving as public point man and city budget director Ben Noble running financial analyses on the bids, it would be Seattle Center director Robert Nellams and his team actually writing most of the RFP.

From the outset, they agreed this would be the city's one chance to go big. The RFP had to command greatness from bidders, stating that a typical renovation akin to the mid-1990s one at KeyArena was out of the question. If this were to work, then KeyArena needed to be gutted and completely rebuilt.

"What I told my team and our staff was that the way we got into trouble on KeyArena before," Nellams said, "was that instead of redoing the arena in a way that increased space and made it grand, we did it—I wouldn't say on the cheap because you spend $100 million and that isn't cheap—but that we did it in a way that we could as a public entity.

"But that is not something that a private entity would have done in terms of trying to renovate an arena. And the thing that I was trying to convince our team about was that if we went partway again, it may work for a few years but then we'll be right back to where we are right now. And that can't be where we want to be."

Not only that, but public funding for construction was out. The city's RFP team realized they had a chance to do something unique within the American sports landscape. Sure, some cities had built all-private arenas. Construction on Chase Center in San Francisco for the Golden State Warriors was about to get underway and its financing through corporate sponsorships was something Leiweke's company was taking a keen interest in. But Chase Center would be owned by the team itself. In Seattle's case, the city would retain ownership of KeyArena. Despite all its flaws, KeyArena still turned a small annual profit on behalf of the taxpayers who'd funded its construction in 1962 and paid for the mid-1990s renovation as well.

The arena showed profits of $632,000 in 2012, $1.2 million in 2013, and $579,000 in 2014. For all the disparaging comments directed its way, the venue still hosted more than 100 events a year and wasn't a drain on the city's economy.

But now, those profits were about to vanish unless somebody pumped hundreds of millions of dollars into restoring KeyArena to something more usable. The previous year's AECOM report had shown that. So, here were companies willing to do it. Now, the trick would be to safeguard the profits KeyArena had been turning. Sure, the developer and any NHL or NBA teams they attracted would expect to keep the bulk of monies from an arena they were paying hundreds of millions to upgrade.

The RFP would just need to guarantee that the city would be made whole on what it had already been bringing in. And there would need to be a profit-sharing mechanism down the road for the city to grow its stake. After all, while KeyArena wasn't much, the land it was sitting on adjacent to downtown and Amazon headquarters in South Lake Union was actually quite valuable.

Hansen had spent millions buying up the SoDo land to build his arena on. With KeyArena, the land was already there and owned by the city. So, whoever won the bidding would be getting a break on not having to buy the land. It was up to those crafting the RFP to use that leverage to negotiate a better deal for taxpayers.

Meanwhile, the traffic and parking issues hadn't exactly gone away. They'd gotten worse. A rallying cry for SoDo supporters stated that KeyArena becoming the new major sports venue would cause untold bottlenecks and traffic paralysis throughout entire city neighborhoods.

Any bidder would need to present a comprehensive plan to deal with that. It was a lot to ask. But the city was banking on Leiweke needing KeyArena to launch his envisioned OVG empire. They knew he couldn't begin to rival AEG and its vast array of global venues without a flagship arena to call his own.

Also, they assumed AEG wouldn't let that go down without a fight. This wasn't only about arenas and sports. Behind the scenes, things were getting nasty between AEG and OVG over music. AEG was a concert-promoting behemoth, given the arenas it controlled. And its biggest rival was Live Nation. Relations between the two had become so cutthroat that music artists were reporting being blackballed from the arenas owned by each company if they played at venues controlled by the other.

It just so happened that Leiweke's group already had serious connections within the music and concert industry. It started with his co-founder, Irving Azoff, legendary manager of the Eagles going on a half century and a growing music industry mogul. His ties to the Madison Square Garden group and James Dolan led to that company financing OVG's launch period. But the opening salvo in Leiweke's coming war with former employer AEG was when OVG and Live Nation joined forces. Under the deal, Live Nation would supply artists to perform in OVG venues.

Thus, the Seattle fight over KeyArena wasn't just about sports. Smaller-city venues were also part of mini skirmishes between Live Nation and AEG, and it was Philip Anschutz's company feeling the squeeze. Already, the city's landmark Showbox venue, an intimate music facility for 1,100 patrons built in 1939 across from Pike Place Market, was facing financial hardship.

AEG had purchased the Showbox in 2007, opening a sister 1,800-patron venue in SoDo not far from Hansen's planned arena site. But Live Nation was siphoning away acts from both places.

Now, the fight was on for music survival in Seattle. Whether it was AEG or Live Nation through its OVG partnership, whoever won the rights to transform KeyArena into the region's premier sports and concert facility would control music in Seattle for years, possibly decades to come.

Those crafting the RFP knew this. And it was their job to get the competing groups to throw everything they could at one another to the city's benefit.

Leiweke knew the city's ongoing relationship with AEG at the time could prove tough to overcome. AEG's local president, Bob Newman, had already held discussions about KeyArena the prior year with Victor Coleman, the Canadian-born real estate mogul from Los Angeles who'd visited the city and Mayor Murray with NHL commissioner Gary Bettman two years prior seeking to become a hockey owner. The rumor was AEG and Coleman would be teaming up on a joint KeyArena bid.

But Leiweke had some of his own personal cards to play. He was well known to Seattle's sports power elite, having made the moves that helped Joe Roth and Adrian Hanauer land a Sounders MLS franchise, then getting Pete Carroll and his brother, Tod, together at his house so the former USC Trojans coach could join the NFL Seahawks.

"We had a unique relationship with Seattle," he said. "My old company, AEG, managed KeyArena because that was an old account I helped get when I was still there. So, we did have a history. And I think that helped us a little bit.

"But I also had my brother's reputation," Leiweke said.

The younger brother he'd helped nurture in Missouri following the devastating death of their mother had, during his time running the Seahawks from 2003 through 2010, become arguably the most universally liked and respected sports executive in the city's recent history. And Tim Leiweke planned to use that to his advantage.

"That was an immense help that everyone felt as strongly about Tod as they did," Leiweke said. "They probably figured that apple couldn't have fallen too far from the tree."

Perhaps not. But as the OVG–AEG showdown in Seattle officially got underway, plenty would try to paint Tim Leiweke as a runaway train even his younger brother was powerless to stop.

Chapter 27

PEEING ON THE PARADE

To the surprise of absolutely nobody, the only responders to the City of Seattle's Request for Proposals (RFP) to overhaul KeyArena were the Anschutz Entertainment Group and Tim Leiweke's new Oak View Group. With them in the hunt, there wasn't much room for less-experienced arena builders to sneak into the fray. Spectra took a gander and passed.

AEG also brought along additional artillery. Victor Coleman, who'd met with Mayor Ed Murray nearly three years prior in May 2014 hoping to become a Seattle hockey team owner, had joined forces with AEG's local president, Bob Newman. Coleman's Hudson Pacific Properties company and AEG formed a bid group officially known as Seattle Partners.

Coleman's company was publicly traded with a large Seattle presence. His British Columbia roots and longstanding hockey fandom had led him to attempt to team up with Chris Hansen at his SoDo arena. When that failed, he'd approached Newman and AEG in 2015 to discuss KeyArena and that year's AECOM report stating the venue could be repurposed for NHL and NBA teams despite its 44-million-pound roof being historically protected.

The RFP process had finally been launched in January 2017, roughly two months after Leiweke had come out mentioning OVG's interest.

It offered two choices: demolish and completely rebuild KeyArena or attempt to overhaul it with the roof intact. Technically, the roof had yet to attain landmark preservation status. But everybody connected with the city and arena expected this would happen—and it eventually did—so any bidder pitching a complete demolition was required to submit two separate plans in case roof preservation was indeed required.

Neither OVG nor the AEG–Coleman partnership wanted entanglement in historic preservation red tape for years. So they both, to their credit, determined the best possible bid was just the one in which the roof was left intact while the arena beneath was redone.

Both had three months to submit final bids. And to win over a skeptical Seattle public already incredulous anyone wanted to renovate, overhaul, restore, or do anything to KeyArena other than level it and pave it over into a parking lot.

AEG had work to do locally, as Leiweke had gotten out ahead of the process more than two months prior, after Hansen's preemptive attempt to direct attention back to his stalled SoDo project. Coleman wasn't a public factor in the RFP process, but delegated a lieutenant, Alex Vouvalides, to speak on behalf of Hudson Pacific Properties within the partnership.

That left AEG's local president, Bob Newman, effectively running point on the Seattle Partners bid. I met with Newman a handful of times during that period and had him on a sports business podcast I was then operating for the *Seattle Times* newspaper. Newman was the opposite of Tim Leiweke. He didn't walk into a room and dominate. Rather, he tried a softer, gentler approach.

One of Seattle's better-known communications strategists, Roger Nyhus, had been engaged by Seattle Partners to promote their KeyArena bid. Nyhus accompanied Newman to his public speaking engagements and meetings with newspaper editorial boards. On one occasion, Newman met my paper's editorial board, which asked me to sit in so they could ask me contextual questions later.

Several times that meeting, Nyhus interrupted Newman as he attempted to answer the board's questions. I tried to imagine Tim Leiweke allowing a subordinate or hired PR gun to do that. It was a moot question, as none would have dared.

Still, there were advantages to Newman's approach. Newman knew Seattle and how nails got hammered down if they stuck out. If Leiweke sometimes played as the proverbial bull on a china-shopping expedition, Newman was more the storekeeper gently pointing out the best plate, saucer, and serving bowl options.

In a close bid, Newman's approach might have won. He'd merely need to turn some folks off the more bombastic Leiweke. And Leiweke early on was living up to his showman reputation. His pitches, unlike Newman's, seemed more rehearsed. I'd heard him utter the same lines time and again. And his "you can't get ahead of commissioners" line when it came to publicly lobbying for sports teams was becoming a running joke within media circles. I knew of some city officials rolling their eyes at hearing it for the umpteenth time. Of course, it was true. Leiweke knew exactly what league commissioners wanted. He had them all on speed-dial and was soft-playing his demands for teams because he didn't want to blow what he felt was a winning hand.

He just needed to say it a little less. Or maybe not. In the end, it didn't matter. The AEG–Coleman team lost the bidding the minute it submitted its proposal.

It wasn't necessarily the bid itself, an ambitious $520 million offer nearly double what the AECOM report had suggested KeyArena could be upgraded for. Seattle Partners would increase KeyArena's square footage from 400,000 to 600,000 without rotating the rink floor as AECOM had suggested. And it pledged to do it by October 2020, in time for the 2020–21 NHL season.

That was all well within what the RFP had asked for. There was one deal-breaking problem—Seattle Partners was seeking up to $250 million in public bond funding to help pay for construction.

All around city offices that day, loud thumping could be heard as jaws hit the floor.

"I was beyond surprised," said Robert Nellams, the Seattle Center director who'd crafted the RFP. "I was amazed."

Brian Surratt, the mayor's point man leading the bid process, agreed. "It was a non-starter," he said. "An absolute non-starter."

The RFP language specifically stated the construction needed to be privately funded. This was no accident, as Tim Leiweke had indicated in initial discussions that OVG was prepared to go that route. Now, here was the AEG–Coleman tandem telling the city it wanted up to $250 million in what amounted to a public loan. Even if it was merely using the city's bonding capacity and would pay back the relatively low interest rate, it was still a public subsidy. One reason the SoDo project pitched by Chris Hansen had been so controversial was its provision for up to $200 million in bond funding from the city and King County.

Now, Seattle Partners wanted $50 million more than that. Besides disregarding the RFP provisions, it would be a tough sell to an already skeptical public that distrusted city politicians and bureaucrats. For one thing, SoDo arena supporters could rightfully ask why Hansen's project was being ignored in favor of a KeyArena process where Seattle Partners wanted even more public money.

It didn't help the AEG–Coleman tandem's cause that Leiweke and OVG had returned a bid pledging $564 million of all-private money to build a 660,000-square-foot facility. Their bid would not only produce a bigger venue but spend more money and use none of the city's bonding capacity.

"We're looking at them going, 'Um, the RFP specifically says do not ask for funding from the city,'" Leiweke said. "So, we were mad because they didn't follow the rules."

Even to the uninitiated, it was game over.

To the initiated, seasoned city officials running the RFP, the Seattle Partners bid seemed like a practical joke.

"What I was trying to understand was, what are you telling us? Are you telling us that you just don't want to do this?" Nellams said. "Are you telling us that you believe this is the only way to do this? Because I've got another entity that doesn't believe that."

Even Seattle Partners seemed to know their proposal was shaky. They'd touched on their bonding request during a public unveiling of their bid while declining to mention how much money they wanted. It was only later, when Newman and Nyhus visited the *Seattle Times* editorial board, that I pressed on the amount. It was then and there that Newman dropped the $250 million figure. Even our editorial board members, hardly experts on arena financing, seemed visibly flabbergasted.

Those newspaper men and women in the room may not have known how to secure a nine-figure bridge loan. But they could read. And add, subtract, and divide. The $250 million represented nearly half of the entire Seattle Partners bid. And the editorial board members had been very familiar with Chris Hansen's SoDo project, as they'd opposed it for years. One reason had been its $200 million public bond funding element.

Now, Hansen had dropped that and was pledging to go all-private on his SoDo arena if anyone in city government ever wanted to listen to him again. But here was this AEG–Coleman tandem and point man Newman arguing for even more bond money than Hansen once had. It didn't make sense.

Newman told us the $250 million amount wasn't set in stone. That Seattle Partners would be willing to go all-private if the city rejected its initial bid. He explained that public bonding would help his group generate even more money for the city long-term. But all the tap dancing in the world couldn't get around the basic premise—the city's RFP had demanded an all-private construction bid. And Seattle Partners came back with a bid asking that nearly half be funded with public bonding.

It turns out, city planners discussing the bids internally were just as dumbfounded. Speculation was rampant as to what was fueling it. Seattle Partners communications strategist Nyhus had been a longtime ally of Mayor Ed Murray—perhaps he'd felt he could lean on that relationship?

Also, behind the scenes, Seattle Partners was aggressively questioning whether Leiweke's group could live up to its promises. Seattle Center director Nellams said everyone could sense "some bad blood" between AEG and its former boss Leiweke.

"We were kind of in the middle of a personal duel there between Tim and AEG because Tim had come from AEG," Nellams said. "And so, we didn't know what was going on or how people were playing this. But we knew we didn't want to be in the middle of something like that."

AEG even flew in Dan Beckerman, Leiweke's former subordinate and the man who'd replaced him as president and CEO, to make a last-ditch pitch to the city. It did not go over well. Leiweke attributes the moves to AEG patriarch Philip Anschutz wanting to defeat him at all costs.

"Needless to say, they were out there trying to drag me through the mud," Leiweke said. "It didn't make me real happy, some of the things they were out there saying. I built that company for the guy and then he in turn tries to go out there and badmouth me. That was unfortunate.

"But we stayed above it all."

The city had already asked Seattle Partners to rework both the financing and the physical details of its renovation proposal. Part of the group's bid had involved extending the KeyArena roof over the arena's east side to allow for more space to be created beneath.

One official likened it to an ugly "mullet" design that would never fly. Ultimately, Seattle Partners did some design reworking but their "best and final" offer still involved the public bond funding. A person working closely with the bid described AEG's attitude as, "We're the global experts in arena building. If we say it can't be done without this public money, then it can't be done. Take it or leave it."

For context, AEG had just built the new T-Mobile Arena in Las Vegas for the NHL's expansion Golden Knights at an all-private $300 million cost. With KeyArena, they appeared to view their up-front investment as capped by that figure.

For Nellams, the man whose team had crafted the RFP, the final Seattle Partners submission was akin to a surrender.

"They never really explained it in a way that I bought, let's put it that way," he said. "They said that this was as far as they could go. And they didn't see doing any more than they had said."

Just days before the bid winner was to be announced, the city planned to inform the AEG–Coleman tandem that its bid was non-responsive to the RFP and would be left on the presentation table. That's when Seattle Partners decided to scorch that table and any earth beneath it.

The group announced it was withdrawing its bid and pulling out of the process. A letter to Mayor Murray, made public by the group, stated, "We fear the City is driving toward an unrealistic financing structure, and we believe the City has failed to conduct a sufficiently thorough, objective, and transparent process to properly evaluate the respective strengths and weaknesses of the two proposals and, most significantly, to identify the proposal best positioned to deliver a project consistent with the community's interests."

The letter was somewhat stunning, given AEG's longstanding ties to the city in having run Seattle Center and KeyArena's marketing. It had practically accused the city of running a rigged RFP process.

"I did not see that coming," Nellams said. "After all those years of working with them and being partners and all that, having them throw their hands up and say they can't do this was very surprising.

"I thought that they knew about our market. They knew about the opportunity that was there. They knew that this was going to be something that was not only going to work, but was going to be a pretty grand thing for the city and the sports and the entertainment community and they just walked away."

Nellams still takes the whole thing somewhat personally.

"When I say that they just 'walked away' that's the way that I have to say it," he said with a chuckle. "Because they know me and that's not something we do. We don't play games. We don't lie. We don't cheat. We don't steal. We don't do anything but tell you flat out what we're doing.

"Their frustration was that Tim [Leiweke] was saying he was going to do stuff that they didn't believe could be done."

And so, they handed Leiweke his greatest personal and professional triumph by default. Today, Leiweke, softened by five additional years of perspective, isn't bitter about being denied his moment of celebratory triumph in as brutal a fight as he'd ever engaged in. Ultimately, he had his arena. That mattered more than settling old scores.

"It wasn't personal until they made it personal," he said, adding that the final open letter to the city was the worst blow. "I took it as it was a question of our ability and of my character. And I didn't like it. That's when it became personal. When they took their ball and went home. They felt like they had to pee on the parade before they left.

"I felt that was a low-class thing to do," he said. "I built a hell of a company and then they did that. I'm like, 'Alright, I get it. They're going to fall victim to the vindictiveness of a billionaire. I get it.'"

Leiweke that day, literally and spiritually, left AEG behind. His vision of a better company was finally taking shape.

Chapter 28

A HOLLYWOOD BEGINNING

Jerry Bruckheimer wasn't always a household name as a producer of block-buster Hollywood movies such as *Top Gun*, *Flashdance*, *Armageddon*, *Beverly Hills Cop*, and *Pirates of the Caribbean*. Once upon a time, he was a young, hockey-loving kid in Detroit, whose clothing store salesman father occasionally got tickets to Red Wings games at the old Olympia.

"We didn't have any money," Bruckheimer said. "Whenever somebody gave him tickets, we'd go and sit up in the rafters. I just remember those great nights with my dad watching the Red Wings play."

The Red Wings of Bruckheimer's early-1950s youth were a dynasty led by Gordie Howe, with fellow Hall of Famers Ted Lindsay, Alex Delvecchio, and Terry Sawchuk. They won four Stanley Cup titles in six seasons from 1950 to '55 and were regular season league champs seven straight years starting in 1949, when Bruckheimer was five.

One of Bruckheimer's earliest hockey memories was seeing Detroit beat Montreal when playing for the title. That could have happened in 1952, 1954, or 1955.

"It wasn't the game they won the Cup, I don't think," Bruckheimer said. "I just do remember going to those games and it was always Montreal and Detroit, and one of those years Detroit wins the Cup."

Later, he'd learn to skate and organize neighborhood kids into a team. He attended Arizona State University, majoring in psychology, then took an advertising job in New York in 1968, starting out in the mail room and working his way up to producing a Pepsi-Cola commercial. That begat offers to move to California to co-produce films. His love for hockey followed. He took skating lessons for the first time and began organizing a game among local celebrities by the 1990s that eventually drew NHL players and became a charity event.

"We had a lot of pros from the Kings come and play," he said. "It was a good time slot, Sunday nights at 6:15."

"And it's still going on," he added. "Guys have changed, and we have their kids playing now."

It was inevitable Bruckheimer and NHL commissioner Gary Bettman would cross paths. And that came in handy when Bruckheimer decided he wanted to pursue an NHL franchise.

Bruckheimer was friendly with businessman Harry Evans Sloan, originally an entertainment lawyer. Sloan had founded SBS Broadcasting in Europe and Bruckheimer helped him open several television stations. By 2005 he'd become chairman of Metro Goldwyn Mayer studios, a sizeable chunk of which was owned by businessman David Bonderman through his TPG Capital investment company.

Bruckheimer and Sloan began talking sports investments. Sloan was interested in football and baseball, but Bruckheimer suggested hockey was "very undervalued" and there were major cities that could support an NHL franchise.

Disney had just put the Mighty Ducks of Anaheim up for sale.

"I think at the time, the price wasn't very expensive," Bruckheimer said. "So, we looked at the Ducks."

But Henry Samueli, a deep-pocketed investor who controlled the team's arena, was also interested and Bruckheimer figured he'd be the one getting the Ducks. "If you buy the team, you want to have a piece of the arena anyway," Bruckheimer said.

So, the duo moved on. A sports agency Sloan had ties with suggested looking at the Pittsburgh Penguins, which had been put up for sale by owner Mario Lemieux. But then, the Penguins drafted Sidney Crosby and soon pulled the team off the market.

Shortly after, Sloan introduced Bruckheimer to Bonderman. He was already a Boston Celtics minority owner but was interested in becoming the majority stakeholder in a team.

"So, we went on this quest of finding him a team," Bruckheimer said. "And the place that always came up—because he owned a piece of Caesars— was Vegas. This was in '07 or '06. We struck a deal with MGM to build an arena and made a deal with [NHL commissioner] Gary [Bettman] to buy a team for about $265 million. But then, the 2008 recession happened. And everything dropped out and we couldn't get an arena built."

By 2010, the trio abandoned their Vegas dream.

But they kept trying. Several years passed before Tim Leiweke approached both with a plan for Seattle. Bruckheimer had long held Los Angeles Kings season tickets in the lower bowl corner a row up from the Staples Center ice. They happened to be next to where AEG and Philip Anschutz had theirs. When Anschutz didn't attend games, the seats would typically be filled with celebrities and other VIPs. As president of the Kings, Leiweke was busy running all around the building on game day but occasionally used the seats right next to Bruckheimer. The pair quickly got to know each other.

"We had a long relationship," Bruckheimer said. "We'd chat about the team and trades and things he was thinking of doing with coaches. So, this went on for years. The whole time he was in L.A., we were very friendly."

Bruckheimer told Leiweke about his desire to own a team alongside Bonderman and Sloan.

"I can't remember exactly when he came to us, but he said, 'I've got a great idea: I've been working to get an arena built in Seattle.'"

Bruckheimer was sold. He knew the Sonics had left in 2008, right before his Vegas deal had fallen though. In the interim, the Sounders had joined MLS in 2009, immediately becoming the league's attendance leader. The Seahawks then won a Super Bowl in early 2014, spotlighting the city and its rambunctious "12s" fans.

"I'd always told Harry [Sloan] the one market that I'd really always felt strongly about besides Vegas was Seattle," Bruckheimer said. "It's underserved in the winter and it's a great opportunity. There're just crazy fans in Seattle. I mean, you see all the teams they support. Plus, they lost their basketball team. So, he had a winter sport and there was a hole."

Not only that, but the vision aligned perfectly with what Bonderman wanted. He'd grown up in California, but graduated Phi Beta Kappa from the University of Washington's College of Arts & Science in 1963, majoring in the Russian language. In 1995, he'd created the Bonderman Fellowship for the university's business school, allowing 16 to 18 students annually to travel the world independently for up to eight months.

Bonderman as a student had even earned money as an elevator operator at Seattle's Space Needle. The towering landmark overlooked the arena Leiweke wanted to overhaul. Now, the billionaire owner of Texas-based TPG Capital was being offered a chance to own a team in KeyArena, as well as an equity partnership in revenues from events within it.

So, Bonderman, Bruckheimer, and Sloan "went along for the ride" with Leiweke. Partway through, Sloan left their group to to start the process that by 2020 helped take DraftKings fantasy sports public through a merger. But Bruckheimer and Bonderman waited in the wings while Leiweke set out to win the KeyArena bid.

Once that happened, Bonderman and Bruckheimer were unveiled as future team owners on June 7, 2017. That day, Leiweke vowed to bring an NHL team to Seattle. "We're going to get you a team," Leiweke said. "Mark it right here. I promise you…we're going to get you at least one team."

Leiweke was quick to mention the NBA was still a long way from granting anyone a team. That was greeted by skepticism and suspicion by local Sonics fans. They worried Leiweke would make KeyArena a hockey and music venue.

And Leiweke had trouble on another front in those initial days of the Bonderman–Bruckheimer potential ownership.

Among numerous positions held by Bonderman, whose company seemingly had a piece of something within every American industry, was a seat on Uber's board of directors. Uber had come under fire for alleged corporate misbehavior and sexual harassment within its ranks and Bonderman didn't help things at an all-company staff meeting. Sitting onstage with another Uber board member, publishing magnate Ariana Huffington, the 74-year-old Bonderman attempted a bad joke. It went over about as well as a defenseman firing the puck into his own net.

Huffington had mentioned that having one woman on a company's board often leads to more women joining it. Bonderman then quipped, "Actually, what it shows is that it's much more likely to be more talking."

Attendees were outraged. Many fired off emails to company leaders after the meeting. Somebody posted cell phone video of the exchange online, where it went viral.

Bonderman immediately resigned, posting a statement apologizing that he "came across in a way that was the opposite of what I intended, but I understand the destructive effect it had, and I take full responsibility for that."

But it wasn't over. His resignation set off alarm bells back in Seattle, where city officials knew they had a serious problem. It had been only 13 months since female Seattle City councilmembers had been harassed with misogynistic comments and threats following their votes to defeat the SoDo arena proposal from Chris Hansen.

Now, the main owner of a future Seattle NHL team and financial backer of a proposed KeyArena overhaul was embroiled in a national scandal over a sexist remark. Mayor Ed Murray, Leiweke, and others knew they had fence-mending to do. And fast. Leiweke and Bonderman spoke individually with council members, apologizing for his remarks and explaining they did not define who he was or had been.

Fortunately, the overtures worked, and council members moved forward. Had they not, the KeyArena effort might have died there.

Instead, Leiweke threw himself into getting a memorandum of understanding done with the city that would enable him to secure the NHL team he'd promised Bonderman, Bruckheimer, and Seattle sports fans. The council would need to vet and finalize the interim deal, so it set up a Select Committee on Civic Arenas, co-chaired by future Seattle Mayor Bruce Harrell and Debora Juarez.

Brian Surrat, the Murray aide who helped spearhead the Request for Proposals process, was now running point on negotiations to get the preliminary deal with OVG and Leiweke in place by fall for the council to finalize before its winter break.

Parking and traffic were two primary areas of concern. The Mercer Corridor project and the "Bertha" tunnel dig had caused traffic chaos all over the Queen Anne, South Lake Union, and Belltown neighborhoods adjoining KeyArena. Residents and commuters from elsewhere were understandably concerned about any further disruptions caused by 18,000 people a night attending major winter sports events at the venue.

Among the more controversial items was a proposal to incorporate the city's aging, underused monorail system as a solution. It all would require major investment dollars poured in by Leiweke's investors on top of the $564 million arena pledge and the half billion or more needed to buy a team.

While those negotiations were underway, Bonderman and Bruckheimer waited anxiously for the NHL to allow them to apply for an expansion squad. Both knew it would take an interim deal with the city. From there would be a number of financial hoops to jump through before the NHL would approve an expansion bid. But one thing at a time.

Bonderman's company at the time had been valued at $2.6 billion by Forbes. Bruckheimer's net worth was pegged at $900 million. Leiweke's fledgling company had Madison Square Garden Company underwriting its KeyArena overhaul with guarantees of up to $1 billion and was working behind the scenes for additional capital from Silver Lake.

Everything seemed in order. But Bruckheimer had been down this road with Bonderman before, only to have their Vegas deal fall apart. He knew they still had a long way to go.

"It's a marathon, it's not easy," Bruckheimer told me. "I had a relationship with [NHL commissioner] Gary [Bettman] for a long time before all of this. I used to come to New York and call him and we'd have lunch.

"And I'd sit down with him and say, 'We're going to get a team now.' And he'd look at me like I was nuts."

Chapter 29

MONORAIL FOR DUMMIES?

There's an old *Simpsons* episode from January 1993 written by Conan O'Brien titled "Marge vs. the Monorail" in which Homer's wife saves Springfield from the foolish purchase of a faulty train system sold to the town by a con artist.

Naturally, when Tim Leiweke and his Oak View Group began suggesting Seattle's traffic woes in and around KeyArena could be resolved by the existing monorail, cartoon enthusiasts quickly dusted off their old VHS cassettes to find the Simpsons episode. Initial references to the monorail fitting within a broader transportation strategy had been contained in OVG's winning $564 million bid to overhaul KeyArena. By mid-summer 2017, as OVG and the city worked on their memorandum of understanding for a permanent development deal, Sonics fans and other supporters of the by then stalled SoDo arena plan used the monorail idea to publicly lampoon and undercut the KeyArena efforts.

Few could blame them. The monorail, as the *Simpsons* episode duly noted, had long been trumpeted by cities globally as traffic salvation. Why stay snarled in logjams below when you could pass above it all on uninterrupted monorail tracks? It wasn't all that different, in theory, from the light-rail system Seattle was then implementing on a vastly bigger scale.

I'd seen an effective monorail system when visiting Bangkok, Thailand, in 2004 and used it daily to explore that congested city's neighborhoods. The Seattle Center Monorail, unfortunately, looked nothing like its Thai counterpart.

For one thing, it didn't go all across the city. Indeed, that might have made it a key transit asset in Seattle's ongoing fight against traffic. No, the Seattle version, built for the 1962 World's Fair, only had one starting and stopping point stretching across 0.9 miles of track. It began downtown at Westlake Center and took commuters out to the former World's Fair site at Seattle Center. Then, it turned around and went back downtown.

For a half century, that one-stop reality had proved its downfall. Sure, pretty much anyone in Seattle could have used a car-free ride to the site while the World's Fair was actually going on. Many of those folks happened to be tourists staying in downtown hotels within a few blocks of the monorail station. The problem came after the World's Fair. Seattle residents typically didn't live in downtown hotels. And unless there was a Seattle Totems hockey game at what later became KeyArena, they had no reason to go to Seattle Center. Even if they found one, they'd need to be downtown to begin with just to be close enough to the monorail.

So, there really wasn't much need for the monorail among city residents. As with Marge Simpson and the fine residents of fictional Springfield, they'd been sold a big white elephant.

Naturally, it hadn't started that way. No, when pitched to the good folks of Seattle in the late 1950s, it was just the latest in a long line of monorail propositions.

A New York City inventor named William Boyes in 1910 pitched the idea of a monorail between Seattle and the city of Tacoma some 34 miles to the south. That never happened, nor did the handful of other ideas to use monorails to replace Seattle's streetcar system.

Then, in 1957, as the city was planning its second World's Fair, a five-mile monorail was proposed between the Seattle Center fairgrounds and auxiliary parking lots in Interbay and other attractions along the Elliott Bay waterfront. Such a plan might now be helping modern Seattle enormously, as Interbay has become the site of Expedia headquarters and a string of retail and warehouse outlets underserved by mass transportation. Alas, that 1957 proposal was dramatically scaled back.

Alweg Rapid Transit Systems was awarded the bid to build the monorail when it agreed to underwrite the entire $3.5 million construction cost. Six months later, the event was done, eight million people had used the two red and blue trains on adjoining tracks, and Alweg had recouped its capital expenditures and turned a small profit.

Century 21 Center, which had operated the fairgrounds, took over management of the monorail as prearranged at no cost, but soon ran into financial problems. It began negotiating with the City of Seattle to take over all fairground operations. By 1964, it sold it the monorail for $600,000.

The first serious monorail accident occurred in 1971, when brake failure on the red train caused it to slam into a girder at the end of the track at Seattle Center. The train was going between 15 and 20 miles per hour and 26 of its 40 passengers were injured.

Then, in 1979, 15 people were injured in a similar incident involving the blue train at the same station. The accident was blamed on driver error.

By 1994, the city had contracted out the system's daily operations to Seattle Monorail Services.

Then, on May 31, 2004, the blue train caught fire in the middle of a late-afternoon Memorial Day passenger run with 150 people onboard. The train had just left Seattle Center after the final day of the Northwest Folklife Festival and was headed south toward the downtown station when a loud *pop!* was heard. Flames six-to-eight-feet high shot out of the rear compartment.

Power went out and the train halted on an elevated, banked curve of track positioned 25 feet above 5th Avenue. Panicked passengers watched black smoke billow into the rear cars. They quickly heeded the driver's instructions to move toward the front. The Seattle Fire Department arrived within minutes; doors were opened; and distraught, coughing passengers, unable to see more than a few feet, raced over to breathe in fresh air.

A ladder was hoisted to the stuck train to evacuate passengers one by one. The second train, this one operational, pulled up in the northbound tracks alongside the burning one. Metal planks were inserted between the trains to enable about 50 additional passengers to escape. The tracks had been designed to allow for such rescues and likely saved lives that day.

But they couldn't save the monorail's reputation.

Forty people were treated for minor injuries at the scene and released. Eight others and one firefighter were treated for smoke inhalation at a local hospital and released that day.

Service halted for seven months pending repairs and an outside investigation. The fire was later attributed to a broken low-speed drive shaft on the third of the four cars. It caused the high-speed drive shaft to speed up and break off, damaging the train's energy collector shoe. From there, sparks flew and ignited with grease and oil on the tracks, causing flames that spread to foam pillows within the car and tripped circuit breakers that shut the train down.

It was the first fire in the train's history. The investigative report recommended the train's electrical system be overhauled.

The red train resumed service December 31, 2004, while the fire-damaged blue train returned May 2, 2005. But just less than six months later, the two trains struck each other while passing in separate directions on the adjoining tracks. The blue train's driver was blamed for failing to yield at a "gauntlet" section of track where it was dangerous for both trains to pass at regular speed.

Two of the 84 passengers were hospitalized with minor injuries. All of those aboard again had to be rescued with fire truck ladders, given their precarious perch high above ground. The system was shut down for nine months while the trains were repaired.

The two high-profile accidents and dramatic fire truck rescues months apart did little for the monorail's image. Numerous expansion studies and initiatives had come and gone, most recently a $4.9 billion, 10-mile line proposal rejected by city voters in a November 2005 ballot initiative just 17 days before the two-train collision.

The latest mishap ended further expansion talk. For years afterward, the monorail operated as somewhat of a tourist attraction—a salute to the city's distant past, but not a functional means of transit. Its trains were incompatible with other modes of transit passes and needed to be paid for separately. And in cash only, as it had no means of accepting credit cards. So, commuters lined up single file in front of a ticket window and purchased fares with hard currency for the 90-second ride in either direction.

Naturally, when Leiweke and OVG suggested the monorail as part of their plan, eyeballs rolled. But it made all types of sense. Though still trapped in the early 1960s, the monorail actually served a vital transportation route from downtown out to a part of the city snarled by traffic chaos.

And it was about to become even more vital as Seattle's slowly unfolding light rail system took shape. Leiweke knew that by 2021, about a year after he'd hoped to reopen an overhauled KeyArena, the light rail system would be connected from the city's northern suburbs to a downtown station at Westlake right below the monorail.

An additional station was planned for right outside KeyArena, but not for at least another 18 years. So, Leiweke needed to get light rail users that final mile from downtown to the arena. And there was the monorail staring him in the face.

Not only could riders heading in from the north use it, but those from the south could as well. Also, by 2023, an additional light rail connector to Westlake Station from affluent Bellevue on the other side of Lake Washington was to become reality.

Therefore, he reasoned, Seattle already had its answer to mass arena transit. All it needed was to integrate the monorail into the light rail plans.

Arena opponents would not let this go lightly. It didn't help that Tom Albro, the owner of the Seattle Monorail Services company privately operating the system, had been elected a Port of Seattle Commission president.

The Port had lobbied extensively against Chris Hansen and his proposed SoDo arena, claiming it would impede industrial traffic within the neighborhood and put unionized jobs at risk. Naturally, a KeyArena overhaul would end any talk of a SoDo venue and so Port officials quickly aligned with Leiweke, OVG, and the city.

But here was Albro, his company turning yearly six-figure profits off the monorail, standing to make money if KeyArena drove more passengers to his monorail. Albro had anticipated the conflict when the city launched its Request for Proposals process on KeyArena. In January 2017, he'd written the commission's board recusing himself from all KeyArena discussions.

Still, in March 2017, his position running Seattle Monorail Services came to light in a handful of news reports. Albro's ownership of Seattle Monorail Services hadn't exactly been hidden. It was just that nobody had really cared enough about the monorail to bother connecting the dots before OVG and Leiweke came along.

So, now, as talks continued between OVG and the city on bolstering the monorail as part of an overall KeyArena deal, opponents alleged the SoDo arena proposal was being deliberately shortchanged for ulterior motives. Through it all, OVG and the city ignored the barbs and plowed ahead, knowing time was of the essence. The longer it took to get a KeyArena deal finalized, the more ammunition opponents could gather to torpedo it politically.

Chapter 30

MAYOR ED MURRAY RESIGNS

Seattle mayor Ed Murray had awakened to sunshine in his Capitol Hill home on September 12, 2017, excited about closing a file that had dominated his lone term.

His first daily item was a press conference at a Seattle Center outdoor courtyard adjacent to KeyArena. He and Tim Leiweke would announce a memorandum of understanding between the city and Oak View Group to renovate KeyArena for an amount now expected to exceed $600 million.

Sure, the preliminary deal still needed to be ratified by the Seattle City Council. Its members could be tough and weren't exactly enamored with Murray by then, given four people had come forward against him with sexual assault allegations. But no criminal charges had been filed, a civil lawsuit had been dropped, and Murray's contention of innocence was out in the public domain.

Though he'd made the agonizing decision months back not to seek November re-election, polls still showed he might win if he did. As is,

Jenny Durkan was squaring off against Cary Moon to be his successor. All that remained for Murray was to get lingering items off his plate.

So, he headed downtown to his sixth-floor office at city hall, briefly checked his agenda, then called for his car to take him to Seattle Center. That's when a phone call stopped him cold: another sexual assault allegation, this time by a male cousin who'd been 13 at the time.

Over at Seattle Center, Leiweke; his daughter, Francesca Bodie, then a rising OVG star; legal counsel Lance Lopes; and lobbyist Emilie East had arrived early for the press conference. They'd walked through the setup of folding chairs and a podium, where reporters and photographers were gathering, and headed inside KeyArena to a windowed "green room" staging area to await Murray's arrival.

"I'd walked through the press conference to look at the setup, so I knew everyone was out there," Leiweke said. "And then I went back to the green room and kind of remember looking out and going, 'Uh-oh.'"

Leiweke could see the folding chairs being hastily packed away and confused reporters unsure what to do next.

Brain Surratt, the mayor's point man on the Request for Proposals process and negotiations on an interim deal with Leiweke, had attended a 7 AM meeting tying up loose ends regarding organized labor for the KeyArena rebuild. An hour later, the city's labor representatives and legal counsel finalized that part of the OVG deal. Everything was good to go for the press conference.

Surratt raced back across the street to city hall and up to the office of Benton Strong, Murray's communications director. "I'm pumped, because I knew we had the presser coming up that morning," Surratt said. "I told him, 'We're done! Labor's signed off. We're good. We're ready to go.'

"And Benton looks at me and he's like, 'We can't do the announcement.'

"I was confused. I went, 'Why? What's going on?'

"And he goes, 'There's another accusation.'

"So, I'm like, 'Oh, shit!'"

Both men knew this was the end of the line. Murray was unlikely to last the day.

Surratt immediately phoned Seattle Center director Robert Nellams, asking to help escort the Leiweke contingent out through a back entrance so they wouldn't bump into media members.

Leiweke had seen the press conference being disbanded and warned his entourage "something's up" even before getting told. "Then finally, somebody pulled me aside—I can't remember who—and told me the mayor can't come, there's an issue and we've got to delay this," Leiweke said. "And actually, there was a debate about whether we should announce this without him. And I'm like, 'Well, my guess is there's something going on with him and I don't want to get in the middle of it.' I'm not going to go out there and announce it without him if it puts us in the middle of a controversy."

Leiweke promptly phoned NHL commissioner Gary Bettman and NBA commissioner Adam Silver to tell them why the announcement was delayed.

"We were actually pretty calm, cool, and collected, which is unusual for me," Leiweke said. "We knew this was going to get done because it was the right deal and the right idea. I always used to tell people, 'If you want to debate whether they'd change their mind, let's review the deal.'

"We're going to build the arena. We're going to pay for it. We're going to take all the risk. And they don't have to do anything? Who in their right mind is going to turn that down? I don't care who replaces the mayor."

But back at city hall, things weren't so calm. This was Seattle, after all, and no deal was finalized until ink went to paper. Those crafting the KeyArena deal had already seen the project nearly torpedoed by an off-handed joke from prospective team owner Bonderman at an Uber staff meeting.

They'd seen Chris Hansen's arena project for the SoDo district shut down by the city council when the vote seemed in the bag. Now, the current mayor was about to be replaced by a new one. Mayoral front-runner Durkan was a sports fan and seemed onboard with the KeyArena overhaul. But no one really knew what more progressive-leaning Cary Moon might do if she won.

Not to mention, there'd be a temporary new mayor if Murray stepped down. Bruce Harrell was council president and would automatically assume the role for at least five days as per the city's charter. But he'd voted in favor of the SoDo project 16 months prior. So had Tim Burgess, assumed to be next in line for mayor if Harrell left after the five days.

While Harrell and Burgess seemed favorable to the KeyArena proposal, no one really knew. And the rest of the council? Kshama Sawant had made it clear she felt sports team owners were cretins on the evolutionary scale. And it would be the council deciding whether this KeyArena package lived or died. If they started making even more demands of OVG ahead of time, there was no telling how Leiweke would react.

Murray that morning spent time on his private office phone with *Seattle Times* reporters Lewis Kamb and Jim Brunner, who'd broken the story about his latest accuser. Meanwhile, Murray's most trusted confidants were being called in and waiting for him to get off the line.

When Murray finally did, he met in his office with chief of staff Fred Kiga, who'd only been on the job a week replacing the departed Mike Fong. Deputy Mayor Hyeok Kim was there as well, as was Sandeep Kaushik, Murray's outside political consultant.

They all told Murray he needed to resign. Murray still thought the allegation would be among the easier ones to refute. But his advisors weren't listening. To them, the time for fighting was over. Murray broached staying on for the rest of the week but was advised the public backlash would threaten his ongoing deals. Those included the KeyArena overhaul, where a press conference had just been cancelled because OVG and Leiweke didn't want to get ensnared in Murray's mess.

"It was clear this project was probably in jeopardy," Murray said.

Moments after Murray's top advisors left the room, councilmember Burgess went in and offered the same resignation advice. About 15 minutes after that, Harrell made the same plea.

Harrell left and Murray, alone in his office, mulled whether anything was salvageable. Everyone warned there was no hope of finishing projects he'd hoped would salvage his legacy.

"I said, 'The deal is still there, right?'" Murray said of KeyArena. "And I was assured the deal was still there. But it wasn't going to happen if I was still around. I realized windows were going to start to close."

His hope of staying around until Durkan or Moon took office now seemed unrealistic.

"To sit there for three and a half months could mean this deal would unravel," Murray said. "They could ask for more. The hockey team might not happen. It was just not a good scenario. As you know, it was fragile. It was touch-and-go all the way and probably was even before I came into office. But from the moment I came into office until my last day this was a big deal to me…. And it was one aspect of many things that caused me not to stay in office."

Roughly an hour after skipping the press conference, Murray decided he would indeed resign—effective at 5 PM the following day. Kaushik and communications officer Josh Feit prepared Murray's resignation letter and sent it out. Murray left the building and never came back. His personal items were shipped in a box.

Harrell was named interim mayor the following day. He served his mandatory five-day term and then Burgess was chosen to fill the final two months until a new mayor was elected in November.

Still, that two-month period was critical. The city wanted the KeyArena deal approved by the council no later than year's end. Any longer and OVG, Leiweke, Bonderman, and Bruckheimer might start having second thoughts about doing business in such a chaotic place.

Also, KeyArena's enemies were never far behind. Murray's resignation, the very day the KeyArena interim agreement was to be announced, was seen as another setback for the project—another reason the SoDo arena pushed by Chris Hansen was the way to go.

Harrell would play a key role in the year ahead. Not accepting the mayor's chair beyond his five-day requirement left him free to return to his council seat. He resumed duties as co-chair of the council's Select Committee on Civic Arenas along with Debora Juarez. Their committee was the one vetting the memorandum of understanding with Leiweke's group. It needed their support to pass.

Leiweke watched events unfold from a distance with detached fascination. But he remained optimistic he had a "right place, right time, right deal" that whoever succeeded Murray would support.

"The unique situation in Seattle is, it's a council form of government," Leiweke said. "The mayor has some power, but the council has more. So, we'd gone through that process already of meeting with the council and knowing where we stood there. We knew we were going to get this done.

"Did we like the delay? No one wants to go through that kind of change. But the reality is, we knew Bruce Harrell well. And I had a lot of faith in Bruce, I really did. I was really comfortable with Bruce and felt confident in his legacy, even if it was temporary."

In Burgess, the ensuing temporary mayor, Leiweke also saw an ally who "still guides us to this day." Leiweke's lobbyists, Tim Ceis and Emilie East, seemed to have good relations within city government.

"Did we enjoy the bumps in the road? No. But that's what happens. We were a young company and I had been through an awful lot in my time building AEG. I had thick skin."

PART FOUR

Sprint to the Finish

Chapter 31

THE VIEW FROM 27 STORIES UP

NHL commissioner Gary Bettman seemed relaxed sitting across from me on a sofa in his window-lined office 27 floors above the start of Manhattan's afternoon rush hour. The sprawling room offered a commanding view of Midtown, with the Hudson River off in the distance.

Bettman had moved in a few months prior to start the 2021–22 season, on the highest of five floors forming the league's new headquarters in an office complex a block away from Madison Square Garden. This was the first time I'd been to the NHL's new digs, having met Bettman on a handful of prior occasions in conference rooms of the league's former base several blocks north.

It being a Friday, Bettman's major business was done. He had a party to attend that evening honoring retired New York Rangers goaltender Henrik Lundquist. But otherwise, he seemed eager to chat about a Seattle file he'd spent the prior decade on.

As much as Bettman's workspace had evolved since our earlier New York visits in 2014, 2015, and 2016, so had the league. It had been Bettman's vision to expand to an untapped U.S. portion of the Pacific Northwest, completing what he'd started in the Southwest in June 2016 by awarding a Las Vegas franchise.

Bettman could have expanded to Quebec City, which had paid a non-refundable $2 million expansion application fee and had an almost-completed arena about to open back then. But Bettman and NHL owners that summer had taken the unusual step of balking at awarding expansion teams in pairs.

They'd wanted Seattle. And they were willing to live with an unbalanced 31-team league until Seattle figured out its arena problems. Sure, there'd been disappointment when three Seattle-area arena groups in SoDo, Bellevue, and Tukwila failed to make expansion bids by the July 2015 deadline. But it was short-lived. And now, with seven years of hindsight, Bettman insisted he'd been confident all along a bid would materialize.

"We were very focused on Seattle being a great opportunity," Bettman said. "Seattle is a great sports town. Although ancient, there is a hockey history there. Filling in the Pacific Northwest is something that always intrigued and excited us.

"So, with the Sonics leaving, we believed that we could really make an impact. But the one issue that always had to be solved was the arena."

Bettman knew Chris Hansen had an arena exclusivity deal with the City of Seattle. And as long as that deal remained intact, the NHL's only shot at expansion within the city itself and not some suburb was through the SoDo project.

But Bettman had also spent years working in the NBA as an understudy to commissioner David Stern. He knew as well as anyone that Hansen's chance of landing an NBA franchise was years away from even being explored.

Bettman told me he'd tried to talk Hansen into accepting that an NHL team should come to his arena first. That his deal with the city should be altered to allow for that. He'd even brought in prospective owner Victor

Coleman in May 2014 to meet with Mayor Ed Murray about nudging the arena file forward.

Coleman had a non-binding deal with Hansen to examine bringing an NHL team into the SoDo project's fold. But nothing was happening. And Murray reaffirmed to Bettman nothing really could happen until Hansen landed his NBA franchise.

"I think Chris consistently misread the situation," Bettman said. "Maybe perhaps to this day, although I've stopped following his exploits. But at the end of the day, whether it was his [SoDo] building or the transformation of what used to be known as KeyArena at Seattle Center, we were looking for a building.

"We had looked at Las Vegas for years," Bettman added, alluding to the prior failed David Bonderman–Jerry Bruckheimer effort from 2007. "But it wasn't until a building was coming out of the ground and we knew it was coming out of the ground that it could happen. So, we knew the dance. And so, it was really a question of making sure there would be an arena."

Bettman held multiple meetings with Hansen, some face-to-face in his New York office. And he'd emphasized that bringing in an NHL franchise first would be the SoDo arena group's best option.

When Coleman was looking to be an NHL owner in 2014, there'd been a suggestion of him partnering 50-50 with Hansen on SoDo project construction. Bettman said the plan would have seen two identical leases— one for NHL and one for an NBA team. And with a contingency plan, he added, that if the NBA team never came and Hansen wanted out, his interest in the arena would be bought out by the ownership group.

"I suggested this to Chris repeatedly, although he never really got it," Bettman said. "I said, 'If you knew you could get a team if you had the arena, your likelihood of getting the arena might have been enhanced.'

"And he was like, 'I'm not going to build an arena for a hockey team. You're wrong. That's not how it's going to work.'"

Bettman said he'd replied to Hansen: "You know, I've done this a bunch of times before."

But Hansen wouldn't hear it. "He goes, 'The NBA's guaranteed me a franchise,'" Bettman said. "So, I told him, 'It's been a long time since I've worked there, but I doubt that would be the case.'"

Ultimately, Tim Leiweke and his Oak View Group would use Bettman's suggested playbook with KeyArena. Bettman had known Leiweke for decades, dating back to their NBA years followed by Leiweke's time serving as Los Angeles Kings president and running the Toronto Maple Leafs' parent company.

And though Bettman couldn't officially guarantee Leiweke a franchise, he'd told him the league was waiting on Seattle. Bettman had said much the same thing to Murray in their conversations, which caused Seattle's mayor by early 2015 to abruptly shift his public stance in favor of the NHL coming to town ahead of the NBA.

So, the city and Leiweke were aligned. Both knew a serious upgrade of KeyArena was likely to beget an NHL team. And that the NBA would almost certainly follow.

"There's a way to do this," Bettman told me. "There's a process when you're dealing with cities, when you're dealing with funding, when you're dealing with boards of governors of leagues. There's a process. And if you take the right steps, in the right order, you can get from point A to point Z."

Leiweke's first step was finalizing a memorandum of understanding he'd drafted with Murray's team before the mayor's resignation. Work continued through fall of 2017.

What they came up with was a 39-year lease with two eight-year renewal options covering a 55-year period. OVG would assume all project costs and overruns—that latter point would ultimately prove critical—and put $40 million into a transportation fund for the city's use. Leiweke's group also pledged an additional $20 million toward a community fund, with half of it going to the nonprofit Youth Care program for homeless teens and young adults.

In addition, OVG would pay a rent amount equal to revenues the city currently generated from KeyArena, its parking garage and on-campus sponsorship rights. The city in the first 10 years would also earn a 25 percent share of any "upside revenue" beyond what the deal forecasted and 50 percent after that.

It wasn't an easy negotiation. And the envisioned project cost kept rising. The agreement would see OVG preserve the arena's 44-million-pound roof while doubling the venue's square footage.

All the while, the project continued to come under public scrutiny. Chris Hansen complained the city was ignoring his stalled SoDo project, creating unnecessary red tape to ensure KeyArena received preferential treatment. That part was obvious, given the city was protecting its own KeyArena asset to prevent it from being rendered obsolete by Hansen's project.

But still, Hansen's supporters viewed this as an attempt to crush the city's NBA dreams. Some even suggested racist motives—that the city was favoring a mostly white sport like hockey to the detriment of BIPOC communities where basketball was adored.

The SoDo group continued to insist KeyArena would become a "music only" facility unlikely to attract NHL or NBA teams. That music would feature prominently was beyond dispute: OVG had been co-founded by Leiweke and music mogul Irving Azoff, who had the Live Nation concert promotions group as an equity partner in the arena plan.

Concerts would help KeyArena survive on nights teams weren't playing. The arena's acoustics would be designed with input from a select advisory board run by Pearl Jam manager Kelly Curtis.

So, there was no way around music being the only guarantee OVG could offer at an overhauled KeyArena. There'd be no way to disprove the

SoDo group's claims that sports teams would balk at coming there. That is, until the NHL or NBA said something out loud.

There were signs they would. That September, two weeks after Murray's resignation as Seattle mayor, I'd flown to OVG headquarters in Los Angeles to see Leiweke's company.

One of the first people I met at OVG was Peter Luukko, the Florida Panthers executive chairman and representative on the NHL's board of governors. We talked hockey a bit and he guaranteed me the league was coming once an arena deal was struck.

Later, I met Azoff, who'd popped up from his downstairs offices. Azoff was a powerful figure within the music industry, a legendary manager of the Eagles I'd just seen featured a few nights prior in a Netflix documentary about the group. OVG was promoting an Eagles concert in Seattle later that week at T-Mobile Park in conjunction with the Mariners baseball team.

Mariners owner John Stanton had been a longtime friend of David Bonderman, the envisioned majority owner of a Seattle NHL team. And it turns out Stanton wasn't the only sports pal OVG had.

At the Eagles concert later that week, OVG had a private suite next to Stanton's that turned into a party for the who's-who of the local sports scene. Seahawks president Peter McLoughlin was there with Leiweke. So was Sounders owner Adrian Hanauer. Luukko also was there, as was Azoff. Stanton was hosting a group of political movers and shakers in his own suite. But he stopped by partway through to greet the Leiweke entourage, his concert co-promoters.

Before long, Leiweke's longtime buddy Al Michaels showed up, as did NBC cohort Cris Collinsworth. The duo was in town for a *Sunday Night Football* telecast the following evening.

Partway through the night, Leiweke's nephew, Dan, guided a group of suite-goers down to the stadium's floor to give them an up-close, unauthorized view of the stage. He'd headed straight down the aisle to within feet of where Don Henley was belting out tunes, with Michaels, Collinsworth, and a handful of others in tow. But Collinsworth, at 6'5", quickly attracted the attention of stadium ushers, who sternly advised the group to leave.

It did, but then kept stopping at other vantage points, where ushers again saw Collinsworth's towering presence and urged the group onward. At some point, the 72-year-old Michaels got separated from the group. I found him wandering the floor later, struggling to locate the suite elevators, but smiling and having a grand old time. We got back to the elevators in one piece.

But that night summed up OVG for me. It was chaotic at times, stepping out into the unknown. But confident, even when it made others nervous. And connected too. No sports entity in Seattle, even billionaire Paul Allen's Vulcan company, exerted that much influence over sports, politics, and business on a nationwide scale.

It was clear to me then that Leiweke would get his NHL team.

Two months later, I was in Toronto to see Adrian Hanauer's Seattle Sounders play Leiweke's former Toronto FC team in the 2017 MLS Cup Final.

Just before I flew out, on a Wednesday that week, the Seattle City Council approved the memorandum of understanding with Leiweke's group by a 7–1 margin, with only Kshama Sawant opposing. On the Thursday in Toronto, I was an in-studio guest on Sportsnet's nationally televised *Tim & Sid* hockey show.

Sid Seixeiro was hosting and his guest co-host was Sportsnet columnist Stephen Brunt, who'd worked for the *Globe & Mail* while I'd covered the Blue Jays for the *Toronto Star* a decade prior. On air that night, they asked when I felt the NHL might indicate Seattle expansion interest with the interim city deal approved.

I told them it was imminent. That if nothing happened within a few weeks, I'd be shocked. Brunt disagreed, saying the NHL doesn't move that quickly.

We were both wrong. The next day, two days after the council's approval, NHL commissioner Bettman announced the Bonderman–Bruckheimer group could officially apply for NHL expansion. No other bids would be taken.

Years later, sitting in his new office in January 2022, Bettman told me he'd seen no reason to wait.

"David [Bonderman] was interested and OVG was making it clear that this wasn't some pipe dream, that this was for real," Bettman said.

He also felt the timing would send a strong signal to Seattle civic leaders and the general public about the NHL's interest at a time the Hansen-led SoDo group continued to cast doubt on whether sports leagues would want to play in KeyArena.

"It was consistent with what I'd told [Hansen] all along," Bettman said. "If people believe you're going to have a team and not just smoke and mirrors, but a team that's coming, they will engage you on the building a lot more readily."

The city had engaged. And now, the NHL had opened its door.

Chapter 32

HOW FAST CAN YOU COUNT TO 32,000?

Word the NHL would take a Seattle expansion application from the David Bonderman–Jerry Bruckheimer ownership group set off a wild, yearlong scramble lasting throughout 2018. It was one thing to have a league ready to take your $10 million application money, quite another to jump through needed hoops to prove your viability to other NHL owners.

Sure, those owners wanted Seattle. And yeah, Bonderman was a legit billionaire while everybody who'd ever eaten popcorn at a megaplex knew his business partner Bruckheimer. But there was still the question of paying for it all—funding the KeyArena overhaul and ensuring enough local interest to keep the whole thing running without an NBA franchise in the short term.

After all, the NHL now wanted a $650 million expansion fee from the so-called "NHL Seattle" group. That was a significant jump from the $500 million demanded of the Vegas Golden Knights only a few years prior and even that was staggering compared to past NHL expansion demands.

But Vegas had no major professional sports competition at the time. NHL Seattle would be jumping into a market populated by the NFL Seahawks, MLB Mariners, MLS Sounders, WNBA Storm, and lesser pro teams. Not to mention the NCAA Washington Huskies football program, which was the equivalent of a pro squad.

Also, it was clear an NBA team was envisioned by Tim Leiweke and his arena partners, Bonderman being one. So, the NHL had competition in securing the hearts and minds of local sports fans, not to mention winning over any league owners skeptical that major pro hockey could make it long term within the market.

The NHL was already dealing with a disastrous situation in Arizona, where the Coyotes were burning through owners unable to make a go of it in Glendale. Nobody wanted a repeat farther north.

One of the first things Leiweke did after the NHL allowed Bonderman's group to apply for a team was lease two floors of office space in a semi-residential part of Seattle's Queen Anne neighborhood known as Uptown. The two-story building was a five-minute walk from KeyArena, but non-descript enough that sports fans passed right on by it without noticing. There was no security guard at the entryway, just a lone glass door kept locked at all times. With no intercom, you'd have to make a cell phone call upstairs first and have somebody jog down the stairwell to let you in.

Eventually, a small "OVG Seattle" sign was taped to the inner portion of the doorway. But unless you had business inside, it was easy to miss from the street. It was on the final day of February 2018 that Tim Leiweke took my call and hustled downstairs to hold the door open so I could head up and be introduced to Bonderman and Bruckheimer.

The next day was huge for NHL Seattle. That's when a season ticket deposit drive was planned, in which interested hockey fans could plunk down $500 for a regular seat and $1,000 for a more expensive "club-level" version. Even if the franchise got approved, there would be no actual games at least until NHL Seattle's targeted October 2020 debut more than two and a half years away. But the deposit drive, as in Las Vegas, was viewed as a major test of local NHL interest.

The Vegas Golden Knights back then were completing a debut regular season unlike any prior expansion team. They were contending for the playoffs, being watched by sold-out home crowds, and ticket demand was soaring on various online resale exchanges. They'd had their own season ticket drive in February 2015, to gauge market interest ahead of applying for expansion later that summer. The NHL had considered 10,000 deposits a strong benchmark. But the Vegas group led by Bill Foley secured 5,000 deposits in two days and 9,000 within a month, surpassing its goal of 10,000 shortly after.

By September 2016, with the franchise awarded and a year ahead of launching, the Golden Knights announced they were capped out at 16,000 deposits.

NHL Seattle knew they'd be measured against everything Vegas did. So, they too had a minimum benchmark of 10,000 deposits. But they didn't just want to reach it. They wanted to shatter the time it had taken Vegas.

Bonderman and Bruckheimer were in town as part of OVG's effort to drum up deposit drive interest. Through OVG's partner, Ticketmaster, the deposits would start being collected at 9 AM the following morning.

I was ushered through a vast room of empty cubicles and desks not yet occupied by soon-to-be-hired employees and over to where Bonderman and Bruckheimer were sitting. Bonderman's TPG Capital firm at the time, among its many holdings, owned a minority stake in a multinational company of 40,000 employees at which my wife was a mid-level executive. So, I used that as an icebreaker between us, telling him we had a conflict because she indirectly worked for him.

"What's her name?" he said, feigning menace and pretending he was going to write it down.

We all laughed.

While I'd met plenty of men worth hundreds of millions of dollars, Bonderman was the first billionaire. Not surprisingly, as I'd found most men and women of significant wealth to be, he leaned toward understatement. His handshake had been steady, but without attempt at a harder grip the wannabes sometimes make to exemplify power.

Bonderman already had power. He didn't need to prove it.

He'd had the Rolling Stones play for him at a birthday party. But there'd be no name-dropping with me. Very few mentions of his companies or holdings unless directly asked. Only a genuine willingness to tell fans how interested he was in a team.

Seattle Center director Robert Nellams would later tell me of a similar impression when first meeting Bonderman.

"Tim Leiweke said, 'Bonderman wants to take a tour around campus; can you grab a golf cart and take him on a little tour?'" Nellams said. "So, I got a golf cart and took him on a tour and talked about the things we were doing and how the campus worked. But I'm sitting there next to this billionaire and he's just an everyday guy. And he was so gracious and so nice when I took him around. I was a little taken aback because I expected him to be a little more on point—what's going to happen here? What's going to happen there?

"But that's not how he was. And I really, really appreciated the fact he was so gracious."

And Bonderman came off that way to me as well. So did Bruckheimer. He was known throughout Hollywood as a guy who shunned parties—a man who believed your work spoke far more about your measure of success than who you were seen with.

It's probably why the pair hit it off so quickly. Neither had any interest in outshining the other. Only in getting this franchise landed. In the months and years ahead, Bonderman remained in the background while Bruckheimer occasionally did any rare speaking required of ownership.

"I've looked at franchises from time to time, but I haven't been in the right place at the right time until now," Bonderman told me that day. "I think of it as a personal opportunity, as they say. But it's a different opportunity in some ways than what I've done before. What I do for a living is make investments, and this is a big one."

Indeed, the $650 million franchise fee, on top of the $600 million pledged by OVG on the arena—which Bonderman was covering a chunk of as an equity investor—was quite the sports gamble. But Bonderman was quick to point out the Kraken would get the same favorable expansion draft rules the Golden Knights had.

"We've had some discussions with the commissioner on this," Bonderman said. "And the idea is they want to keep the same format as they did in Las Vegas, which was a little more favorable to the Golden Knights than people expected. It shows you what you can do to make an expansion team a real player in the game."

No one yet knew that Vegas would go all the way to the Stanley Cup Final that first season. The Golden Knights still had two months of regular season play to go by then, but still, everybody could see they were superior to prior expansion squads from the major pro sports.

And for NHL Seattle, getting to 10,000 season ticket deposits quicker than the month it had taken Vegas became an obsession. Even if the ensuing comparisons they used were somewhat suspect. For starters, the Vegas deposits had been refundable only if the Golden Knights weren't awarded a franchise.

But NHL Seattle had guaranteed fans that the $500 and $1,000 deposits it was collecting were completely refundable at any point, even if a franchise was secured. That made them less of a commitment in Seattle's case than they'd been in Las Vegas.

Still, the Golden Knights had also been the first major pro sports team in Las Vegas at the time. NHL Seattle was a newcomer in a market already dominated by legacy teams, with the Seahawks just four years removed from their Super Bowl title.

So, OVG and NHL Seattle faced struggles for local sports market share that Vegas never had to contend with.

The morning after my meeting with Bonderman and Bruckheimer, deposit day finally arrived in Seattle. Tim Leiweke, Bonderman, Bruckheimer, and a handful of others gathered in front of a computer in a private office at OVG Seattle's new headquarters.

Ticketmaster had set a 10 AM start time for fans to enter an online portal to make their deposits. The time came and went. Every few minutes, an employee would enter the office and announce a certain threshold had been surpassed.

"We had to get 10,000," Bruckheimer would tell me years later, describing that morning. "And at first there were 3,000, then 4,000. And then before we knew it, they were over 10,000, which was unbelievable."

It had taken just 12 minutes to vault through the 10,000-deposit threshold. Vegas had needed just over a month. The initial surge temporarily crashed Ticketmaster's servers. Fans kept hitting the refresh button, hoping to get on the portal. Within the first hour, 25,000 deposits had been taken.

"It was a terrific experience, I've got to tell you," Bruckheimer said.

By the time it was over roughly 31 hours later, the group announced it had secured 32,000 deposits.

"I think at one point, they told me we had between 50,000 and 60,000 people that were trying to get in," Leiweke said immediately after. "It was crazy."

Future NHL Seattle CEO Tod Leiweke had been sitting with NFL commissioner Roger Goodell in his office when the deposit drive began. Leiweke was still about a month away from leaving his NFL executive position to join the hockey team and had agonized over whether to switch jobs. The ticket drive helped sell him.

Leiweke said his brother, Tim, phoned him twice during his meeting with Goodell. On the third call, he told Goodell he'd better take it and see whether anything was wrong. "I said, 'Hey, I'm meeting with Roger, what's up?'" Leiweke said. "And he said, 'We just crossed over 15,000 deposits.'

"I literally remember getting chills. And I went home and said to my wife, Tara, that this has the potential to be so great."

Leiweke may have been stunned by the speed in which the deposits were gathered. But NHL commissioner Gary Bettman said Leiweke had told him ahead of time the NHL Seattle effort would easily surpass the 10,000 threshold in less time than it had taken the Vegas franchise.

Bettman had known Leiweke well from his years working as a Vancouver Canucks executive in the 1990s and later as CEO of the Tampa Bay Lightning for five years before taking up his NFL post in 2015.

Bettman would tell me years later, in our meeting at his new Manhattan office, that despite Leiweke's optimism, he'd actually been quite surprised by how many deposits were gathered.

"That, I was really pleased by," Bettman said. "And I can't deny saying, 'Wow. That was great!'

"Tod all along had said that would be the case. I knew I believed—and we had seen this in other places when bringing in a team—that they would have no problem selling out the building. That was never an issue.

"But the fact that there was this much demand? It said, 'Hey, we made the right decision.'"

Chapter 33

THE FEATHER MASSAGER

From the moment Tim Leiweke announced plans to seek the KeyArena bid contract, it was evident his younger brother, Tod, would head up expansion operations. Tod Leiweke had been arguably the most popular sports executive in Seattle history as CEO of the Seahawks from 2003 through 2010, including their first Super Bowl appearance in January 2006 against the Pittsburgh Steelers.

After leaving for a president and CEO role with the Tampa Bay Lightning, he'd spent five years overhauling that NHL team's business operations. One enticement in leaving Seattle for Tampa Bay had been the small ownership stake he'd been given. A similar carrot would be dangled his way before Leiweke returned to Seattle and the NHL.

Upon leaving the Lightning following their failed 2015 Stanley Cup Final bid against Chicago, he'd re-joined the NFL as its chief operating officer. That July 2015 move came only days after the collapse of a Bellevue arena bid orchestrated by his longtime associate Jac Sperling to bring NHL expansion to greater Seattle. I'd never believed Leiweke's assertions he wasn't intending to be part of an NHL team playing out of a Bellevue arena.

It's something I'd kidded him about in the years since. But it seemed clear late in his Tampa Bay tenure that Leiweke was on the lookout for more. The NFL gig seemed the perfect placeholder for a few years until Seattle figured out its arena situation.

At times, the role appeared too good. Leiweke relocated to New York City, where some viewed him as the NFL's No. 2 executive—and at worst No. 3—behind commissioner Roger Goodell. The pair hit it off well and even had gone hiking together up 14,000-foot-tall Mount Rainier. There was a point in 2016 when it appeared Goodell might not stay on as commissioner. Leiweke began to be rumored as his successor.

But it didn't last. By December 2017, Goodell finalized a new contract extension paying him roughly $40 million annually in base salary plus incentives through 2024. That extension was announced the day before the NHL gave the David Bonderman–Jerry Bruckheimer group permission to apply for a Seattle expansion franchise.

Not long after that, NHL Seattle made its move.

"We were looking for a CEO and Tim said, 'Talk to my brother,'" Bruckheimer said. "So, I called him cold. I told him I'd be in New York soon and would love to sit down and talk."

They set up a Manhattan dinner meeting, which Leiweke's brother and Bonderman also attended. Leiweke immediately found a sweet spot with Bruckheimer the lifelong hockey fan. "He's got such life experiences," Bruckheimer said. "And he talked to me about Tampa. He talked about Minnesota, about Vancouver. About all the teams he'd been involved in and for me it was like a hockey history lesson."

Leiweke loved telling stories about his presidency of the NHL expansion Minnesota Wild. He greatly admires the team's former coach Jacques Lemaire and enjoys imitating the Hall of Fame centerman's thick French Canadian accent in describing their conversations.

Leiweke also gets emotional describing his Canucks executive years, where the late Pat Quinn, a tough, cigar-chomping former NHL defenseman, was the team's president and general manager. Quinn gruffly referred to Leiweke as a "marketing puke" the first time he saw him playing recreational hockey. Leiweke later sat in Quinn's office regaled by stories about the old NHL, bonding with a man who'd once knocked Bobby Orr out of a playoff game with a thunderous bodycheck.

Leiweke repeated these stories and more for Bruckheimer. But the deal wasn't sealed. Not long after, Bonderman wanted to meet Leiweke one-on-one at his Manhattan office and set up a meeting.

Leiweke was in Minneapolis speaking to a large group ahead of that year's Super Bowl. He'd planned to fly to New York immediately after to meet Bonderman at 9 the next morning.

Just before his Minneapolis talk, Bonderman's assistant phoned to give Leiweke the office's door code for the meeting—which she reminded was that morning, not the next day. Leiweke panicked, realizing he'd been double-booked. The assistant suggested he call Bonderman personally to break the bad news. "So, I called David, apologized profusely and we rescheduled for the next day. So, I went there the next day and immediately hit the carpet and gave him 15 push-ups.

"And he laughed."

It took even more meetings before Leiweke accepted. He'd gotten used to the idea the NFL job would cap his sports career.

"My brother was super enthusiastic, but this was not necessarily going to be with him," Leiweke said. "And I wondered what their objectives were beyond the game of hockey. Were they going to be patient? Were they going to let us build? What did they think of the arena project? There was a lot to get to know."

Leiweke was officially named CEO in April 2018 at a press conference at the Chihuly Garden and Glass pavilion at the Seattle Center public park, a short walk from KeyArena. The pavilion exhibits the works of renowned blown glass artist Dale Chihuly. Staging the press conference there sent a not-so-subtle signal the powerful Wright family, which owned the Space

Needle and the blown glass exhibit, was firmly behind the KeyArena and NHL efforts.

There'd been rumors David Wright, a son of Space Needle builder Howard S. Wright II, might head up a local minority ownership group alongside Bonderman and Bruckheimer. Wright attended the press conference, as did his brother, Jeff, managing partner of the Chihuly exhibit.

Others there included Bonderman and Bruckheimer, Mariners owner John Stanton, Sounders owner Adrian Hanauer, Seahawks president Peter McLoughlin, and former Seahawks coach Mike Holmgren. Former Sonics player and coach Lenny Wilkens was also there along with onetime team executive Chris Ackerley. His father, Barry, had owned the Sonics through some of their greatest years.

Those in attendance represented as broad an array of sports power figures as possible in Seattle. And the basketball presence delivered an additional message that this wasn't only about the NHL.

Tod Leiweke, after all, had started off as a vice president of marketing with the Golden State Warriors. He later became interim Portland Trail Blazers president as that Paul Allen–owned NBA team fell under the Seahawks' corporate umbrella.

"I couldn't believe that the Sonics left," Leiweke said during the press conference. "And I couldn't believe that there wasn't a solution for an arena."

Leiweke added, "I think it's a logical thing for the NBA to be here. And I think our building will be not only a great home for NHL hockey, but those same principles will be there for the NBA."

But he quickly added the NHL team wasn't a "consolation prize" until the NBA showed up. That perception among some fans was one the NHL Seattle group would devote much energy to counteracting.

Privately, OVG, NHL Seattle, and city officials were frustrated by continuous references to the Sonics on social media whenever KeyArena got discussed. There still was much public resistance to the KeyArena plan, framed by opponents as circumventing an NBA return by importing the

NHL. And though the NBA made clear it wasn't adding new teams for several years, organized Sonics fans held out hope the stalled SoDo arena project pitched by Chris Hansen might somehow be revived for basketball.

But the tide was turning. The presence of Wilkens and Ackerley at Leiweke's press conference showed some local NBA establishment figures were backing the KeyArena bid. But the Leiwekes knew talk was cheap.

While Tim Leiweke threw himself into finalizing a KeyArena development deal with the city—which he felt was key to securing the NHL franchise—Tod Leiweke began building a hockey team.

The differences in style between the Leiwekes were evident. Tim was the global mover and shaker who did whatever it took, no matter whose feathers got ruffled. Tod, the sports executive nobody in Seattle seemed to dislike, was there to massage those feathers back into place.

"He's kind of similar but different than Tim," Bruckheimer told me. "You can tell he's got the same conviction. But he's not as bombastic as Tim is. He's very settled, deliberate, funny."

Tod Leiweke's first bold move as CEO was hiring former Arizona Coyotes coach Dave Tippett as an NHL Seattle senior advisor. Tippett was beloved in hockey circles, a former Hartford Whalers mainstay in the 1980s and 1990s. That team won no Stanley Cups but spawned the NHL's greatest coaching tree.

Tippett had resigned from the Coyotes the previous summer, feeling burned out. But he'd since played a lot of golf near his Scottsdale, Arizona, home and was eager to return to the game somehow.

Tim Leiweke approached Tippett about the job. They'd worked together with the Los Angeles Kings when Tippett was an assistant coach and Leiweke team president. Tippett flew to Los Angeles, met with both Leiweke brothers and Bruckheimer, and accepted the job.

Tippett and I first met over lunch at Petit Toulouse restaurant in Uptown. His job had not yet been announced, though I'd break the news in my *Seattle Times* column. The restaurant was a few blocks from OVG's local headquarters. With Leiweke's arrival, the building was now being split with NHL Seattle offices on the top floor and OVG Seattle beneath.

Either way, Tippett was now an employee there. His job? Consulting on player spaces at a revamped KeyArena and a planned practice facility at the old Northgate Mall location. Tod Leiweke also envisioned building a full-fledged season ticket preview center with replica suites inside. Nothing could happen just yet. The NHL, after all, had yet to officially approve a team. But NHL Seattle needed to hit the ground running once that took place.

"There were a lot of things they just needed a hockey opinion on," Tippett said. "Facilities were one thing. But just organization-wise, the makeup of a hockey staff…they needed somebody that'd been in the routine of it day-to-day. They had great ideas but then they said, 'How does that look from a hockey player's perspective?'"

Tippett was also not a man who enjoyed the first word in any conversation. But his approachability often guaranteed him the final word.

A man like that was exactly the ambassador NHL Seattle needed as a liaison with the area's Seattle Thunderbirds and Everett Silvertips major junior squads, as well as minor hockey programs. His name carried hockey credibility and clout in a state that had produced but a handful of NHL players.

Tippett's hockey and NHL knowledge was also in short supply in the NHL Seattle offices. Even once the company expanded beyond 100 employees, few knew the league's history. Certainly not as Tippett did. His insights added badly needed hockey perspective to an organization grappling with what it wanted to be.

It would be Tippett going on a weekly Sports Radio KJR segment with popular host Dave "Softy" Mahler. KJR was losing a ratings battle with rival 710 ESPN Seattle and wanted major pro sports on its airwaves. Though KJR had the MLS Sounders broadcast rights, 710 ESPN had the NFL Seahawks and MLB Mariners.

Naturally, KJR had been huge supporters of Hansen's proposed SoDo arena, feeling it the quickest way to land NBA team rights.

Now, Tippett's forays with Mahler were the first attempts at a union between the station and potential NHL team. It eventually led to a much bigger relationship. One that would see KJR—onetime fierce critic of a KeyArena remodel—becoming the hockey team's radio broadcast partner.

But that was a way off. If anything, the biggest accomplishment of Tippett's KJR forays with Mahler was legitimizing the NHL and KeyArena project for a portion of the Sonics-loving KJR audience that wanted little to do with either.

That was Leiweke's doing. He'd started a "Tuesdays with Tod" segment with Mahler shortly after being named CEO. Then, he'd passed it off into "Tuesdays with Tip" once Tippett was hired in July 2018.

Meanwhile, Leiweke and Tippett weren't the only things on the rise. NHL Seattle's planned arena was soaring in cost. By mid-summer, Leiweke's brother, Tim, had revised OVG's KeyArena cost projections. The initial $564 million bid had jumped to a $700 million estimate. OVG was still planning to pay for it all. But as costs mounted and plans grew even more lavish, the NHL itself began to take notice with crunch time looming on awarding a team.

Chapter 34

MAYOR JENNY DURKAN GOES ON THE POWER PLAY

The sudden resignation of Mayor Ed Murray in September 2017 sent chills through those hoping to overhaul KeyArena and land an NHL team. It wasn't necessarily Murray's contributions they'd miss. Everything since the summer had mostly been in the hands of Brian Surratt, Robert Nellams, and the Seattle City Council.

But what stirred up OVG and city angst was the unknown. Namely, whether Murray's successor might muck everything up. Among mayoral finalists was Seattle-born Jenny Durkan, a former federal prosecutor hailing from a political family. Her father, Martin, had been a Democratic state senator and lobbyist with two unsuccessful runs for governor.

Early on, the corporate power brokers decreed Durkan the safest "establishment candidate," which provided reassurance to those hoping to rebuild a sports venue and add major professional teams.

All told, Durkan's corporate backers gave her a record Seattle mayoral war chest of over $1 million, more than $600,000 coming from a political organization created by the Seattle Metropolitan Chamber of Commerce and funded by large corporate donors she'd courted. Durkan would outspend challenger Cary Moon 5-to-1 and win with more than 60 percent of the vote.

Still, you never could tell what a mayor might do in office. Throughout her campaign, Durkan refused to take sides in the debate between overhauling KeyArena and reviving Chris Hansen's stalled SoDo bid.

But her background yielded one indicator Durkan was somebody OVG and the city could literally play ball with. She'd been a very good high school basketball player at Forrest Ridge of the Sacred Heart in Bellevue. Good enough that, upon enrolling at the University of Notre Dame, she'd tried out for their women's basketball team. Once cut, she became the team's statistician.

"I traveled with the team," Durkan told me for this book in February 2022. "The men's team would fly to wherever the destination was. And the women's team would take little vans. It was a different world then."

But basketball never left her. Two decades after graduating with honors from Notre Dame with her B.A. in English, she became an original season ticket holder of the WNBA Seattle Storm for their 2000 debut.

"I'm a big sports fan and I'm a huge Sonics fan," Durkan said. "They were such an important part of my childhood growing up. I went to game after game. I had posters of Lenny Wilkens and Xavier McDaniel and all that.

"So, that whole time when the Sonics left, for me personally it was hurtful. And I also think it was bad for the city."

She'd been lobbied by all the arena interests. But ultimately, in weighing the SoDo or KeyArena options, she saw only one clear path.

"We had this amazing asset in Seattle Center that had kind of lost its weight when the Sonics left," Durkan said of KeyArena. "And it needed a complete kind of renewal and rethinking. And that would only happen if we had sports teams centered there.

"I personally really wanted to get the Sonics back. And I also was a strong believer that the public shouldn't pay hefty prices for arenas for their sports teams."

At the time, Seattle was spending hundreds of millions revitalizing its waterfront and parts of downtown. Durkan realized a KeyArena overhaul fit within that strategy and could revitalize the entire Seattle Center public park.

"We could do the Seattle Center and as a plus, get ourselves in a better position to get an NBA team," she said. "So, from the very beginning, that relationship was a strong one. But for me, I also represented the people of Seattle to make sure we got a good deal. So, the negotiations were sometimes tough negotiations over terms."

Murray's resignation vacancy meant Durkan had to assume the mayor's chair immediately in November 2017, a month before the NHL officially gave the David Bonderman–Jerry Bruckheimer ownership group permission to apply for expansion. During her initial weeks in office, the city raced to complete a memorandum of understanding with OVG on developing the arena.

But over the ensuing year, that agreement would need to be expanded into a full development deal, then turned over to the city council for approval. "We really had to make sure that whatever deal we struck on the arena, the public was going to be protected for things like cost overruns and the ability to still control the dirt and the future at Seattle Center," Durkan said. "But they at the same time had this real business need that if they were going to spend all of this money on refurbishing and basically building a new arena, that they would have enough control that it worked for them economically."

Surratt had left his city job shortly after Murray's resignation, replaced by Durkan-appointed Marshall Foster. Through summer 2018, Foster,

Nellams, and OVG worked to strike a delicate balance between present and future.

The framework was similar to the interim deal. But bigger elements involved fine-tuning true costs of preserving the roof, gaining an understanding of limits to the types of sponsorships allowed within the public park, and finalizing details of the project's community aspect. Though OVG had pledged millions toward various community programs, some local stakeholders, such as KEXP public radio and the Uptown Alliance community group, were skeptical of Leiweke's intentions.

Foster said the April 2018 arrival of Leiweke's brother, Tod, as NHL Seattle CEO smoothed over those relations. "There had been some real concern and an almost adversarial relationship initially," Foster said. "And Tod has such an incredible civic kind of perspective. He was able to go in and sort of build partnerships with organizations such as KEXP, the Uptown community, which had understandable concerns about the construction impacts."

The differing skill sets and demeanors of the brothers, he added, were an "awesome combination" in what Foster felt was to be a public-private partnership no city and sports group had ever undertaken.

"We were very lucky," Foster said. "Because Tim Leiweke was at a moment in terms of creating OVG as an organization. This was the project that would make that company. That's the way I always perceived it and the way he perceived it."

Leiweke was willing to spend big. The city would own the arena, but OVG was taking all financial risk. But the company needed assurances it could recoup a big enough percentage of arena revenue to pay for everything.

Likewise, the city needed OVG to guarantee at least the modest profits it already made on KeyArena—and additionally, provide a bigger revenue share once NHL and NBA teams arrived and increased OVG's intake.

In March 2018, OVG had secured $100 million from the Silver Lake private equity firm to help pay for the project. Costs were certainly escalating. Part of that was by choice, with OVG using its newfound capital to hire the renowned Rockwell Group to upgrade suite designs and provide higher-end finishes.

And some added costs were by necessity. OVG and its engineers and architects had determined what was planned beneath the 44-million-pound KeyArena roof was unprecedented. The roof would effectively need to be hoisted for months atop high-grade steel posts while the arena beneath it was destroyed and rebuilt.

By July 2018, the projected cost of everything vaulted from $600 million to $700 million. OVG announced a Skanska Hunt joint venture as the project's general contractor. Skanska was a Swedish-based global construction giant that had built Met Life Stadium in New Jersey, where the Seahawks had won their only Super Bowl four years prior. The "Hunt" part of the joint venture involved the AECOM Hunt construction company, which came about when engineering firm AECOM, which had produced the eye-opening 2014 study concluding KeyArena could be overhauled for major pro sports, acquired the Hunt Construction Group.

"OVG was really, really good with bringing us under the tent with their design team," city representative Foster said. "And as we saw the costs escalate, we were concerned they may come back to us to want to reconsider, or ask that some public financing be brought to bear. All I can say is that never happened. And we're glad it didn't because it would have been a very hard thing to contemplate."

The NHL was also concerned. Commissioner Gary Bettman and his entourage weren't convinced a project of this magnitude would finish by its October 2020 target to play the 2020–21 season.

The Leiweke brothers told him it remained on schedule. Timing was critical because Seattle had yet to officially be awarded a team. Some owners already felt NHL Seattle was getting a break on the expansion fee of $650 million. They'd seen how quickly the Vegas Golden Knights had capitalized financially on their opening season.

Bettman was in a tough position. If owners wanted launch date certainty before awarding a franchise, he couldn't waver between 2020 and 2021 and risk opening more topics, such as the franchise price tag, for discussion.

OVG also needed its development deal with the city finalized ahead of the league's owners approving a franchise at its December board of governors meeting in Sea Island, Georgia. Actually, they needed the deal done much sooner. The league's powerful, nine-owner executive committee first would hear NHL Seattle's expansion pitch at an October 2, 2018, meeting in New York before deciding on whether to even schedule a full December vote.

This was where Seattle's franchise would truly be awarded or rejected. NHL Seattle would give a presentation and whatever these kingmaker owners recommended would be rubber-stamped in Georgia.

Tim Leiweke had taken a calculated step toward ensuring executive committee support. A year prior, OVG signed a deal with Delaware North to serve as lead concessionaire of an overhauled KeyArena. It so happened Delaware North was controlled by Boston Bruins majority owner Jeremy Jacobs, the most senior NHL executive committee member.

But there were eight more members. Some had questions about Seattle being as viable as the city's real estate prices suggested. And whether local politicians were truly on board. The Sonics debacle had occurred just a decade prior. City, county, and state politicians had balked at subsidizing a public-funded arena that might have saved the team.

At one point, the October 2018 meeting with the NHL's executive committee came close to not happening. OVG and NHL Seattle first had to head off disaster. A pair of apartment complexes adjacent to KeyArena had sent a lawyer's letter that June warning that an environmental impact study on the project and potential noise disruptions was "inadequate" and implied they'd challenge it before a coming deadline.

Any challenge would delay the study several months and push back OVG's development deal with the city. NHL Seattle needed that development deal before meeting with the league's executive committee.

"It went down to the final minute where we thought they were going to file a challenge," Tod Leiweke told me years later. "And…we reached a deal at the very last minute and there were no challenges. It was a big, big, important moment."

The development deal was ratified by the city council a week before the executive committee meeting. Also right before, NHL Seattle announced local minority owners headed by David Wright, from the powerful family that owned and operated the city's landmark Space Needle.

They also included Andy Jassy, soon to succeed Jeff Bezos as Amazon CEO, as well as Sounders owner Adrian Hanauer and the Acklerley brothers, Chris and Ted, whose father once owned the Sonics. Also, Jay Deutsch, who'd founded a corporate branding empire. And Tod Leiweke and his wife, Tara.

Those owners, combined with Bonderman, Bruckheimer, and other investors scattered nationwide, formed a corporate entity dubbed "Slapshot" through which the partnership funneled money.

And, as the league's executive committee would discover, OVG, Slapshot, and NHL Seattle also had Durkan in their corner. She'd headed off to New York with a Seattle contingent that included Bonderman, Bruckheimer, Wright, the Leiwekes, Francesca Bodie, and Len Potter, a longtime Bonderman adviser and strategist.

I'd chatted briefly with Durkan that October 2018 morning in her Manhattan hotel lobby, about 45 minutes before NHL Seattle's presentation to the committee. She'd seemed fired up, fueled by caffeine from an early breakfast with Tod Leiweke.

The pair looked on quietly as New York Yankees legend Reggie Jackson sauntered through the lobby. Both took in the message without speaking: this was New York. They were on the big stage now.

NHL Seattle's plan was Durkan winning the owners over with her sports background and energy for the project. Then, they'd roll out star power with Bruckheimer delivering closing remarks on his personal tale of growing up poor in Detroit, but loving hockey.

"It was such a positive feeling," Durkan said. "Because I'm a Seattle chauvinist. I don't think there's anything we can't do and can't get."

She and the NHL Seattle delegation stood at the front of the boardroom, using video and slide presentations highlighting the city and its sports tradition. The Leiweke brothers both spoke, then Durkan. She energetically described Seattle as not just a sports town, but a city of innovation that "punched above its weight" in terms of companies it produced, such as Costco, Starbucks, Microsoft, Expedia, Nordstrom, and Amazon. "I mean, we have built really innovative companies," Durkan said. "They all capture the spirit of a city that believes it can really build the future."

Durkan remembers there being one, maybe two other women in the room. And she's long felt that being a female mayor likely resonated with the male owners. That they'd gotten a glimpse of the modern, progressive future they envisioned for their league.

"She nailed it," NHL commissioner Gary Bettman would tell me years later. "I've seen mayors and government officials make presentations. She gave the executive committee all the reasons that—if you're making a decision to come to Seattle—you want to have.

"And, as importantly, she made clear that this project had her support and the support of the city.... We were going to be welcomed with open arms."

With Durkan done, Bruckheimer hammered things home.

He was nervous as he stood before the owners.

"Of course I was," he told me. "I told them how I grew up watching the sport. How my dad used to take me to the Olympia and watch the games. And what we could bring to it with my knowledge of entertainment and getting people excited about things.

"It was just talking about the value of the group that we'd put together and Tim's expertise and Tod's ability to run things in a very classy way. It was value added. I think our group was value added to their teams."

Bruckheimer said Durkan certainly helped smooth his entrance.

"She was great," he said. "She's got a big smile and she was great. Politicians tend to be great speakers, so she was going to help. Her excitement for the city and excitement for the team really came through."

Within a couple of hours, the executive committee rendered its unanimous verdict—they'd recommend the full board of governors approve Seattle as the league's 32nd franchise.

Chapter 35

GEORGIA BOUND

Jenny Durkan and Jerry Bruckheimer aside, the hockey gods weren't about to give NHL Seattle the smoothest ride into expansion franchise acceptance. First, there was the small matter of the tornado that struck just outside Sea Island, Georgia, as NHL owners began arriving for two days of December meetings.

The meetings began on a Monday, followed by the expansion vote Tuesday, December 4, 2018. But the prior Sunday, an EF-3 tornado touched down along a seven-mile path, injuring five people. The King's Bay tornado was one of the region's largest in recent memory, with 144-mph winds causing widespread destruction along the area's First Coast, just north of St. Mary's and south of Brunswick and St. Simons Island adjacent to Sea Island.

I'd overnighted in Jacksonville, Florida, about 80 miles to the south and cautiously driven up early Monday. Alongside the highway lay felled tree limbs and other visible damage from the prior day's tornado. My car radio warned further tornados could be coming.

Sea Island isn't so much a town as one giant resort. Driving up to it, I marveled at the golden marshes on both sides. This wasn't what your average hockey fan typically got to see—and I don't mean just the wild, untamed seaside forests. This was old, big money. Reinforcing that, a security gate and guard booth appeared on the main road. Not for any one hotel, but the entire island.

Guests have a choice of hotel accommodations—The Cloister, The Lodge, or The Inn. The Cloister was the old money-burner, a Forbes Five-Star resort set along 50 lush acres. This is where the NHL meetings were held as millionaires and billionaires wandered its hallways. I'd bit the bullet for two nights there, offset by the cheaper Jacksonville hotel on the trip's front and back ends. I wanted to experience the NHL team's birth in all its lavishness.

Though I'd had little time to appreciate them, The Cloister's rooms were huge, with tastefully appointed southern charm. Mine had a patio overlooking the marsh, which, on my first morning, served as the setting for a peaceful 20-minute cup of coffee before the chaos.

Drinking my brew, it seemed surreal this steamy place was where Seattle's NHL franchise would be birthed. The state of Georgia is hardly hockey heaven, despite the NHL twice sticking a franchise there with the Atlanta Flames from 1972 to 1980 and then the Atlanta Thrashers from 1999 to 2011.

Despite it being December, the weather was humid and, apparently, prone to tornados. But it was a wondrous setting. I'd been to The Oriente in Ecuador and Kruger National Park in South Africa. But the forests of Sea Island, so opulent, yet wild in their own way, were something I'd never imagined existed in the United States. I'd half-wanted to grab one of the hotel's free bicycles and pedal along the nearby trails, hoping to stumble across a wayward gator or pelican. Of course, there was bigger business to tend to.

On that first day, it was figuring out exactly when this future NHL team would actually begin play. Once again, nothing was being made easy. NHL commissioner Gary Bettman and his deputy, Bill Daly, had sent ominous media signals that Seattle's launch might be delayed a year until October 2021. Tod Leiweke had originally hoped to go in front of the full board of governors six months prior. But Bettman had told Leiweke his group didn't yet have its "ducks in order" on the arena and he wasn't about to rush things with NHL governors only to have them raise doubts.

So, he'd bought NHL Seattle six additional months to see where arena plans were in terms of finalizing a development deal with the city. And with contractor Skanska Hunt on estimating the venue's reopening date.

"Gary kept sending messages, signals that he didn't think the arena would be done," Leiweke told me in March 2022. "Bill Daly was much more direct. And he just said, 'I don't think the arena's done and I don't think you should count on 2020.' It seemed like that extra year was just going to be a long time."

Nonetheless, Leiweke and NHL Seattle had gone to the Sea Island meetings with an outside hope of still making an October 2020 launch.

After trying all day, I'd gotten hold of Leiweke late that first Monday afternoon when he'd finally been freed from meetings. Leiweke was very much in demand at the hotel, where the hockey world's media had gathered. Some of those seeking him out were acquaintances from my former Toronto media days, such as *Hockey Night in Canada*'s Elliotte Friedman and Pierre LeBrun of The Athletic. Emily Kaplan of ESPN, who I'd been introduced to for the first time, had been seeking Leiweke out as well. Then, finally, he emerged via text message. Leiweke asked me to jump on a hotel trolley and meet him at The Lodge, one of the resort's other properties he had a late-afternoon meeting at. The trolley ride took 40 minutes through what passes for rush-hour traffic on Sea Island. By the time it got there, Leiweke's meeting was already finished and he'd left. He told me to turn around and come back and meet him in the Cloister parking lot away from prying media eyes.

There, with the sun already set, he let me know the NHL had delayed the team's launch by a year. The good news: the franchise would be awarded the following morning. But it was nearly three years away from playing.

I felt disappointed hearing that and could tell Leiweke was as well. Three years was a long time. NHL Seattle had generated serious momentum for hockey within the city. It had shaken off the negative talk surrounding the lack of an NBA franchise and the fact that a SoDo arena wasn't getting built. But now, hockey fans needed to wait. And wait. Then wait some more.

"We were a little worried about how people would react," he'd tell me years later. "But we quickly realized it was going to be a stretch to get the building done."

Bettman would come to view it as one of the luckiest calls of his tenure. After all, in December 2018, nobody had yet heard of COVID-19 or global shutdowns. Those were more than a year away. But Bettman knew all about Seattle's construction industry, where customers were gouged and things rarely got built on time. Already, OVG was butting heads with its Skanska Hunt contractor over costs inflating well beyond initial projections. Now, OVG was being told the original $564 million project would surpass $800 million. And, as Seattle homeowners often do, OVG was shopping around for a replacement contractor. It was clear Tim Leiweke's vision and Skanska Hunt's were not aligned.

"Listen, they were excited, and they were anxious," Bettman said of OVG and NHL Seattle. "And putting COVID aside, I didn't think they could finish on time. And there were two issues there: one, they had no place else to really play. And two, the risk to the schedule. If they were to miss, it would be too great."

Bettman said Tim Leiweke countered that crews could work triple shifts. But Bettman's "sixth sense" told him no.

"I didn't think there was any way they could get it done in time," he said. "And ultimately, they came to agree with me."

Bettman's intervention, given what later happened with the pandemic, may have ultimately saved the Seattle franchise. And back on that December 3, 2018, evening, the franchise had yet to be officially granted. The board of governors would meet the following morning and vote on it.

Tod Leiweke had already told me the team would be approved. But I was sworn to secrecy until it happened, with NHL Seattle not wanting to upstage its own announcement. Morning watch parties had been planned back in Seattle, including a team-organized event at Henry's Tavern for hundreds of fans. Also, the sports world could be a strange place. Owners were known to change their minds.

Going into that final morning, Kraken owner Jerry Bruckheimer wouldn't allow himself premature celebrations.

"There's always suspense," he said. "You never really know. The owners had to vote. We had no idea what was going to happen. It looked good. We did everything according to what the NHL asked us to do. But you never know. Maybe Vancouver doesn't want the competition. Who knows?"

It turns out Vancouver did indeed want the competition. So did the other 30 teams. Any personal suspense ended when I walked into the hotel ballroom staging the post-meetings press conference.

There, I spotted a TV camera and a teleprompter reading, "Good afternoon everyone. Today is an exciting and historic day for the National Hockey League. I am delighted to announce that, this morning, the Board of Governors unanimously approved a plan of expansion that will bring a National Hockey League team to…"

The teleprompter cut off there. But it was clear what the decision was. Not long after, the room filled up and commissioner Bettman entered and read those very words aloud.

Back in Seattle, the celebrations began. A decade since the NBA Sonics had left for Oklahoma City, Seattle had a major winter sport again. It was also the first time in nearly a century that top-flight pro hockey was returning.

Disappointed as NHL Seattle was about the added year's delay in launching, they were nonetheless grasping the day's historical significance. Leiweke and the owners had even flown down Beverley Parsons, the 83-year-old niece of Lester Patrick, from Seattle for the event. Lester and his brother, Frank, had first brought pro hockey out west back in 1911 with the Pacific Coast Hockey Association. Four years later, the Seattle Metropolitans had been born.

Parsons still worked as a real estate agent in the Seattle suburb of Bellevue, where Mayor Jenny Durkan had played her high school basketball. And though Parsons couldn't remember much about "Uncle Lester," she told me she'd long hoped to see pro hockey's return to Seattle.

"I've wanted it for years and years and years and always dreamed about it," Parsons said. "It didn't seem as if we would ever do it. So, I'm so thrilled with the men that have made it happen."

Being there for the franchise's birth had been a blur. There were interviews to do, stories to write, and a drive back to Jacksonville for a flight home early the following morning. It was an exhausting day, but then again, what part of this arena ordeal hadn't been a test? Tod Leiweke had been misty eyed when I met him for a few moments, away from the television cameras and microphones. He was still disappointed about waiting the additional year. But at that very moment, the magnitude of the day had overtaken him. He and his brother had fought so hard to get to this point. Now, it was at hand. No matter what else happened in coming months and years, they'd landed the NHL's 32nd franchise.

And on that day, Leiweke took a moment to celebrate. "We did it," he told me, giving me one of his too-hard back slaps. "We fucking did it!" He'd meant the "we" part to be about him, his brother, and their team. Though I'd been there to see everything unfold, every step of the way, this was their project. And with that ownership victory being celebrated came a staggering responsibility even Leiweke couldn't yet fathom.

The reality was they weren't out of the woods yet. Everything could still go wrong. And that would be theirs to own as well. The Leiweke brothers had made history. And they alone would be responsible if they screwed it all up.

Chapter 36

WHEN DREAMS BECOME REAL

John Barr rose before sunrise and headed to the South Lake Union branch of Henry's Tavern, arriving at about 6:30 in the morning. No, Barr wasn't an alcoholic, though there'd been days the prior eight years when a drink might have helped. Barr was a business intelligence consultant who, in 2010, had taken up the lonely role of forming a website and movement devoted to bringing the NHL to his transplanted home city of Seattle.

And on this day, December 4, 2018, an early watch party had been planned for local hockey fans waiting to see whether NHL owners meeting in Sea Island, Georgia, would finally award a Seattle franchise. For Barr, this day was years in the making. One he'd only dreamed of without allowing belief it might happen. So, he wanted to savor every minute, arriving hours early to ensure a prime seat.

"It was incredible," Barr said of seeing the franchise announced on the bar's TV screens. "I've had a lot of great milestones which felt like dreams had come true. But that is one of the days where literally, my dream was coming true.

"And it's a dream that seemed so far off," he added. "That I could influence or even have a part in this thing of bringing an NHL team here. And I think it's debatable—the team probably comes here without me. But at the same time, I probably made it easier. Just maybe a little bit."

Barr indeed made it easier. Much as with Brian Robinson and his Sonics Rising website, Tim Leiweke recognized Barr was key to connecting with local hockey fans. Leiweke and his Oak View Group felt Seattle was a "sleeper" town of hockey supporters. He knew it had two major junior teams in nearby Kent and Everett, a thriving adult league, and youth programs already established. All that was needed was a connection to tap in to their hockey enthusiasm.

Barr had recognized much the same thing about hockey and Seattle upon moving there in 2005. He'd grown up in the Bay Area, discovering hockey in 1991 when the San Jose Sharks joined the NHL. Barr was hooked by the sport's fast-paced energy.

But in Seattle, he'd found an existing hockey infrastructure so much deeper than San Jose's prior to the Sharks' creation. Right there, Barr felt Seattle was primed for expansion.

So, he did what any tech savvy entrepreneur would. He formed a website to share his vision with like-minded hockey fans. Naturally, he'd named it "NHL to Seattle." His following was nowhere near what Sonics Rising had with NBA supporters, but the sites complimented one another and often shared posts. After all, they had a mutual interest in an arena getting built.

Still, as the city's arena debates raged the next decade, NHL to Seattle often watched from the background as Sonics Rising and basketball dominated fan conversation. That is, until Tim Leiweke showed up in late 2016 offering to overhaul KeyArena. Suddenly, it seemed the NHL could actually arrive ahead of the NBA.

"The one thing I'll always be impressed about with Leiweke is that I met with Tim before he even bid on the arena," Barr said. "Tim, not anybody else. So, all of those other ownership groups, I was dealing with a staffer.

A really low-level person. Maybe a couple of emails or something every once in a while. It wasn't me demanding it. I had nothing to really gain by forcing a meeting. But that is testimony to their broader success."

Leiweke's daughter, senior OVG executive Francesca Bodie, also attended their meeting. So did OVG Seattle legal counsel Lance Lopes and publicist Steven Gottlieb. Leiweke told Barr he wanted to overhaul KeyArena to bring an NHL team there and needed his support.

Barr had previously supported Chris Hansen's bid to build an arena in the city's SoDo district. But that was more a marriage of convenience.

"You know, I'm not really a basketball fan," Barr said. "But I knew the key to getting an NHL team here was having an arena. And in the beginning, when they originally launched that concept, hockey was part of the messaging from the Hansen camp. And so, the fact that they were even acknowledging hockey or the NHL was pretty encouraging."

But he felt no true loyalty to Hansen's group, especially as years passed without an arena. And with the NHL not being prioritized. So, while the SoDo project's defeat in the May 2016 council vote left Barr discouraged, he quickly shifted focus elsewhere.

And when Leiweke showed up six months later, the timing could not have been better. Even before Leiweke invited him to meet, Barr had been approached for a sit down by Brian Surratt, the man tabbed by Mayor Ed Murray to help lead the KeyArena bidding process. A meeting was set between Surratt, Barr, and Sonics Rising counterpart Robinson to discuss fan resistance to KeyArena.

"My message in there was, 'Hey, I'm not an urban planner, I don't know how things work but if the arena can support NHL, then I'm in,'" Barr said. "I will support anything that can bring an NHL team to Seattle."

Not long after, Barr met with Leiweke and told him the same thing. From then on, Barr would be the one helping relay OVG's message to the local hockey community. After OVG won the bids process in June 2017, the company began arranging public hockey fan gatherings or NHL game watch parties. And Barr would be the one helping ensure crowds of hockey fans knew where to go.

This included at city council meetings throughout 2017 and 2018 as OVG worked to secure a temporary development deal, followed by a final one just before the franchise was awarded. After all, it wouldn't look good if the council was debating measures for an NHL arena with no hockey fans showing up to watch. So, Barr and his allies were continuously there.

It wasn't always an easy ride. Many of his loyal hockey followers, as had been the case with Robinson and Sonics Rising, felt betrayed by Barr supporting the KeyArena plan.

"I took some arrows, too, just for supporting the Seattle Center Arena," Barr said. "People thought I should turn over my NHL to Seattle Facebook page, which at the time was like 10,000 strong or something like that. They were like, 'No, we should not be supporting this arena.'"

The preliminary KeyArena construction deal was agreed to by OVG and the city in December 2017 and signed off on the next day by new Mayor Jenny Durkan. Barr felt it was important step in what he knew would be a long process. But he wasn't prepared for the phone call he got the following day, from a Durkan staffer, telling him to rush over to city hall.

"He said, 'Hey, John, the NHL's going to make an announcement about Seattle. Can you get down here with a Metropolitans sweater or some kind of hockey sweater that the mayor can show at a press conference?'"

Barr obliged, bringing with him a replica Seattle Metropolitans jersey.

"I literally wasn't sure what was going on," Barr said. "And on my way taking an Uber downtown to the mayor's office, my phone starts blowing up. That's when Bettman said publicly that they are accepting an application for NHL expansion from the Seattle group.

"So, you can imagine, I was freaking out. But I was literally on my way to city hall and pretty much walked upstairs. It was a Friday and super quiet walking in there. But it was probably one of the best days of my life."

Durkan was photographed at the press conference holding Barr's hockey sweater.

Even then, Barr wasn't prepared to let himself think a team was coming just yet. But all that changed on March 1, 2018, with the season ticket deposit drive and the Bonderman–Bruckheimer group attracting 32,000 paid deposits in slightly more than a day.

"That's where I just felt that it could not be ignored," Barr said. "And you always worry. You've seen enough and I've seen enough in this process that you're never sure. And part of it's my ignorance of the political process… and where things could go wrong. I was going through that for the first time because I'd never been political until I understood this process."

But for the first time, he felt the ticket drive, itself delivering a political message, was something the NHL could not ignore. And it kept his faith going that year, through OVG's tough negotiations with the city and concessions on public infrastructure. By the time the Sea Island, Georgia, vote on approving a franchise rolled around, he'd gone to Henry's Tavern with confidence.

"It was just great to see a dream come true," Barr said. "And it was also cool to be around so many fans that were fired up. There'd been a lot of people that were supportive along the way. So, that was pretty fun to be celebrating with them instead of watching at my house on my couch.

"So, it was a great day. And as you know, the rest was history."

Well, maybe not quite yet.

Chapter 37

BUILDING
THE VISION

Even while the Sea Island vote was going down, OVG was switching KeyArena general contractors. The team was at odds with the Skanska Hunt group over whether the project could get done on time. Meanwhile, projected costs were skyrocketing. By the time the NHL vote took place, they'd surpassed $800 million.

With the franchise approved, the NHL Seattle contingent flew back for a groundbreaking ceremony with OVG at the KeyArena site. Preliminary demolition had already gotten underway. But OVG's deal with the city required the franchise be approved before serious demolition began. Now, it could start. But again, things were delayed. Word soon got out that Skanska Hunt was removing itself from the project and would be replaced by the Mortenson construction firm. Unlike the Skanska Hunt deal, which was pay-as-you-go, the one with Mortenson offered more of an "all in" price. But it would take several more months of fine-tuning the project's scope. In the meantime, NHL Seattle hired longtime local construction consultant Ken Johnsen as its project executive. Johnsen had actually consulted for the city during the KeyArena bids process and had been particularly aggressive in grilling Tim Leiweke about the complexity of OVG's intentions. So, when Leiweke wanted somebody overseeing OVG's interests with its general contractor, Johnsen topped the list.

By spring 2019, full work had resumed. But the project's price tag now was $930 million. Also, the arena's reopening had been pushed back from October 2020 to June 1, 2021. And that was a floating target. Nobody could really say for certain. When I spoke to NHL Seattle CEO Tod Leiweke at the time, he told me he'd been assured the reopening would be no later than August of 2021.

That was problematic. For one thing, the WNBA Seattle Storm already planned to be displaced for two seasons. Any reopening beyond May 2021 would keep the Storm out for at least part of a third season. And OVG in its contract with the city had agreed to pay the Storm penalties of up to $2 million depending on how many games were played elsewhere.

But also, an August 2021 reopening bumped up perilously close to the start of the NHL's 2021–22 season. There was no suitable substitute arena in the region, so this was a concern. But OVG and NHL Seattle had assurances the arena would be done.

While the full arena demolition began in earnest, the Slapshot owners and NHL Seattle sought out a general manager for the team. They'd had senior adviser Dave Tippett aboard for nearly a year and nailed down a finalist list of GM candidates by spring 2019. A front-runner quickly emerged: Tippett's former Hall of Fame teammate from the Hartford Whalers, ex–Carolina Hurricanes GM Ron Francis. The Hurricanes had changed owners and let Francis go a year prior.

"I think we had maybe a dozen names to start with and then that got whittled down to a final three and Ron was in that mix," Tippett said.

Tippett initially wasn't sure his old pal would want the gig. Francis had strong ties to the Raleigh-Durham area and was involved in a new business venture there. So, before including him on their list, Tippet phoned Francis to gauge interest.

"I wasn't sure whether he was going to retire or looking," Tippett said. "So, I was pleasantly surprised that he had a great deal of interest in the job."

Francis seemed a good fit. He was level-headed and respected throughout the league. The last thing the expansion team wanted was a temperamental GM who risked becoming a sideshow. It was too important to sell the team to a new NHL market without a background circus.

Not to mention, Francis had been receptive to incorporating analytics within his Carolina front office, bringing on one of the game's better minds in Eric Tulsky, who'd become a Hurricanes vice president. NHL Seattle wanted a GM at the forefront of analytics, feeling it critical in the tech-laden market. But Francis also had some old school in him, coming of age in the 1980s NHL with Hartford before winning Stanley Cups in Pittsburgh alongside Mario Lemieux in the 1990s.

"One of the prerequisites we'd talked about for the GM was you had to have somebody that's got good experience," Tippett said. "And he's had great experience from playing, to coaching, to GM."

Tippett said the team had a handful of assistant GMs on its list, but worried that running an expansion team might overwhelm them. NHL Seattle CEO Tod Leiweke had once launched the Minnesota Wild as their president and agreed with Tippett about the immense job ahead.

"It was going to be a big job and it's hard to have a first-time GM," Tippett said. "There's so much interaction with the GMs in the league. Both Tod and I thought that it was imperative to have somebody that had a rapport within the league already."

Francis had some initial discussions, then flew to Seattle in early June 2018 to meet with Leiweke, minority owner and Amazon executive Andy Jassy, and Kraken chief operating officer Victor de Bonis. His first night in, Francis dined out with Leiweke, discussing their long-term visions. The next day, Francis met again with Leiweke and de Bonis in the team's Uptown offices. After that, Leiweke drove Francis to Amazon headquarters in the South Lake Union district for an afternoon meeting with Jassy. At the time, Jassy was still Amazon's No. 2 executive and had yet to replace Jeff Bezos as CEO. But his time was nonetheless in short supply, given his responsibilities running one of the world's largest companies.

Amazon's headquarters were less than a mile from KeyArena. The area had terrible rush-hour traffic on the best of days. But it also happened to be raining and Francis was learning firsthand that wet weather and Seattle drivers don't mix.

"We got stuck in traffic and I literally jumped out of the car and ran the last three blocks to get to the office," Francis said. "I didn't know where I was going. But I managed to get to Andy's office. We ended up starting the meeting about 30 minutes before Tod was able to get in there."

But during their alone time, Jassy and Francis hit it off. It turned out Jassy had grown up an avid New York Rangers fan. His father, Everett, a prominent Manhattan lawyer, had been a Rangers season ticket holder who'd once tried to buy the St. Louis Blues. Jassy knew all about Francis and his on-ice exploits, and their conversations varied between business and personal. "It was a lot of different questions on my philosophies on building a team, the development process, analytics, some questions on Carolina," Francis said.

Not long after, the team invited Francis back for a second round of meetings. Most of Slapshot was there for a quarterly team board meeting, meaning Francis could meet Bonderman, Bruckheimer, and more local and non-local minority owners. It was clear by the end of those meetings that NHL Seattle had its GM. But the team had also scheduled interviews at the upcoming NHL Draft later that month in Vancouver, B.C. They told Francis they wanted to get through those before deciding.

Bruckheimer and Leiweke made the trip, initially planning to stay throughout the two-day affair. Instead, they got all they needed on Day 1. By the end, they'd figured out Francis was their man. A handful of conversations pushed them over the top. The biggest was with Hurricanes head coach Rod Brind'Amour, who stood in a quiet arena corridor and gave a glowing review of Francis, declaring he'd walk through a wall for his ex-teammate and that NHL Seattle would be foolish not to hire him.

But Francis wasn't the employee Leiweke and Bruckheimer hired that trip. Leiweke told me he'd be checking out early the following day and had me meet him and Bruckheimer for coffee at their hotel. Seated between them was a woman I'd never met. They introduced me to Alexandra Mandrycky, who, I was informed, was in the process of leaving the Minnesota Wild and would soon be introduced as NHL Seattle's very first hockey operations staffer. Mandrycky would head up the team's analytics department and be given "a seat at the table" alongside any GM eventually hired.

The team clearly knew Francis would be getting the job. It seems unfathomable they'd hire an employee to such an important position without giving the future GM a heads-up. I'd heard stories about what had gone down with the analytics group in Minnesota. They'd been installed by former Wild GM Chuck Fletcher, who was subsequently fired and replaced by Paul Fenton. The Fenton regime was tumultuous, lasting just 14 months. But in the interim, he'd managed to alienate the Wild's entire analytics team. I couldn't imagine Mandrycky signing up to work for another GM coming in completely blind to who she was.

Partway through our coffee, Bruckheimer turned and asked me who I thought the GM should be. At the time, Francis was clearly the most experienced candidate out there who was known for using analytics in decision-making. I told Bruckheimer I'd pick Francis.

"Interesting," he said, nodding his head.

I decided to push my luck, asking Bruckheimer what he thought of "Kraken" as a possible team name. He feigned annoyance. It wasn't the first time. The prior year, he'd scoffed at the name in a phone conversation we had while he was standing on an aircraft carrier filming a sequel to the *Top Gun* movie from 30 years prior. Bruckheimer had included a Kraken giant sea monster in his *Pirates of the Caribbean* movie. So, it surprised me he continued to seem so put off by using it as a team name. Turns out, as I'd later hear from those making the decision, Bruckheimer truly wasn't an early fan of the Kraken name. But at that point, in June 2019, there was time to change his mind.

But first, the yet-unnamed NHL Seattle team still needed a GM. And a few weeks after that Sunday morning in Vancouver, Francis was indeed unveiled to an eager Seattle media as the team's second hockey ops employee and first GM. Now, the reality of an NHL franchise coming to Seattle was beginning to feel tangible. After years of intense fighting over arenas and debating the hypotheticals, the actual Seattle NHL franchise had an actual GM to go along with its actual analytics department head.

Francis and Mandrycky spent his initial days on the job doing a traveling media road show. Though the team was still more than two years from taking the ice, there was plenty to do. Francis would be at the center of it all. Not only with picking the players to form Seattle's first team, but helping design the interiors of both a revamped KeyArena and a state-of-the-art practice facility.

Oh yes, and the team name. Francis would be dragged into that as well. And for those already familiar with Seattle's NHL venture, that was a whole other debate unto itself.

Chapter 38

WHAT'S IN A NAME?

Months before the NHL officially even granted Seattle a team, the "debate" over a name began. And, given the internet's ignorance of subtlety and nuance, it was a debate about as sophisticated as the years of prior local arena wars.

Some fans wanted "Metropolitans" in an ode to the city's Stanley Cup legacy. Others preferred "Totems"—remembering the teams of Guyle Fielder, Don Ward, and Rudy Filion back in their minor professional WHL heyday. The local geography and wildlife buffs insisted the name needed links to the Pacific Northwest. This brought cries for Sockeyes, Steelheads, Cascades, Emeralds, and even Sasquatch—though that last one was controversial, as folks debated whether something could be part of Northwest heritage without proof it actually existed.

But if Sasquatch got fans up in arms, that was nothing next to tentacles waved in anger over the most controversial suggestion of all. No one is certain how "Kraken" got thrown into the mix. But the name evoked love or hatred, no in-between. A local bookstore owner near KeyArena would later tell me he'd overheard OVG executives—he thinks one was

Tim Leiweke—discussing the Kraken name over coffee. This was shortly after the bid process was won by Leiweke's Oak View Group in June 2017. The store owner told me he'd recommended some Kraken-themed books for the group to check out.

Then again, John Barr, owner of the NHL to Seattle fan website, told me he remembers "Kraken" being tossed around online by somebody in 2015. Barr even tweeted "Let's release the Kraken!" shortly after. "You know, Twitter is full of things and I'm pretty sure it wasn't me who started it," Barr said. "But I liked the concept. I do like *Pirates of the Caribbean* and that was before we knew Jerry [Bruckheimer] was involved in the team.

"But I tried to distance myself from having any one conviction about the name," Barr said. "Because I wanted to get the team first. So, I was able to be relatively neutral."

Not everyone shared his neutrality. Seattle city councilmember Debora Juarez, who'd co-chaired the Select Committee on Civic Arenas, which vetted and ultimately approved the arena development deal with OVG, had choice words about the future team's name when first introduced to NHL Seattle CEO Tod Leiweke in 2018.

"I'd barely gotten two words out and she looked at me and said, 'You'd better not name them the fucking "Totems,"'" Leiweke told me.

Juarez, a member of the Blackfeet Nation, had been the first Native American elected to the council. And she knew totem poles were not indigenous to the the local Duwamish and Suquamish people. They'd been imported and were viewed by local tribes as a sign of great disrespect.

So, Totems, unbeknownst to those who'd continue arguing ferociously for years that the team should pick that name, was already out. Nobody wanted the sharp-tongued Juarez for an enemy.

Ultimately, she'd prove a staunch ally, getting the NHL to town and the team's eventual practice facility built in her home district. But it would never be a "Totems" team if she was still breathing.

Online polling by NHL Seattle and local media organizations typically had Totems, Sockeyes, Sasquatch, and Steelheads among name finalists. The "Kraken" name usually lagged behind that initial group, seemingly with more of a cult following than mainstream support.

The *Seattle Times* ran weeks of bracket voting in which "Sockeyes" won out. Some fans had written in declaring they'd never support the team if a "cartoonish" name like Kraken prevailed. Some wondered about "Kraken under pressure" jokes when the team went on a losing streak. Or of KeyArena being nicknamed the "Krak-house" or "Krak-den."

Inside NHL Seattle offices, the debate was just as impassioned. GM Ron Francis remembered the team paring the short list to 10 to 12 names when he began helping the search in mid-2019. Initially, the team planned to release the name later that year. By that point, "Kraken" hadn't made the short list. Some owners, including Bruckheimer, worried the name was too gimmicky. And he'd produced the *Pirates of the Caribbean* films containing Krakens in them.

Soon after, Francis got to talking with Heidi Dettmer, the team's vice president of marketing. As with so many locals, she was of Scandinavian descent and remembered her grandparents telling her about Kraken folklore as a child.

"She was telling me the whole story about how she was talking about it as a kindergarten person," Francis said. "I thought it was pretty cool."

The team eventually cut the shortlist to five or six names. Kraken still wasn't one of them. They were sent to designers for logo mock-ups. Later, Tod Leiweke asked Francis which names he liked.

"I said, 'Honestly, you're going to think I'm nuts but I like Kraken,'" Francis said. "He said, 'Really? Why?' And so I told him the story about Heidi. And as we kept going, the Kraken seemed to come back into the mix.' I remember having a discussion with [NHL commissioner Gary] Bettman at one point and he thought the Kraken was interesting. He liked it."

By that point, the team had owners, marketing personnel, Francis, and some other hockey ops staffers involved as well. Francis by then had hired Ricky Olcyzk as his assistant GM and rounded out his scouting department. Things were taking shape, but the team was being extra cautious researching trademark issues on name choices. One by one, they came back with issues. And as that happened, Kraken kept gaining in stature amongst the group.

One thing they'd noticed: nobody debating the Kraken name was ever passive about it. Love it, or hate it, Kraken was often the first name candidate that jumped to fans' minds. The team liked that recognition factor. They wanted the name to evoke feelings.

Finally, they reached a point where everyone agreed "Kraken" seemed a logical choice. They asked for logos and designers came back with a stylized "S" everyone in the room felt was perfect. But then, before they could wrap things up, majority owner David Bonderman had a late suggestion.

"Mr. Bonderman looks up and says, 'I think we should put a red eye right here,'" Francis said, adding that Bonderman wanted the red dot placed in the upper fold of the "S" design. "And when you looked at the design people around the room, it was almost like they were kind of deflated. But when they came back with it, it made so much more sense. And it's a huge part of the logo today."

Fellow Kraken owner Bruckheimer loved the color red. He might have installed red seats at KeyArena had he not been warned about that while touring other venues as part of his ownership research. He'd learned red seats are a no-no in the arena industry because it makes it more obvious on television when those seats are empty. So, that was out. But Bruckheimer wanted red incorporated in the logo somehow and Bonderman's suggestion made that happen.

The trademark delays and late name switch meant NHL Seattle put off announcing the name until the first quarter of 2020. That wasn't all bad, as it enabled the team to keep building suspense through newly up-and-running social media channels. The great name tease was one of the biggest marketing coups NHL Seattle would pull off ahead of the team's launch. Somehow, they kept it a secret. But every now and then, somebody came close to leaking it.

In late January 2020, Josh Hoven of the Mayor's Manor website, which follows the Los Angeles Kings, reported that an unnamed source told him "Kraken" would be chosen. That set off a firestorm of speculation, which NHL Seattle spent the rest of that day defusing without outright lying and saying Hoven was incorrect. So many at the time still refused to believe "Kraken" would be chosen by an actual professional team, so the rumor quickly went away.

By then, the team had already started selling club-level season tickets. It planned to release general season tickets for sale by March 2020 and was putting final touches on its preview center across the street from the arena site. The arena itself had been knocked down by September 2019 and the 44-million-pound roof was being propped up by 72 giant pole-like support beams. Construction to rebuild the outer shell would take all of 2020 and then the interior and finishes would be done in time for the September 2021 NHL preseason.

The plan was coming nicely to fruition on all fronts. And then, it wasn't.

By late February 2020, as the team was about to announce season ticket sales, concerns about a novel coronavirus emerging out of China became impossible to ignore. In fact, what was believed to be the very first North American case of COVID-19 had been detected right in the Seattle suburb of Bellevue.

News changed by the hour. And with just days to go before the ticket launch, NHL Seattle made the gut-wrenching decision to postpone it indefinitely. Same with the name announcement. At that point, people were worried about dying from an incurable coronavirus. Images filled TV screens of patients gasping for breath on ventilators. Nobody, rightfully, was thinking about sports. By early March 2020, it was evident Washington

Governor Jay Inslee planned on shuttering all non-essential business activity statewide. This included construction sites, with limited exceptions.

OVG and NHL Seattle needed to be among those exceptions. The timeline for KeyArena to be completed had little margin for error. Halting construction indefinitely risked the arena not being ready for the NHL's 2021–22 season.

"We were very concerned—the city and the ownership group—when the pandemic hit," Seattle Mayor Jenny Durkan told me. "You'll remember we had to stop construction for a period of time. And we didn't know what that was going to look like and how long. Every day lost is like five days lost on the opening. Just because of the complexity of bringing in different trade groups and where you are and resources."

That week, intense dialogue flew between the mayor's office, the governor, King County public health officials, OVG, Mortenson, and NHL Seattle. Durkan had three major construction projects she needed open: efforts to repair the closed and crumbling West Seattle bridge, the city's yearslong waterfront restoration venture, and the KeyArena overhaul, which was already running late.

Inslee outlined needed steps for those projects to continue. OVG and Mortenson took notes. Safety measures were implemented. Shift changes were made so workers weren't bumping up against one another. And it was all implemented within days of construction halting. After about a week, the KeyArena overhaul was back on.

Durkan said what happened at KeyArena will likely become a pandemic model for other companies to use years from now.

But Durkan felt keeping those projects going was vital to more than just getting them done on time. She realized that once the pandemic ended, however long it took, a depressed and exhausted citizenry would need things to look forward to.

"People were going to need a way to come together," Durkan said. "And if you could keep this thing moving and have people kind of rise out of the ashes of COVID and have something really positive, that was going to be important."

And within months, with the COVID death count reaching six figures, the country engulfed in nationwide protests over the police killing of George Floyd in Minneapolis, and a divisive federal election campaign about to be unleashed, Seattle's yet-unnamed NHL team decided to offer up some of that hope.

What's in a name? Seattle's new NHL team was about to find out. After keeping their "Kraken" choice a secret for months, it was time to release it.

Chapter 39

TOO MUCH PANDEMIC, TOO LITTLE TIME

By mid-summer 2020, NHL Seattle CEO Tod Leiweke knew a couple of things. One, the COVID-19 pandemic wasn't going away. And two, NHL commissioner Gary Bettman had saved him and his brother from possible career ruin by launching the Seattle team in 2021 instead of 2020.

KeyArena's outer shell by summer 2020 was still being built in one of the most complex arena projects ever attempted. The engineering alone, carried out by Thornton Tomasetti, had been unprecedented in keeping the venue's 44-million-pound roof propped for months on 72 temporary posts. From a distance, it looked like one of those popsicle-stick houses. But it had been serious business and was finally done. The cement columns surrounding the venue had been reattached to the roof and the temporary support posts removed. Nobody had ever tried anything like it. And it's possible no sports franchise ever will again.

So, OVG and the hockey team were breathing huge sighs of relief. They could finally focus on building up the arena's walls, add inner grandstands and luxury suite finishes, and be done. Oh yeah, they could also get on with selling and marketing the actual team. Or could they?

Leiweke faced an agonizing choice. He'd worried about appearing tone deaf by making NHL announcements during the pandemic. The George Floyd killing by Minneapolis police officer Derek Chauvin in May 2021 had only exacerbated nationwide tensions. Leiweke knew his staffers were mentally drained, worried about their physical health, the country's future, and their own employment. He understood his NHL team was trivial in the grand scheme. But trivial or not, that team was launching in just over a year and still didn't have a name.

Neither did KeyArena. OVG and the team had tried temporarily dubbing it New Arena at Seattle Center, which caught on nowhere except their corporate press releases.

But everybody agreed Key Bank's decade of free naming rights publicity had run its course.

Right after the April 2018 press conference announcing his hiring as team CEO, Leiweke and his brother had hopped in a chauffeured SUV and headed to Amazon headquarters for a business meeting. A few months later, Amazon No. 2 Andy Jassy became one of the team's local minority owners. And now, in June 2021, Amazon was to be KeyArena's new naming rights partner. And they wanted to announce it.

If anything, this made for a perfect trial balloon on whether the public was ready for announcements related to the team. The arena was technically OVG's project, and it was possible the public would be more tolerant of something seen as a corporate announcement rather than sports related.

It turns out, not surprisingly, people were indeed ready to discuss something other than the pandemic, the racial crisis gripping America, and whether Donald Trump could keep his presidency. They really wanted to discuss Amazon's arena naming choice—some more kindly than others.

The new "Climate Pledge Arena" name was a mouthful. And it certainly had mouths gaping wide enough in astonishment to stuff plenty of words inside. No corporate entity had ever done this. Companies simply didn't commit tens of millions of dollars to naming rights without splashing their brand all over buildings.

But if any company had spare cash to try something different, it was Amazon. The "Climate Pledge" was a strategy the company had devised to counter criticism its delivery vehicles and mechanisms burned too much fossil fuel globally. Cynics accused the company itself of not doing enough to honor its own "pledge" to become carbon neutral by 2040. Still, it was a lofty goal. And companies doing business with Amazon were urged—sometimes strong-armed—into signing on.

But this was more than just a name added to an arena. Climate Pledge Arena would be the world's first to earn a net-zero-carbon certification from the International Living Future Institute. It was to run entirely on renewable electric energy, collecting rainwater in an underground cistern to freeze for its ice rink. All concessions inside would be strictly sourced. And the arena would rid itself of all plastics by its second year.

Again, cynics and Amazon-haters labeled it a PR stunt. But others argued that, whatever Amazon's motives, the name raised awareness of an important issue. No other sports venue could say that.

The debate over the name was about as friendly as prior team name discussions. But it signaled to Leiweke and others the community could discuss things beyond the nation's multiple crises. Leiweke kept telling me, as the team secretly planned its name reveal, that fans needed something to be happy about.

NHL Seattle had done an incredible job keeping "Kraken" a secret. But then, in a sign of pandemic delivery woes that would plague Climate Pledge Arena right on through its reopening, an errant package nearly blew their name reveal.

GM Ron Francis was home in Raleigh, North Carolina, staying put during the pandemic, when the team set July 23, 2020, as its naming announcement date. Leiweke and Heidi Dettmer, the team's marketing VP who'd told Francis about hearing folkloric Kraken stories as a child, would make the live-streamed announcement alongside construction workers on the arena's floor.

Francis, meanwhile, would be ready to speak on the livestream from North Carolina. But the team wanted him wearing a golf shirt with the new Kraken logo, the stylized "S" with David Bonderman's red eye inside the upper curve. So, a bag of golf shirts was prepared and shipped to his home.

To be safe, the team put a combination lock on the bag. They'd scheduled it to arrive the morning of the announcement. Only it never did.

"It was supposed to arrive at my house at a quarter to eight," Francis said. "So, I'm sitting on my porch waiting and nothing shows up. So, about eight o' clock I go and start driving around the neighborhood thinking maybe somebody else had gotten it.

"So, I'm driving around and there's nothing. I call and they say, 'No, the package has been delivered.' So, I get hold of the driver and we find out the package has been delivered to a medical supply store about an hour north of where I live.

"It was a good thing we had a lock on the package."

The driver went back to retrieve the unopened package. Finally, it arrived at his house just as Francis was preparing to start livestreamed interviews.

"If they hadn't put a lock on it, it could have been opened and the name could have been out before the actual release later that morning," Francis said.

Back in Seattle, bullet dodged, Dettmer stepped to the microphone and mouthed the words that transformed NHL Seattle into the Kraken. The reaction was explosive. The team had wanted a name that would trigger something in fans and got exactly that. Some loved Kraken, some hated it, but nobody was caught in the middle. Still, even among those hating it, the venom was muted. The Kraken, for better or worse, were now Seattle's team.

"It was exhausting," NHL to Seattle fan website creator John Barr said of the name debate. "It was easily the most contentious issue facing the team and the fanbase. I don't think they ever were pleased.

"One time, I was hoping they would go completely off into left field and pick a team name nobody was thinking of. But that would have probably pissed off more people.

"And believe it or not, I think the Kraken is probably the best they could have done. Because people seem to have kind of embraced it."

Indeed, within days, nationwide sales of Kraken merchandise would shatter records on the website of national online retail giant Fanatics. Two weeks in, Kraken merchandise across all Fanatics platforms was selling at roughly four times the rate of the Vegas Golden Knights during their opening period.

The Kraken also had the No. 2 and No. 3 best-selling items across all Fanatics sports platforms, a navy logo T-shirt and a branded tri-blend T-shirt.

Not only that, but the Kraken's season ticket waitlist had expanded by 13,300 people since the naming announcement and was up to over 51,700. Selling those season tickets was the next order of business. The team had put that off for months but was now ready for its biggest remaining step that year.

On August 20, 2020, the Kraken finally released general season ticket prices for the majority of arena seats. As expected, they were pricey. And the team was requiring a minimum commitment of three years. Fans could also buy in five- and seven-year plans.

It was an ambitious undertaking. The Kraken planned to walk each prospective buyer individually through the team's season ticket preview center, past the replica Guyle Fielder locker, and on into the theater room where a model of Climate Pledge Arena awaited, replete with a laser light show. From there, fans could view 3D renderings of views from their future seats.

The pandemic ruined all that. Fans on the season ticket waiting list, by and large, were too skittish for in-person appointments. So, the Kraken got creative. They transitioned everything to a personalized online experience, providing the same virtual glimpses of seat views from home computers. Instead of hurrying deposit holders through the process in groups, they stuck to the personalized approach.

One consultant suggested that streamlining could complete the process in five weeks. Instead, the Kraken did it one by one over five months. By spring 2021, the sales were done. The team had guaranteed sellouts of 17,151 for every game.

Meanwhile, arena progress continued. But at a slower pace than anyone wanted. It wasn't until April 2021 that the first shipment of 700 seats manufactured by an Australian company arrived on-site.

The seating design by Populous and architects Chris Carver and Geoff Cheong had called for steep seating grades akin to old-fashioned arenas in Toronto, Boston, and Montreal. Once the first seats were installed, it was evident how good views of the rink were from the steep sections. The big question was whether they'd all be installed in time.

OVG construction executive Ken Johnsen assured me things would be done. There were more than 1,000 workers on-site daily scrambling to the finish line. Only problem was, none of them drove delivery trucks. All the seats, Johnsen said, had actually arrived in Seattle and would soon be delivered to the arena. The arrival part was true. But delivering them to the arena amid pandemic delays was not an easy task.

By June of that year, the Kraken's state-of-the-art practice facility at the site of the Northgate Mall, several miles north of downtown, was nearing completion. The budget had soared from $50 million to $80 million as pandemic costs and lavish upgrades kicked in. And shipping delays prevented a planned restaurant inside the three-ice-rink facility, dubbed the

Kraken Community Iceplex, from being completed for the September start of training camp.

Everything, it seemed, was in a state of flux. But at least the Kraken finally had a head coach. On June 24, 2021, the Kraken stunned the hockey universe by naming onetime Philadelphia Flyers coach Dave Hakstol the first bench boss in team history.

Nobody had Hakstol among the list of rumored candidates. As with their team name, the Kraken had proved their ability to keep secrets was greater than their penchant for getting on-time deliveries. But by July 2021, they had a practice facility with ice being poured on the three rinks. They had a semblance of a main arena with some seating, a northern wall of windows that glanced out into the street, and high-end interior finishes with tiles continuing to arrive by the week.

They also had a coach in Hakstol. All that was needed was players. And enough fortitude to make it to the opening night finish line.

Chapter 40

WINNING THE LONG GAME

The sun-kissed afternoon of July 21 was arguably Seattle's most beautiful of 2021. Pleasing high-70s temperatures and nary a cloud in sight. Enough to make years of toil feel worth it for the Kraken and those who'd created them.

The NHL expansion draft had arrived, the Kraken this day selecting players from 30 other teams. An elaborate, made-for-TV show was planned for scenic Gas Works Park, offering ESPN's live broadcast a downtown backdrop across glistening Lake Union, replete with boaters and kayakers basking in late-afternoon sunshine.

The outdoor event came together in mere weeks. It had been touch-and-go whether public health officials would allow such a mass fan gathering of thousands. But coronavirus caseloads dropped, and civic leaders and the Kraken viewed the draft event as a celebration of Seattle's emergence from the pandemic.

That the Kraken's player selections had been surreptitiously leaked to the media hours earlier was a headache for the NHL and its new ESPN TV partners. But for Kraken owners and executives, they couldn't have picked a better day for 4,000 people on picnic blankets to see those players announced one by one.

Some, such as future Kraken captain Mark Giordano, had flown in that morning to be introduced on the outdoor TV stage. I'd met Kraken CEO Tod Leiweke and his wife for dinner the Friday five days prior and he'd confided it was his first private moment in weeks. Early the following morning, Leiweke would be at his office as the Kraken received the confidential list of draft-eligible players left unprotected.

The remaining pre-draft days were dominated by talk of the Montreal Canadiens leaving star goalie Carey Price exposed. Price played his junior hockey across the state for the Tri-City Americans. His wife, Angela, was from Kennewick, Washington. But the Kraken never seriously contemplated selecting Price and his bloated salary. Instead, a few days after the draft, they did a free-agent deal with former Colorado Avalanche netminder Philipp Grubauer.

In hindsight, those summer days were the highlight of the Kraken's debut season.

If the Kraken were one of Jerry Bruckheimer's Hollywood movies, their tale would have ended with captain Giordano hoisting the Stanley Cup. Or perhaps with a trademark Bruckheimer explosion, caused by an F-18 taking out the enemy's anti-aircraft position. Whatever the plotline, it would have ended with a bang, not the whimper produced by the real-life Kraken, minus Giordano, who was traded at the March 2022 deadline.

But that's why happy endings are sometimes best left for movies. This book's happy ending is where the Kraken's on-ice journey begins. And that beginning wasn't very good, despite media pundits, statistical analysts, and oddsmakers pegging them as a 90-point playoff contender.

In the grander scheme, the 30th-place-overall Kraken's first season closed out the epic battle to birth Climate Pledge Arena. The venue's overhaul came in at $1.15 billion, double the $564 million winning OVG bid five years prior. But all was covered, as promised, with private money.

And on October 23, 2021, that billion-dollar arena was unveiled to the sports world in the Kraken's home opener against the Vancouver Canucks. The arena had technically opened earlier that week with the "soft launch" of a Foo Fighters concert followed by a harder Friday opening by Coldplay. But sports were the reason for Climate Pledge Arena's rebuild, and the Saturday night hockey game was the test.

The Kraken had dropped their franchise opener in Las Vegas, overcoming a 3–0 deficit only to lose 4–3 to the Golden Knights on a late, kicked-in goal the video review experts somehow allowed. They'd notched the franchise's first win two nights later in Nashville, lost in overtime at Columbus, then dropped two more road games in regulation to sit 1–3–1 heading home.

Outside Climate Pledge, the smooth-flowing traffic on nearby streets was an early victory. The team had spent years devising a smart phone application to help fans prepay for parking at neighboring lots. An additional light rail line now connected northern suburbanites to downtown. From there, the monorail, upgraded with $6 million in OVG funding, carried those fans the remaining distance to the arena. The Kraken included free transit passes within their phone app for fans with game tickets.

Thus, the feared "Mercer Mess" redux, played up by opponents during years of endless arena debates, never materialized. Sure, there was some traffic, as at any arena in the country. But everyone got to the game on time.

In fact, had the story ended that home opening night, with those who'd toiled on Climate Pledge and the Kraken basking in their achievement, Bruckheimer himself might have signed off on the big-screen adaptation.

As it happened, Bruckheimer attended the Canucks game. For the child from Detroit who'd sat with his salesman father in the Olympia's cheap seats watching 1950s Red Wings greatness and dreaming of more, being an honest-to-goodness NHL owner in an arena he'd helped plan and pay for was overwhelming.

"It reminded me kind of like when I was making a movie," Bruckheimer told me. "What you go through to get the movie made: to find the material, to convince the talent to get involved, to get the studio to put in hundreds of millions of dollars.

"And then, you have opening night. And on a movie, it's either a hit or a flop and you know pretty quickly. This is a long-term situation with an arena and a team. But it was that same kind of feeling. It was opening night. This was our unveiling. And it couldn't have gone better."

The 17,151 fans seemed enthralled by the intimacy of the arena bowl and spaciousness of the concourses. The north end wall of windows peering out to the street flooded the venue with natural light, even after sundown. This was beneficial beyond aesthetics. The arena's footprint had doubled to 800,000 square feet mainly because Populous architects devised a plan to dig down 53 feet and widen the venue, mainly below street level. From the street, the arena appeared only slightly bigger. But below ground, it was nearly double the size. Arena entrances let fans into the highest seating sections and most would take escalators down to their seats. But the incoming natural light gave patrons the illusion of being at street level and not encased in an underground tomb.

So, the Kraken and OVG had reached the finish line. But the pandemic had flared back up, bringing arena vaccine and mask mandates. Nightmarish shipping and planning delays were a daily reality. Anybody peering around corners or through curtains might have spotted ongoing arena construction hidden from view. Those watching the in-game entertainment and on-ice product with a more critical eye could also tell they lacked polish.

The Kraken couldn't even skate at their arena until the morning of the home opener. And it showed in a 4–2 loss. Kraken head coach Dave Hakstol in ensuing weeks conducted more practices away from the team's $80 million Community Iceplex and at Climate Pledge instead to get players acclimated.

But they never regained footing and 2021–22 quickly became akin to a practice season.

The "competitive" team GM Ron Francis expected kept losing. Francis attributed that to more than just an expected lack of goal-scoring. The goal-tending wasn't sharp. The team's solid defensive corps still made a handful of critical nightly mistakes. And then there were the off-ice issues.

"The pandemic, really," Francis told me. "I think everyone thought that was behind us."

Instead, the Kraken couldn't get players skating together until right before training camp. COVID-19 protocols and precautions also limited practice time.

"Most importantly, we had events planned for our players and their families at the end of the preseason," Francis said. "They're trying to learn about each other and become a team. They're trying to learn a new system.

"And with COVID still going, we couldn't do that. We had to cancel events. We have a bunch of players we think our fans would love to get to know if we could get them out into the community. We couldn't do that."

By the March 21, 2022, trade deadline, Francis had traded away captain Mark Giordano; forwards Calle Jarnkrok, Colin Blackwell, Marcus Johansson, and Mason Appleton; and defenseman Jeremy Lauzon for forwards Daniel Sprong and Victor Rask as well as 10 draft picks in Rounds 2–7 in coming years. The team finished relatively strong, playing its most extensive stretch of .500 hockey after the deadline.

Nonetheless, the Kraken finished with a dismal 27-49-6 record—30 points below those lofty 90-point preseason projections. Francis vowed to use some of the draft picks garnered to make summer improvements via trades.

But if sports were all about a lone season, nobody would invest in them. Certainly not invest $2 billion on an arena, team, practice facility, and farm club.

Those who'd waged this battle to land the Kraken were playing the long game. Sure, there were on-ice issues. But they'd have time to fix them. Through years of struggle attaining a Seattle arena, there'd never been time. Everything was a deadline, a ticking time bomb.

And it took a toll.

The Kraken wound up playing home preseason games at major junior hockey arenas throughout Washington while Climate Pledge raced toward completion. The first exhibition was in Spokane against the Canucks. Two hours before puck drop, having arrived early to soak in the historic event, I felt a tap on my shoulder. It was Tim Leiweke saying hello, accompanied by his brother, Tod.

The head of OVG, the man most responsible for this night, looked tired. I asked how he was.

"Well, I've managed to finally start sleeping again," he quipped.

Leiweke told me he'd taken an apartment in Seattle through October to supervise final construction and planned the same for New York in November. His new UBS Arena on Long Island was also running behind due to COVID-19 shipping delays. The New York Islanders would spend weeks on the road before their new home was ready. I could tell Leiweke felt the weight.

"This job isn't for the faint of heart," he told me.

That night, no matter the private jets Leiweke flew, the celebrities he called friends, or the money he'd ultimately make off his company and projects, I realized I'd never trade places. I lacked the stomach for it. Everybody wants to be there when you succeed. But when failure is possible, it's scary at the top. The Oak View Group was Leiweke's dream, but it was never guaranteed. Had it failed, as it might have without him working political angles and corporate pocketbooks to get both arenas built during a pandemic, livelihoods might collapse. His own daughter, Francesca, had bought into her father's vision as much as he had. The circles under Leiweke's eyes told me the stakes.

We discussed having dinner in Seattle to talk for this book. But everything got busier once the season began and the Omicron variant struck. We didn't speak until three months later by phone in December 2021. By then, Leiweke was more candid about Climate Pledge's harrowing debut.

"When you take the first four or five issues that we had to deal with and then add to that COVID, shipping, labor, and put all of that in there, it's by far the hardest project I've ever been a part of and it's not even close," he told me.

Leiweke added: "We were scrubbing things clean the [opening] day of. And we're still going through our punch list. We finally have the lights working on the campus. We finally have our directional signage almost all up and operating. There's still a lot of work that we're doing in the building. And so, it was and continues to be a tight turnaround."

Leiweke told me the arena's "finishes, tiles, light fixtures, deep fryers, our LED boards" had always been "somewhere, someplace, some ship" up until opening week. The final arena seats were installed the week prior. "And as I said, there's still stuff floating around."

The open-ended question of a Sonics return also lingered.

NBA commissioner Adam Silver had finally signaled in 2020 that team owners—their revenues hampered by the pandemic—could consider expansion soon. Former Mayor Jenny Durkan had spoken many times to Silver as Climate Pledge was rebuilt. But when I sought her take in February 2022, she cautioned Sonics fans would need patience with the NBA.

"I think it will still be four or five years," she told me. "It could be sooner than that. But their economic stuff got disrupted by COVID. If not for COVID and this two-year gap, I think we would have gotten a team sooner."

If she "were a betting person," she'd go with a Seattle and Las Vegas expansion pairing. "The NBA, I believe, knows that losing Seattle hurt the league. And that making up for those past actions is important."

Two days later, longtime NBA insider Bill Simmons said on his podcast he'd been "given intel" the league was exploring expansion and Las Vegas and Seattle were front-runners.

Kraken CEO Tod Leiweke told me he knew his team needed firming up within the market ahead of any NBA arrival. Part of that would involve him abdicating his team president's role in coming weeks and ceding it to chief operating officer Victor de Bonis. Leiweke would remain CEO of the Kraken. Left unsaid was that he'd be positioned to become CEO of any joint company managing both the Kraken and any future Sonics team, with both squads retaining separate presidents.

The changeover with de Bonis went into effect by April 2022. At the time, Samantha Holloway, daughter of Kraken majority owner David Bonderman, also assumed the title of chair of the Kraken's powerful executive committee of owners.

Further ownership changes occurred that month when former Seahawks running back Marshawn Lynch and local rapper Macklemore were added as minority owners. Both planned to play public roles in helping the team's community efforts at inclusion and diversity.

Leiweke had already long been on a mission to make the Kraken different in those areas, largely through hiring women and minorities to prominent positions. Leiweke sought to effectuate change the NHL vowed was coming but hadn't always delivered.

Ever an optimist, he added that despite the team's disappointing play, it had taken a first step to forging deeper community ties. And during a global pandemic, at that. "If we can get through this," he told me, "we can get through anything."

We were in a private room inside the restaurant of the team's new practice facility. The restaurant's opening had also been delayed when building materials and furniture arrived late. But it was now operational, as was the three-rink facility, expecting 1 million visitors that opening year.

None of it had been easy, Leiweke said. But the multiple billions in infrastructure was finally in place. From here on, he looked forward to the Kraken simply fine-tuning in the off-season as every other team got to do.

"This has been the hardest thing I've done in my career by far," he said. "But what really motivates me every day is knowing our best days are in front of us."

IT'S HOW YOU PLAY THE GAME

One of those better days envisioned by Leiweke happened soon after. At first, it appeared a cheesy public relations exercise: the team declaring March 2, 2022, as "Kraken Day." The date being the third month and second day equated to the numbers 3-2—which are sacred in team lore. The NHL's 32nd franchise had attracted 32,000 season ticket deposits four years earlier in a day-plus period culminating on March 2. On opening night at Climate Pledge, the Kraken retired the No. 32 in a banner hung from the rafters.

So, "Kraken Day" was a thing, with festivities including an official proclamation by new Seattle Mayor Bruce Harrell, the onetime councilmember who'd helped usher in the city's Climate Pledge development deal just ahead of the Kraken's creation years prior.

"When we look at what the Kraken organization has done, we've made history," Harrell said in a Kraken Day speech to youth hockey players practicing at the team's Community Iceplex facility. "And it's very important that you young folks learned a lesson. We all learned a lesson, too. Sometimes, it's not whether you win or lose in a game, it's what? It's how you play the game."

Harrell was referring to the team and arena being built without public money. Of a historic civic-owned arena being preserved. And of Climate Pledge's environmental message and commitments. Harrell noted the millions spent by the team on community programs and city infrastructure.

Kraken CEO Tod Leiweke was on hand for the proclamation. I knew he took fierce pride in the team's community work in seeking to be different from a typical sports organization. He'd hired the first Black play-by-play announcer in NHL history in radio broadcaster Everett Fitzhugh. A few weeks earlier, Fitzhugh had replaced TV commentator John Forslund for a lone contest in Winnipeg, teaming with analyst J.T. Brown to form the first all-Black broadcast booth for a televised NHL game.

The Kraken also made Cammi Granato the first female pro scout in league history, ahead of her being poached by the Canucks as an assistant GM. The Kraken had Alexandra Mandrycky heading its analytics department. They had a plethora of female and minority executives throughout their ranks. Leiweke knew the Kraken would ultimately be judged by on-ice play. But for him, the off-ice part mattered.

Later that night, I was in the press lounge prior to the Kraken playing the Nashville Predators. Leiweke spotted me and sat down to talk. He told me an unbelievable tale of a Ukrainian singer who'd be performing that country's anthem before the game. Russia had invaded Ukraine the previous week. "Want to meet him?" he said. "Follow me."

We navigated a labyrinth of arena corridors, reaching a private dressing room. Inside, we met Roman Vashchuk, a Kyiv resident who'd been on a lengthy singing tour of churches in multiple states before arriving in Seattle to fly back home. But he'd contracted COVID-19 and been hospitalized with a blood clot and banned from flying by a cardiologist until it cleared. In the meantime, Russia invaded Ukraine, forcing his wife and three children, ages 10, 7, and 4, to flee as refugees to neighboring Poland. Vashchuk showed us cell phone images and footage from his family and friends of the devastation impacting his homeland. He'd been overwhelmed by stress but grateful for the chance to perform and hopefully inspire his people in a small way.

"Here, come with me," Leiweke said.

He led us outside the room and on yet another tour through various corridors, then down a long dark tunnel and out onto the Kraken's bench. Both teams by now were on the ice for pregame warm-ups. Vashchuk stood wide-eyed, then lifted his phone to snap some photos very different from the images of war he'd shown us minutes earlier.

Leiweke motioned starting goalie Chris Driedger over and whispered something. Driedger headed over to Vashchuk, introduced himself, and chatted. Vashchuk handed over his phone and asked me to snap photos of them.

As we prepared to head back to his dressing room, Vashchuck told Leiweke, "Thank you so much for this." Leiweke, visibly choked up, put his hands on Vashchuk's shoulders and patted him gently. "No, thank you for agreeing to do this. You've been through so much."

Vashchuk's stirring rendition of the anthem that night brought the house down. Kraken forward Colin Blackwell said afterward that players felt inspired by it.

I'd found Vashchuk's passionate vocals haunting, given the photos I'd seen on his phone. The arena had been darkened, spotlighting Vashchuk alone on a carpeted corner of the rink as he sang. It's a scene I'll never forget.

The next morning, Leiweke texted me a copy of a text sent by a friend accompanying Vashchuk on his trip. The singer's youngest daughter had received a visa they'd been waiting on and his family would soon join him in the U.S.

Leiweke sent me another text moments later. "The picture in his phone last night," he said of one particularly horrifying image. "Won't ever forget that."

Me neither. The evening reminded me that pro sports, while dominated by money and quest for profit, can be more. The Kraken and the arena they play in had shown it was possible to get big things done in Seattle, a city wedded to process and conventional wisdom that wasn't always the wisest.

But that unlikely success and pulling off arguably the most civic-friendly arena deal in American history was double-edged. It probably contributed to how disappointing the Kraken's on-ice performance seemed by comparison. Even the Leiweke brothers, it turned out, had limits. But the emotional evening prior brought hope. To me, at least, it turned out the team and those running it were still trying to be better and would keep on doing so. One anthem singer at a time.

ACKNOWLEDGMENTS

Researching this book first required living through events spread over several years, starting in 2013 when my newspaper, the *Seattle Times*, asked me to leave a longstanding baseball writing job to take on sports investigative reporting while keeping an eye on the city's quest for a new sports arena.

Executive editor Kathy Best, associate sports editor Bill Reader, and future executive editor Michele Matassa Flores were particularly helpful early on at encouraging me to go against the status quo and get projects turned around. Debunking commonly held beliefs in a devoted sports market such as Seattle is not always easy, and some interim years were quite difficult on a personal level.

I could not have gotten through it without my wife, Amy Grazer, a true friend with a dazzling professional career I take notes from where I can. Amy was also there with feedback, suggestions, and patience as I undertook putting those years into words for this book. She alone fully understands the sacrifice this was beyond the book itself.

Noted sports financial author Neil deMause, whose own *Field of Schemes* book first got me interested in stadium and arena financing way back in 1999, kindly met me for lunch in Brooklyn, New York, at a key point in my reporting where I needed a sounding board for my views on Seattle's arena situation.

Now-retired *Times* sports columnist Steve Kelley has always remained supportive. His gathering and application of institutional knowledge within the sports world is one I've long tried to emulate and served me well in the reporting that led to this book.

And for anyone noticing this book's slightly tongue-in-cheek approach to describing life and history in Seattle, you can thank my former *Toronto Star* baseball colleague and columnist Richard Griffin for instilling some of his wry humor within me for eight years working side by side.

There were countless others along the way who opened doors and provided tips for some of the reporting in this book who prefer to remain anonymous but know who they are.

Finally, none of this would have been possible without the suggestions and willingness of the folks at Triumph Books. Special thanks to book editor Michelle Bruton and senior acquisitions editor Josh Williams, who have now been willing to endure two projects with me in helping fulfill a longstanding dream of writing books I've had since age four. Hopefully, the writing has improved.